The Doctoral
Examination Process

SRHE and Open University Press Imprint
General Editor: Heather Eggins

Current titles include:

The Doctoral Examination Process

A handbook for students, examiners and supervisors

Penny Tinkler and Carolyn Jackson

Society for Research into Higher Education
& Open University Press

Open University Press
McGraw-Hill Education
McGraw-Hill House
Shoppenhangers Road
Maidenhead
Berkshire
England
SL6 2QL

email: enquiries@openup.co.uk
world wide web: www.openup.co.uk

First published 2004

A catalogue record of this book is available from the British Library

ISBN 0 335 21306 5 (hbk)   0 335 21305 7 (pbk)

Library of Congress Cataloging-in-Publication Data
CIP data has been applied for

Typeset by RefineCatch Limited, Bungay, Suffolk
Printed in the UK by Bell & Bain Ltd, Glasgow

To Brenda and John Jackson

Contents

Acknowledgements

This book is the culmination of four years' work on the PhD examination process. During this time many people have supported and encouraged us and, more recently, contributed in valuable ways to the production of this book. Special thanks go to Carol Boulter, Pat Cryer, Miriam David, Rosemary Deem, Pam Denicolo, James Hartley, Stuart Powell, Liz Stanley, Penny Summerfield and John Wakeford. We are also very grateful to Pat Broadhead, Bridget Byrne, Iain Campbell, Amanda Chetwynd, Kate Day, Steve Dempster, Fiona Devine, Laura Doan, Penny Florence, Sue Grace, Howard Green, Maia Green, Peter Halfpenny, Chris Kyriacou, Neil Lent, Diana Leonard, Judith McGovern, David Morgan, Janine Muldoon, Gill O'Toole, Chris Park, Arwen Raddon, Michael Seymour, Malcolm Shaw, Nigel Sherriff, Yvette Solomon, Pat Sponder, James Thompson, Malcolm Tight, Paul Trowler, Stuart Turnbull, Kath Twaddell, Jo Warin and Rod Watson.

We would also like to thank the anonymous candidates, academics and administrators that contributed to the five research projects that we have undertaken. Jenny Van Hooff deserves special mention for interviewing the PhD candidates, as do Alice Jesmont for her speedy transcription and Paula Shakespeare for inputting data. Many thanks also to Mario Chin and Andrew Jackson for the illustrations.

Finally, thanks to our parents and friends for their ongoing support.

1

Introduction to the Doctoral Examination Process

1.1 Introduction to this book

Doctoral education[1] has undergone considerable expansion over the past decade. There are now over 101,000 doctoral/research students in UK universities and, whereas just over 3000 new students started their PhDs in 1992, more than 10,000 started in 1998/99 (Morley *et al.* 2002: 264). In line with this expansion in registrations, there has also been expansion in the number of awards; between 1996 and 2000 there was a 27 per cent increase in the number of doctorates awarded by UK institutions – from 10,800 to 13,670 (Metcalfe *et al.* 2002: 7). In other words, the PhD examination is now a common feature of higher education, one that engages the time and energies not only of thousands of students, but also of thousands of academics as supervisors and examiners.

Whilst doctoral examinations are now more common than they were in the past, they are no less important: PhD examinations have significant implications both for students and for the academy. For students, the examination is the point at which three or more years' work is assessed and judgement pronounced. Success in the examination is also a gateway, potentially, for access into academia and may facilitate promotion in other careers. In terms of the academy, the PhD is the highest formal qualification and the examination process serves as an explicit gatekeeping function and is a marker of standards.

Unfortunately, the PhD examination, particularly the viva, is feared and often poorly understood by many students, and it is a source of concern and confusion for many supervisors and examiners. These feelings and confusions are prompted by three main factors. First, doctoral examination procedures are highly variable – they vary between institutions, between disciplines and between examiners. Second, there are no clearly articulated common criteria or standards for the award of a PhD. Third, the doctoral viva is usually a relatively private affair that takes place 'behind closed doors'; there are only a few institutions in the UK that operate 'public' vivas and even in those universities access is restricted to members of specific academic communities. As such, viva processes are seldom transparent or open to scrutiny; so it is understandable that, for many students and academics, the doctoral examination process, and the viva in particular, is 'shrouded in mystery'.

This book sheds light upon the doctoral examination.

Audiences – who are they and how should they navigate this book?

The book has three primary audiences: PhD students[2], supervisors and examiners. However, the book will also be of interest and use to people who act as independent chairs in vivas, policy-makers and staff development personnel. At the start of each chapter we have identified the primary audiences. In addition, Figure 1.1 provides a visual overview of the relevance of each chapter to each audience, and so provides a guide for how different audiences might navigate the book.

Our approach

*Is **not** about survival . . .*

> Surviving the viva depends fundamentally on preparation and students'
> ability to demystify the examination procedure.
>
> (Burnham 1994: 33)

---

[2] We use the terms students and candidates interchangeably throughout this book.

	Chapter 2 Understanding the doctoral viva – what is it for?	Chapter 3 Understanding the doctoral viva – how does it work?	Chapter 4 Viva preparation – long term	Chapter 5 Selecting examiners	Chapter 6 Who attends the viva? Roles and obligations	Chapter 7 Examiners – should you examine?	Chapter 8 Examiners – assessing a doctoral thesis	Chapter 9 Viva preparation – short term	Chapter 10 Viva preparation – final stage	Chapter 11 In the viva – candidates' perspectives	Chapter 12 The viva – tips and issues for examiners	Chapter 13 Post-viva
Students	☺☺☺	☺☺☺	☺☺☺	☺☺	☺☺☺		☺☺	☺☺☺	☺☺☺	☺☺☺	☺	☺☺☺
Examiners	☺☺☺	☺☺☺	☺☺☺	☺	☺☺☺	☺☺☺	☺☺☺			☺☺	☺☺☺	☺☺
Supervisors	☺☺☺	☺☺☺	☺☺☺	☺☺☺	☺☺☺	☺	☺☺	☺☺☺	☺☺☺	☺☺	☺	☺☺☺
Chairs	☺☺☺	☺☺☺			☺☺☺					☺☺	☺☺	☺

☺ ☺ ☺ extremely relevant;   ☺ ☺ relevant;   ☺ relevant in parts

Figure 1.1 Overview of chapters and their relevance for the key audiences

We agree with Burnham that preparation for, and demystification of, the viva is fundamentally important for candidates. However, this book does not aim to tell students how to 'survive' the viva – our aims are far more ambitious. We do not merely want students to 'survive', we want them to flourish. The viva should be not solely a summative experience, but also a formative one. As such, the book provides students, supervisors and examiners with ways of *understanding* the PhD examination process, and *preparing* for it, that facilitate constructive experiences for all concerned.

Is informed by our empirical research . . .

> What makes this stand out from the other study guides is the research that the authors did, which gives it more weight and makes it more engaging, especially all of the quotes.
>
> (PhD student, Sociology)

An understanding of the PhD examination process cannot be derived from the experiences of a single academic, or based on the policies and practices at a single institution. Examination policies vary between institutions and practices vary between disciplines and individual examiners. Knowledge of examination practices and guidance on how to manage the demands of them – whether as a candidate, examiner, supervisor or independent chair – must be based on insights gained from collective experience. This book is, therefore, informed principally by the empirical research that we have conducted since 1999. Our research, which is outlined later in this chapter, has generated data on the PhD examination process from academics and candidates across disciplines and from across Britain. Importantly, our data sets enable us to provide discussion, illustrations and advice that engage with:

- the diversity of practices that characterize the PhD examination process;
- the different perspectives of examiners and candidates;
- variations within and between disciplines.

Recognizes complexity and variability . . .
It is crucial that guidance about the doctoral examination is not overly general as this can lead to misinformed and ill-prepared candidates, supervisors and examiners. We have been very careful in writing this book not to oversimplify a complex process. Furthermore, we have been careful not to lose sight of the variability of vivas in proposing ways for candidates and examiners to prepare for them. A physics PhD candidate told us: 'from my conversations with other PhD candidates, vivas are so inconsistent that there is no simple advice that can be given'. We agree with this candidate, there is no *simple* advice that can be given, but that does not mean that no useful advice can be provided. We have attempted throughout the book to base our advice on a sophisticated understanding of the examination process, one that recognizes, rather than ignores, the complexity and variability of the process.

Is long-term . . .

> How am I intending to prepare for the viva? Ignore it for as long as possible and then once I have a date . . . I'll run round and get advice . . . At the moment I'm pretty much trying to ignore it and I'll probably deal with it nearer the time.
>
> (Alice, PhD student, Geography)

We do not advocate the approach adopted by Alice – student preparation for the examination process should start on day *one* of the PhD. Long-term preparation for the examination should be integral to the PhD process. Whilst we offer some short-term and final-stage preparations for students in this book, these are to be undertaken in addition to, not instead of, long-term preparation.

What this book is based upon – our research

Empirical research underpins the guidance presented in this book. Since 1999 we have conducted several projects on the traditional research PhD and built up five data sets.

1. *Institutional policy data from 20 British universities.* In 1999 we undertook a survey of 20 universities spread across Scotland, England and Wales. These institutions included 11 'old' (pre–1992 universities) and 9 'new' (post-1992 universities). We requested: the institution's policies concerning the PhD; information and/or guidelines distributed to postgraduate students, supervisors and examiners (both internal and external examiners); details of staff development and postgraduate training courses, and any other relevant information.

   In 2003 we re-contacted the 20 institutions in our initial survey and requested an update of policy materials. In this book we use updated policy materials from the universities that provided them. Where universities did not provide updates, we have used the materials sent to us in 1999.

2. *Questionnaire data.* In 1999 we undertook a questionnaire survey in two old universities in the north of England (Universities A and B). We gathered data relating to the PhD examination process from four perspectives, namely: external examiners ($n = 71$), internal examiners ($n = 66$), supervisors ($n = 61$) and candidates ($n = 88$).

   The academic staff were all based in the arts, humanities or social sciences. The range of departments surveyed was determined by resource constraints which prohibited a university-wide survey. Owing to the small number of potential candidate respondents relative to academics, we were able to include candidates from the natural and applied sciences as well as the arts, humanities and social sciences.

3. *Interviews with doctoral candidates.* In 2001/02 we undertook interviews with 30 doctoral candidates before and then after their PhD vivas (60

interviews in total). Each interview lasted 30–45 minutes and the inter-viewees included candidates from the social sciences, arts and humanities, and pure and applied sciences. The interviewees included students that were full- and part-time, women and men, home and overseas, on-site and off-site, from different age groups, and from two different institutions (Universities B and C).

4. *Interviews with 20 'experts'.* In 2001/02 we undertook interviews on post-graduate examination issues with 20 'experts' from across Britain. These included: deans of graduate schools, senior university administrators, representatives from key national bodies, staff development trainers, and people who undertake research on the PhD.

5. *Information from colleagues – interviews, letters, accounts.* In 2002/03 we gath-ered information from academics from across the disciplines and across Britain about their experiences of the doctoral examination process. This data collection exercise was less 'formal' than stages 1–4 above; however, it produced some interesting and illuminating accounts.

We use our own data throughout the book to inform our discussion and to 'bring it to life'. We also draw upon the research of others in the field. As some information is sensitive in nature we do not disclose the identity of our research participants; the names of our candidate interviewees are pseudonyms.

How this book is designed

We have endeavoured to present clear, research-based information and guidance about the doctoral examination process. With this in mind, we have attempted to make the book reader friendly by:

- clearly identifying the primary audiences for each chapter, both at the start of each chapter and in Figure 1.1;
- providing chapter overviews and summaries for easy navigation;
- presenting clear links between related topics across the book;
- including a wealth of real-life examples and case studies to make the guidance and issues 'come to life';
- suggesting useful tasks and checklists to encourage reader engagement and self-reflection;
- including 'Issue in Focus' boxes to highlight relevant current debates or topics.

What this book does and does not do

There is a range of doctorates on offer. Hoddell *et al.* (2002: 62) identify five categories: (1) the traditional, research-based PhD; (2) practice-based doc-torates; (3) professional doctorates; (4) new route doctorates; and (5) PhD by publication. This book is based upon research on the traditional research PhD and thus relates most directly to students, supervisors and examiners undertaking examinations of this form of doctorate. However, most if not all aspects of this book will also be of direct relevance to those involved in the examination of the thesis and viva elements of practice-based, professional and new route doctorates. We have also included specific discussions about practice-based PhDs in this text. Within these boundaries what the book does and does not cover is listed below.

What the book covers

- The elements of the PhD examination process.
- Understanding the viva – its purposes, components and how it works.
- Who attends the viva – participants' roles and responsibilities.
- Viva preparation for candidates – long term, short term and final stage.
- In the viva – advice for candidates.
- Selecting examiners.
- Examining – deciding whether to examine a thesis.
- Examining – how to assess a thesis.
- Examining – the viva.
- Post-viva.

What the book does not cover

- Undertaking doctoral research – see Cryer 2000; Leonard 2001; Phillips and Pugh 2000.
- Writing the thesis – see Brause 2000; Murray 2002.
- General issues in supervising PhD students – see Delamont *et al.* 1997a.

1.2 Introduction to the PhD examination process

What is a PhD?

It is difficult to write about how PhDs are examined without some discussion of what a PhD is. However, what might seem like a relatively straightforward question – what is a PhD? – is anything but straightforward to answer. Underwood (1999: 1) comments: 'what has been striking' when attempting to answer this question 'has been the complete lack of consensus, not merely between different subject areas . . . but also between different institutions and individuals'.

Definitions of a PhD tend either to be *process* oriented or *product* oriented. For example, process is to the fore in this definition: 'The PhD is a training programme designed to produce a competent and independent research practitioner' (Underwood 1999: 2). But product is emphasized in this one: 'The PhD is a researched piece of work designed to make an original contribution to knowledge. The questions posed and answered by the knowledge would in this definition be "significant" in moving the discipline forward in terms of knowledge or methodology' (Underwood 1999: 2). The main point is that there is no consensus about precisely what a PhD is, and this lack of consensus has implications for the examination process. After all, it is difficult to be sure that a thesis and/or candidate has met the requirements of a PhD when one cannot define exactly what a PhD is in the first place. Examination and definition of PhDs are, therefore, inextricably intertwined; some have gone as far as to suggest 'a PhD is what two people [the examiners] decide it is' (Underwood 1999: 6).

Although we do not subscribe fully to the view expressed in the last quote, we believe that examiners' perspectives about what constitutes a PhD are of central importance. Whilst examiners' views are sometimes informed by institutional policy and usually influenced by discipline knowledges and expectations, examining a PhD is still very much shaped by individual expectations and requirements. As such, the perspectives of examiners are a central concern throughout this book – we explore them and provide guidance to inform them.

An overview of the PhD examination process

The PhD examination process consists of three basic stages: (1) the submission and initial assessment of the thesis and, in the case of practice-related doctorates, practice; (2) the oral examination of the candidate; (3) the examiners' recommendation and the implications of this. In this section we outline each stage.

Stage 1 – the thesis (and sometimes practice)

1. Submission of the thesis and/or other submission.
2. The examiners assess the submission. Depending on institutional policy, the examiners may be required to prepare, and usually to submit, a report on the thesis in advance of the oral examination.

Stage 2 – the oral examination (viva)

There are usually five steps to a viva, although steps 3 and 4 are sometimes omitted if the examiners release their decision to the candidate at the start of the viva. The five steps are:

1. A meeting between examiners prior to the viva to compare views on the thesis (and possibly practice) and to agree an agenda for the viva.
2. The candidate joins the examiners (along with any other observers/participants – see Chapter 6) and, after introductions, they discuss the thesis and related issues.
3. The candidate (and other observers if present) are asked to leave the room. The examiners discuss the candidate's performance in the viva and

their final recommendation about the award. If appropriate, they also agree any amendments required before an award can be made, and a timescale for these.

4. The candidate is invited back into the viva room and the examiners (a) inform the candidate of their recommendation and (b) where necessary, outline additional work and set a timescale for it.

5. After the viva, the examiners complete either single reports or a joint one (depending on institutional policy and whether they agree about the award) and indicate the recommended outcome of the examination. They also indicate, where appropriate, the nature of any amendments or additions required before the PhD can be awarded. The post-viva report(s) is then submitted to a committee responsible for overseeing doctoral awards. Once the committee has considered the examiners' recommendation(s) the university will contact the candidate formally to inform her/him of the outcome.

Stage 3 – the implications of the examiners' recommendation(s)
The third stage is dependent on the examiners' recommendation and the university's policy. Institutions define award categories in different ways; they also vary in the processes that follow the examiners' recommendation(s). The following provides a rough guide to the usual range of possibilities. Candidates, examiners and supervisors are advised to check the policy of the institution at which the examination is taking place.

• *Award forthwith with no corrections.* If the examiners recommend the award of a PhD with no corrections, a committee responsible for overseeing doctoral awards considers the recommendation before an official decision is released.

• *Award subject to minor corrections.* Where examiners request minor corrections before an award can be recommended, the candidate is informed of these corrections orally at the end of the viva, and usually also in writing shortly after. There are substantial variations between institutions about what can be counted as minor corrections and what constitutes a referral. For example, at Lancaster University, 'minor amendments' constitute small corrections that can be undertaken within three or six months. At the University of Manchester, however, corrections are counted as 'minor' only if they can be completed within 'one day'; if corrections are required that will take longer than one day to complete, the thesis is referred. In practice, then, a decision to 'award subject to minor corrections' at one university may be a 'referral' at another.

When the corrections have been completed to the satisfaction of the examiners (frequently the internal examiner takes responsibility for checking minor corrections) the examiners notify the committee responsible for postgraduate awards that they are happy to recommend the award of PhD. The committee then considers the recommendation before an official decision is released.

- *Referral.* In cases where the thesis is referred, the degree of PhD is not awarded, but the candidate is permitted to revise the thesis and resubmit for an award of PhD. The candidate receives guidance on the changes that are required to bring the thesis up to the required level. The amended thesis must then be resubmitted for examination. The re-examination involves reassessment of the thesis by both external and internal examiners (usually the original examiners) and sometimes a second oral examination. See Chapter 13 for discussion of second vivas.
- *No award, or award of a lower degree.* Where the examiners do not recommend the award of a PhD, and they do not permit the candidate to revise and resubmit, they may recommend the award of a master's degree (MPhil). In this case, the recommendation may be that an MPhil can be awarded on the basis of work already presented in the thesis. If so, the committee responsible for postgraduate awards is notified of the examiners' recommendation. The committee then considers the recommendation after which an official decision is released. Alternatively, the examiners may recommend that the candidate do further work on their thesis before resubmitting it for an MPhil. In rare cases, the examiners do not recommend the award of either a PhD or an MPhil and they do not permit the candidate to revise and resubmit for either award.

Note

1. Doctoral study can lead to a range of qualifications 'with a potentially confusing variety of titles' (Hoddell *et al.* 2002: 62). In many cases the award is the generic Doctor of Philosophy, usually abbreviated to PhD although in a few cases to DPhil. In some cases the award is more specific, such as Doctor of Business Administration (DBA) or Doctor of Engineering (EngD). For the sake of clarity and simplicity we use two terms interchangeably throughout the book: PhD and doctorate. See also the later section in this chapter on what the book does and does not do.

2

Understanding the Doctoral Viva – What is it for?

The PhD viva is 'one of the best kept secrets in British higher education'.
(Burnham 1994: 30)

Chapter overview

We aim to provide candidates, supervisors and examiners with ways of understanding the viva that facilitate constructive viva experiences for all parties. Our aim is *not* simply to equip candidates with the tools required to 'survive' the viva. Attempting to understand the PhD viva is a two-stage process. Stage one involves understanding the range of purposes of PhD vivas (this chapter). Stage two involves understanding how vivas work (Chapter 3). Without such understandings it is difficult, if not impossible, for candidates and arguably examiners to prepare for the oral examination in useful and productive ways.

This chapter offers candidates, supervisors and examiners insights into different perspectives on the purposes of the PhD viva. First, we explore purposes of the viva set out in institutional policy. Second, and most importantly, we explore the purposes of the viva from the perspectives of examiners and candidates. Broadly, the key purposes of the viva fall into three areas: examination, development and ritual; each of these is mapped out in turn. We end the chapter by asking whether the outcome of the PhD examination hinges on the viva.

| Students | ☺☺☺ | Examiners | ☺☺☺ |
| Supervisors | ☺☺☺ | Chairs | ☺☺☺ |

Chapter contents

2.1 Why an oral examination? Purposes and importance

> My biggest fear about the viva is not really knowing what to expect.
> (PhD student, History)

Most students are unsure about the purposes of the oral examination, about what will happen in it, and how important the viva is in the PhD examination process. Although supervisors attempt to answer many of their students' questions, the answers are not usually straightforward. Common questions from candidates prior to the viva include:

- Why have a viva?
- What are examiners looking for in the viva?
- In terms of PhD assessment, how do examiners weight the contributions of my thesis and my viva performance?
- Can weaknesses in my thesis be compensated by a good viva performance?
- Vivas seem so variable – why is that?

- If the examiners like my thesis, could I change their minds about the result with a poor viva performance?

These are very important questions, both for candidates and supervisors, and we address them in this chapter. More specifically, we outline and explore the roles and significance of the viva and address the key question, what purposes does the viva serve in the PhD assessment process? In order to answer this question we draw upon two types of data: (1) institutional policy statements and (2) the experiences and views of the different examination participants. Discussion therefore focuses upon the roles of the viva as delineated within university policy and the purposes of the viva from the perspectives of examiners, supervisors and candidates.

Institutional policy

In relation to institutional policy we consider the purposes of the viva by focusing upon two main questions (for a more detailed discussion of institutional policy see Tinkler and Jackson 2000). First, is the viva a compulsory part of the PhD examination? Second, does the viva play a key role in the assessment of a PhD?

The viva is a compulsory part of the PhD examination
The viva is a compulsory part of PhD examinations in Britain (albeit with some exceptions where an alternative examination is arranged alongside the assessment of the thesis). The fact that many institutions stipulate that one cannot fail a PhD outright without undertaking a viva or alternative examination is evidence that the viva is an important part of the assessment process (see Box 2.1 for an example of university policy relating to posthumous vivas).

Box 2.1   Case study

POSTHUMOUS VIVAS

Although university policies usually emphasize the importance of the viva voce in the PhD examination process, we were still rather surprised that quite a lot of institutions have regulations about vivas after death. These regulations provide a rather unusual illustration of the importance that institutions attach to the viva.

The award of Research Diploma and the degrees of MPhil or PhD may be awarded posthumously on the basis of a thesis completed by a candidate who is ready for submission for examination. In such cases the Research Programmes Committee shall seek evidence that the candidate would have been likely to have been successful had the oral examination taken place.

(University of Glamorgan 1998: 18)

What criteria need to be met for a successful viva performance?

If the viva is an integral element in the examination of a doctorate it seems important to consider what criteria candidates should meet in the viva in order to pass the examination. The majority of the institutions that we surveyed offered specific criteria for assessment in the viva and/or provided more general aims for the thesis and the viva in combination. However, a few institutions in our sample identified aims and objectives only for the thesis, and provided no indication of what was to be assessed in the oral examination. Institutions that do provide criteria specifically for the viva usually state that the candidate should be able to locate her/his PhD research in a broader context and display knowledge of their thesis. Apart from these (fairly) common standards, institutional criteria vary considerably. It is important, therefore, to check the criteria of the institution where the examination will take place. However, it is also worth noting that many examiners have ideas about what a viva is for that extend beyond institutional criteria. For this reason, most of this chapter is devoted to exploring the purposes of a viva from the perspectives of those involved in the process rather than from institutional regulations. Nevertheless, it is still important to know what the regulations are at the institution where you will be examined or examine (see Box 2.2).

Box 2.2   Task for candidates and supervisors

CHECKING POLICY AND PROCEDURES

1. Do you know your institution's policy regarding the examination of doctorates?
2. Do you know the criteria that examiners are expected to use in assessing the thesis and viva?

If this information is not made available to you, approach the Examinations Office for a copy of the guidelines that are given to examiners (it is probably best if supervisors do this on behalf of their students).

Can students fail the PhD on the basis of performance in the viva?

> The balance between the assessment of the text and the viva or oral examination is at least unclear and at best ambiguous.
>
> (Morley *et al.* 2002: 266)

If the viva is an integral component of the PhD examination, it would follow that one could fail the PhD on the basis of an unsatisfactory oral examination (even if the thesis is judged to be a pass). At 12 of the 20 institutions in our survey, examiners have the option of requiring a second viva (or sometimes a written examination) if the candidate's performance in the (first) viva is deemed inadequate but the thesis is deemed adequate. For example, policy at Loughborough University (2003: 21) states that: 'If the thesis is deemed to be adequate but the candidate fails to satisfy the examiners at the oral examination . . . they [the examiners] may recommend that the candidate be allowed to sit a written examination and/or undergo another oral examination on one occasion only, within a period specified by the Examiners not exceeding 12 months.' The remaining institutions in our sample made no reference to possible actions in cases where the thesis is deemed acceptable but the viva performance is deemed unacceptable.

In theory, then, in some institutions a candidate with an acceptable thesis could be asked to undergo a second viva (or written examination) on the basis of an unsatisfactory viva performance. In practice though, such a situation is likely to be rare, and in undertaking the research for this book we came across no such cases. However, this does not mean that there are none, and candidates, examiners and supervisors should be mindful of the regulation where it exists.

Limits of a policy perspective

To sum up, the policies of institutions stipulate that the viva is a compulsory component of the PhD examination (albeit with some exceptions). However, institutional policies vary in terms of what criteria candidates must meet in order to satisfy examiners in the viva and in terms of whether a candidate can 'fail' a viva even if the thesis is judged to be a pass.

As far as we are aware, no research has been undertaken in the UK to explore whether external examiners read and take note of institutional policy when examining a PhD. Anecdotal evidence, however, suggests that many do not. Some examiners assume that institutional policies are all roughly the same. They are not. Other examiners work within their own particular framework and are reluctant to work within any others. These points are discussed further in Chapter 5. Research by Mullins and Kiley (2002) in Australia revealed that only one-third of the examiners in their sample took institution-specific criteria into account when assessing PhD theses. The main point to note here is that we cannot rely on institutional policy alone when considering the purposes of the viva. The purposes of a viva are shaped largely by the ways in which examiners approach their role; these approaches may be influenced to some degree by institutional policies, but they are shaped to a larger extent by the examiners' own views about the purposes of the oral. As such, we now move beyond institutional policy to explore the perceptions of examiners. We also explore the views of candidates, as it is important also to consider the ways in which candidates interpret and perceive the viva's purposes – the 'intended' and the 'received' purposes are sometimes at odds with one another. We begin by outlining briefly the main roles attributed to the viva by academics and candidates and then move on to discuss these roles in full.

Academics' perspectives of the roles of the viva

In our research, responses from lecturers to a question about how they perceived the roles of the PhD viva produced an interesting and diverse range of answers. The data suggest that the roles of the viva are not exclusively linked to the examination of the candidate but that they may also be developmental and ritualistic. There was no consensus about the purposes of the viva; no criterion was mentioned by more than 40 per cent of academics. Usually, academics cited a number of roles, the main ones, which are discussed in detail later in this chapter, are listed below (percentages in brackets indicate the proportion of academics in our questionnaire survey who gave this type of response).

- The viva allows the examiners to check the candidate's understanding and ability to produce and present research to PhD standard (36 per cent).
- It clarifies areas of weakness (32 per cent).
- It ensures authenticity (31 per cent).
- It allows the examiners to develop further the candidate's ideas and to provide advice on publication (25 per cent).
- It checks that the candidate can 'defend' her/his thesis (24 per cent).
- It enables the examiners to test the candidate on their knowledge of the broader literature (the relevant sub-discipline field and how they are placed within it) (22 per cent).
- It allows the examiners to test the candidate's oral skills (11 per cent).
- It can be a site of final decision making in borderline cases (11 per cent).
- It acts as a 'rite of passage'/ritual (6 per cent).

Candidates' perspectives of the roles of the viva

> To scare the living daylights out of a poor unsuspecting student!
> (PhD student, Physics)

Like the academics in our research, candidates identified a number of different purposes of the viva. However, what differentiated the responses of candidates from those of the academics was that candidates stressed two roles in particular: (1) authentication of the thesis and (2) a range of examination activities. The responses of candidates suggested quite clearly that, for the vast majority of them, the viva is regarded overwhelmingly as a form of summative assessment – to '*assess* candidate's knowledge without computer/books to aid them. To *assess* authenticity of thesis' (PhD student, Engineering, our emphasis). The emphasis by candidates on examination functions is not surprising, but it is useful for candidates to reflect upon the range of formative roles that the viva may also serve. Whilst most academics undoubtedly saw summative assessment as an important feature of vivas, they were more likely than candidates to attribute formative roles to it as well. Interestingly, although most PhDs in Australia are examined without a viva, Mullins and Kiley (2002) also found a distinction between the views of Australian examiners and candidates about the purposes of PhD examining.

2.2 Exploring key purposes of the viva

In this section we discuss the purposes of the viva that have been flagged in the chapter so far. The section is divided into three parts according to whether the purposes of the viva are principally related to (1) examination, (2) development of the candidate and her/his work, (3) ritual.

Examination

Authentication of the thesis

> It is difficult to cheat in oral examinations.
>
> > (Morley *et al.* 2002: 269)

The viva should always serve as a site for authenticating the thesis. In other words, the examiners should ensure that the candidate is the author of the thesis and that s/he has undertaken the work presented in it. This role of the viva was mentioned frequently by our academics, for example: 'to confirm that the candidate was the author of the thesis' (Lecturer, English); 'test for plagiarism or personation' (Reader, Government); 'To check that the work is their own and not due 100 per cent to their supervisor' (Professor, Accounting and Finance). Examiners are often asked on their final (post-viva) report form to confirm that they are satisfied that the thesis presented is the candidate's own work. In a sense, authentication is a by-product of other viva processes: candidates authenticate the thesis by displaying detailed knowledge of the thesis, discussing methodological issues in-depth, demonstrating specialist knowledge of the area and so on. In Chapter 10 we discuss what it means for candidates to 'know the thesis'.

In line with the views expressed by many academics, most candidates also saw authentication as an important role of the viva. The question 'In your view, what purpose was served by your viva', commonly evoked the following sorts of comment:

> Obviously it confirmed that I did the work – I was able to answer the questions they had.
>
> > (Shaun, PhD student, Engineering)

> (laughs) Well, . . . I was thinking this and really you could actually get somebody else to do it for you couldn't you? I guess . . . it's kind of an

assurance that you are actually *au fait* with the arguments and the material, and the claims you are making are actually stemming from your own thoughts on the matter, rather than you just managed to find a really obscure internet site and downloaded it [the thesis].

(Angela, PhD student, Women's Studies)

Well, to be honest I don't know why we've got vivas apart from being able to see that it's your own work because otherwise anyone could write it, couldn't they?

(Jan, PhD student, Religious Studies)

Can the candidate tell the story? Is it the candidate's own work? And because I work with students as well, I've read pieces of work where I've doubted the veracity of it, [I've thought] that it's been heavily plagiarized and I've had students in and generally my suspicions have been proven correct. And I think you can find out because people just can't tell the story, dead simple. So that's one of the purposes: is it the candidate's own work?

(Douglas, PhD student, Sociology)

First of all it made sure that I wrote the thing and it would have been apparent in the first five minutes if I hadn't written it.

(Bob, PhD student, Chemistry)

Whilst the viva is always important for authenticating the thesis, it is particularly important when the candidate has been conducting her/his PhD research by working as part of a team. Team working is more common in the natural sciences than it is in arts, humanities or social sciences (see Delamont *et al.* 1997b, 2000). In cases where there has been team working the examiners may pay particular attention to the contribution of the individual to the project, and probe the candidate to ensure that her/his contribution is worthy of a PhD. In some cases, examiners are asked explicitly to comment on these issues in their final reports. For example, at the University of Brighton (2002a: 1) examiners are asked: 'In the case of a candidate whose research programme was part of a collaborative group project, did the oral examination demonstrate that the candidate's own contribution was worthy of the award?'

However, whilst team working is more common in natural sciences than it is in arts, humanities or social sciences, authentication is an important role of the viva in all disciplines. In some cases, examiners are concerned to ensure that the supervisor has not been overly involved in the thesis. For example, a lecturer in the social sciences told us a purpose of the viva is 'to establish that the thesis is in fact the candidate's own work. This was important in the case referred to above [earlier in the questionnaire], as the candidate had already published two papers based on her thesis co-authored with her supervisor'. Similar concerns were expressed by a professor of economics who told us that in the viva she is 'looking for confirmation that the thesis is, indeed, the work of the student – that he/she is not simply being told what to do'. See Box 2.3 for a discussion of issues raised about authentication when candidates are notified pre-viva of topics that will be discussed.

Locate the PhD research in the broader context
In our policy survey, those institutions that provided criteria specifically for the viva all stated that the candidate should be able to locate her/his PhD research in the broader context. This was also a purpose of the viva that was mentioned relatively frequently amongst our sample of academics.

> To allow the examiners to question issues arising from the submission and for the candidate to support the thesis in a broader context than is normally possible within the submission (i.e. to discuss and respond to questions and the relevant work of others in the same field).
>
> (Senior Lecturer, Music)

> Ensuring that the candidate not only knows the research reported in the thesis but is able to locate this in a wider field of knowledge.
>
> (Professor, Art History)

> [The] candidate should be able to show general knowledge and be able to explain the contribution of the thesis.
>
> (Professor, Economics)

This purpose was mentioned less frequently by our sample of candidates than it was by our academics, although some candidates did mention it. For example, a pharmacy candidate told us that the viva acts 'as independent verification that you have performed and understood the research within a wider scientific context'. Andrew, a physiotherapy candidate, commented that he was asked very specific, as well as 'broader context', questions: 'It [the viva] was pretty comprehensive, it went down to even the smallest detail of cellular activity of the muscle . . . and to much more global generalization about how in general we thought that might impact on clinical practice.' The 'broader context' is rather difficult to define, and is likely to be conceptualized differently by different people. A candidate from chemistry, Bob, was rather surprised when in his viva one of the examiners got out a research paper and told Bob to read and comment on it. This is one example, albeit unusual, of a way in which an examiner tested, amongst other things, a candidate's knowledge and understanding of the 'broader context'. After this experience, Bob suggested to us that candidates should be aware of general issues that are central to their field: 'People could fall down on the fundamentals of their subject because you've been doing what you've been doing for so long you forget the fundamental points. Make sure you're aware of those as well as what you've done.' Another challenging 'broader context' question was put to a candidate in astronomy; the candidate was asked in the viva to derive Eddington's luminosity limit. According to an established academic in the field, this is a very challenging 'broader context' question even for very strong candidates.

Check understanding and ability to produce and present research to PhD standard
As with authentication and contextualization, displaying knowledge of the thesis is a common requirement for the viva amongst institutions that provide criteria. Comments from academics in our research illuminate and explain what this might mean in practice:

> To test whether the candidate understands and can justify and defend content. To explore and test areas of doubt and uncertainty.
>
> (Professor, Accounting and Finance)

> To ensure that the candidate understood all that he had written and was intellectually original and adroit in his knowledge of the field.
>
> (Professor, Linguistics)

> Test depth of candidate's knowledge.
>
> (Professor, Economics)

> Absolutely crucial for testing candidate's full understanding, for enquiring further about, for example, research methodology and practice . . . for engaging candidate in an in-depth intellectual discussion on her/his subject.
>
> (Professor, Spanish)

> To find out whether they *fundamentally* understand the research they carried out. To distinguish between the roles of 'researcher' and 'research assistant'.
>
> (Senior Lecturer, Economics)

Some candidates in our sample also mentioned this role as a key purpose of the viva. Again, quotes from our candidates give a flavour of what they mean by this and how it was 'tested' in their vivas. The question that we asked candidates (post-viva) was: 'In your view, what purposes were served by your viva?'

> That's a big question . . . the main thing they want you to display is that you understand what you've written and why you've written it and where it fits into the scheme of your discipline.
>
> (Carla, PhD student, Art History)

> Well, pretty much it was all to show that I understood, that I had a clear understanding of what my research was about, where it could potentially go, rather than just getting examined on things which I could have looked up in a library book.
>
> (Dan, PhD student, Chemistry)

Defend the thesis

The notion that students should 'defend' their thesis suggests that it will be 'attacked'; this is not always the case and many examiners (although not all) try hard to make the viva as non-confrontational as possible. However, the viva does provide examiners with an opportunity to attack aspects of the thesis, or, in less aggressive terms, to question, probe and explore. Again, quotes from our academic respondents provide insights into what 'defend the thesis' might mean in practice. How to 'defend' the thesis is discussed further in Chapters 10 and 11.

> To provide the student with an opportunity to defend his or her thesis; to respond to criticism; and to discuss what he or she sees as 'problems' with interested experts.
>
> (Senior Lecturer, Social Policy and Social Work)

> To demonstrate knowledge and defend techniques of hypothesis testing and results.
>
> (Professor, Health Policy)

> To clarify problems arising in the text; to test the student's ability to justify (where there was any doubt in the text) arguments. To vindicate/salvage the thesis if in doubt in the text. To defend the thesis presented in the text, in general and particular.
>
> (Lecturer, Religions and Theology)

> Ability to defend in an articulate manner the case argued in the thesis.
>
> (Professor, Economic History)

> To allow the candidate to defend questionable aspects.
>
> (Senior Lecturer, Music)

Comments from some of our candidates also indicate ways in which they felt that they had been expected to defend and justify the arguments and ideas presented in their theses, and that this defence was a key purpose of the oral examination.

> You have to be able to justify your choices, like where you set the boundaries . . . And if you didn't explore something you have to be able to justify why not. So you have to . . . justify the parameters of your discourse, but also . . . situate it in some way as to 'OK, well why did you do it in the first place?'
>
> (Carla, PhD student, Art History)

> Oral presentation/defence of research undertaken to more experienced peers, who, although only working in related fields, are sufficiently knowledgeable and academically skilled to judge the quality, originality and worth of a student's work as being of PhD standard, based upon the written thesis.
>
> (PhD student, Science)

To challenge students on queries/concerns examiners may have – to assess whether students can substantiate argument and respond to challenges.

(PhD student, Social Policy and Social Work)

To test the candidate's ability to orally defend his/her research and to explore in greater depth some of the ideas presented in the thesis.

(PhD student, History)

At its very core must be a requirement of the author to demonstrate not only that he did in fact produce the thesis but further that the line of argument so advanced is one which he both understands and is capable of defending from reasoned criticism.

(PhD student, History)

An opportunity to both defend and discuss your work with interested and expert parties.

(PhD student, English)

The language of defence does imply a need to respond to aggression, and some candidates experienced an aggressive and confrontational viva that they were unhappy about: the viva was 'not friendly', 'challenging' and 'very confrontational' (PhD student, Biology). However, other candidates suggested that they found the opportunity to defend and discuss their work very beneficial: 'Personally the ability to defend [my] thesis increased my confidence in my work' (PhD student, Biology). Whilst in both of these cases the candidates were required to defend the thesis, whether this is a positive or negative experience depends very often on the tone of the viva and the styles and agendas of the examiners (see Chapters 3 and 12).

The viva as a site of final decision making in borderline cases

Allow 'borderline' students the opportunity to defend themselves.

(Lecturer, Economics)

Later in this chapter we present and discuss our evidence that suggests that the viva is not usually the key site of decision making in the PhD examination process. However, the exception to this is usually cases where the thesis is judged by the examiners to be 'borderline' (the way in which the examiners' assessment of the thesis shapes the viva is discussed in Chapter 4). In these cases, the defence of the thesis (discussed above) may be particularly important: '*If* the thesis is doubtful, to allow candidate to defend it' (Professor, History).

Clarification of obscurities and areas of weakness

Clearing up statements/facts/issues unclear on reading the thesis.

(Professor, History)

Many examiners see the viva as an opportunity for them to probe candidates about areas of the thesis that they consider to be weak or unclear. For example, a professor of economic history saw the viva as important because it allows candidates to 'clarify obscure passages'. Another professor (of health economics) suggested that the viva is important 'to enable the candidate to explain any parts of the thesis that may be controversial/ambiguous/in need of further possible work'.

This purpose of the viva overlaps with the 'defence' of the thesis discussed above. Examiners in the viva can explore aspects of the thesis that they identified as 'weak' when reading it, and ask candidates to explain and clarify and/ or justify and 'defend' these aspects. A professor of social anthropology made this explicit: 'to ascertain whether perceived weaknesses in the thesis are genuine or not, and if they are genuine, to get the candidate to see them and to give advice on necessary revisions'. In some cases, the candidate may convince the examiners that perceived weaknesses are not 'genuine'. The following English candidate seemed rather proud that her 'defence' of the thesis was clearly convincing for the examiner: '[the purpose of the PhD viva is] to allow a defence of the argument and the opportunity for open discussion. I was able to persuade the external examiner that two aspects of the thesis he has reservations about were valid – surely a prime purpose of the viva?'

Checking understanding is not all a one-way process, however. The viva can also serve as an opportunity for candidates to check that the examiners have understood their intended meanings, as a senior lecturer in philosophy wrote: the viva 'satisfies the candidate that the examiners have read the thesis carefully and understood the arguments'. It is important to remember that the viva is a two-way process.

Test oral skills

> To allow the candidate to present key aspects of their work verbally.
> (Lecturer, Psychology)

As the name indicates, the viva is an oral examination. The candidate's verbal skills are, therefore, either explicitly or implicitly crucial to the examiners' assessment of the candidate. The centrality of verbal skills is evident in the frequent reference to the candidate being able to 'defend' their thesis and 'clarify' aspects of their work.

Whether a candidate's verbal skills are interpreted by examiners as an indicator of other competences is not certain. However, a few of our academic respondents did make an explicit connection between verbal and intellectual skills: 'Articulate thoughts mean articulate words, i.e. an oral examination offers evidence of the candidate's ability to think independently and originally' (Professor, Arts and Humanities).

Gatekeeping

The PhD examination is arguably one of the most formal and explicit gatekeeping processes operating within academia. A gatekeeper is a person who 'determines who is allowed into a particular community and who remains excluded' (Becher 1989: 60). A PhD is a gateway into academia; whilst it does not guarantee access to an academic post, increasingly a lack of one bars the path of most would-be academics. The gatekeeping function of the viva was mentioned by a few of the academics in our survey. For example, a professor of history told us the purpose of the viva 'varies between subjects. In my subject, it is to hone research, writing, exposition skills and produce a scholarly piece for *admission to the field*' (our emphasis). Gatekeepers, in this case PhD examiners, can also operate with problematic personal/political agendas – we discuss this further in Chapters 3 and 5.

Box 2.3　Issue in focus

ADVANCE WARNING

Some of you may be surprised to learn that at the University of Brighton candidates may be informed a few days before their PhD viva of the key points that the examiners will address in the examination. Is this a good idea that should be adopted on a widespread basis or does it undermine the examination? As you can imagine, views are divided. At the heart of the debate is the question 'how are the purposes of the viva best met?'

Those in favour of the 'open' practice argue that this practice (1) facilitates informed discussion that enables the candidate to get the most from the experience and (2) makes the candidate more relaxed and allows them to reflect carefully on the principal topics that the examiners want to address.

> What you want to have in the viva examination is a rigorous discussion of issues . . . that shouldn't be in any way constrained by the fact that the candidates might find the format or the occasion or some of the questions so surprising that they couldn't respond . . . If the viva is to debate some substantive issue that you think is weak, the fact that the person has had a chance to think about it beforehand is not necessarily a bad thing . . . You're more likely to have a better discussion and you're likely to be able to tell whether the person is capable of revising the thesis.
>
> (Professor, Media Studies)

BPS/UCoSDA (1995: 13) also suggest that it can be appropriate to make a list of key topics available to the candidate before the viva, 'so that he or she may have a short period of time to reflect alone on these issues, without access to materials other than his/her written submission'.

Arguments against the 'open' practice include: (1) good candidates should be able to 'think on their feet' and respond to questions – this is one of the 'tests' of the examination; (2) a key purpose of the viva is to authenticate the thesis and this may be undermined by pre-release of topics; (3) some candidates may be given more information from examiners than others and this introduces disparities.

As you can see, these arguments often hinge upon different views about the key purposes of the viva.

Development

Basic development – explore ways in which the thesis could be raised to PhD standard
In cases where the thesis is not judged to be at doctoral standard but where the examiners feel that it could be raised to the required standard by extra work, the viva can have a very important developmental role. Morley *et al.* (2002: 270) point out that examiners sometimes complain that the viva is increasingly taking on this developmental role because 'uncooked' theses are being submitted in order to meet research council deadlines. In cases where the thesis is not judged to be of doctoral standard, the examiners might spend a lot of the viva discussing with the candidate aspects of the thesis that are not satisfactory, and exploring ways in which the candidate can work to improve it. This role was reflected in the comments of a number of our academic respondents:

Enable candidate to see ways to strengthen the work.
(Professor, Theology)

To be able to indicate in detail how to improve the thesis.
(Professor, Government)

To give candidate chance to defend position where weak and to help clarify necessary areas for revision where appropriate.
(Lecturer, Theology)

A few of our candidates also felt that this could, in some cases, be an important and productive role of the viva. For example, Andrew (Physiotherapy), who had to undertake corrections to his thesis after his viva, said that:

I think the thesis is now stronger and better because of the viva and you get a certain amount of confidence from having to prove yourself to two people that you can do it . . . I think the ultimate thing is, and I wanted really to hang on to this, that I think the thesis is better, it's a stronger thesis now for having the discussion and also some interesting points they made.

Advanced development – when the thesis meets PhD standard

In addition to acting as an examiner your external will also, if you are successful, act as your publicist. The examination is therefore an opportunity to strike up a good working relationship on which you can later draw for references and in particular for recommendations when approaching academic publishers.

(Burnham 1994: 31)

Advanced developmental roles come to the fore when examiners judge a thesis to meet PhD standards. Many academics in our sample suggested that the viva offers an opportunity for successful candidates to receive guidance on the publication of their thesis or aspects of it: 'to advise on publication plans' (Professor, Archaeology). Publishing is crucial to the development of academic visibility and credibility and is, therefore, an essential feature of establishing oneself within an academic community. In her examination of the processes that are instrumental in determining the publication of research, Spender (1981) identifies gatekeepers as a primary obstacle to publishing. We suggest that PhD examiners, especially external examiners, also serve an important role in fostering or inhibiting the budding academic's attempts to get their work published.

Some of the academics in our sample were quite explicit about their role as a promoter of successful candidates: 'To establish post-viva relationship to help candidate's career' (Professor, Government). Others suggested that the candidate should make the most of this scarce opportunity for career and publishing advice: 'To give the candidate a chance to get feedback from scholars who have read her/his thesis attentively and carefully. This may well be the *only* time she receives such information/advice about future publications etc.' (Lecturer, Art History).

A number of our candidates also commented on the value of the viva for providing advice about publications and future career plans.

I think it's [the viva's] good because it can give you good ideas about future development and future work.

(Silvo, PhD student, Economics)

The external examiner recommended a number of areas that would merit publishing and encouraged me to do it sooner rather than later.

(Nigel, PhD student, Nursing)

I think the very important thing [to come out of the viva] since I plan to publish the thesis is that I got some idea of the way in which I should change it in order to make it better. So that, I thought, was very important, and also some suggestions concerning some other literature at which I can look and whereby I can extend my argument which was also good.

(Sorrel, PhD student, Government)

The viva can also provide a potentially valuable and rare opportunity for a candidate to discuss her/his work with an 'interested expert'. As one history candidate put it: 'To talk about the work of a lifetime!' A geography candidate described it as a 'once in a lifetime opportunity' as 'there are few ways in which you can get someone at the top of your field to spend considerable time evaluating and discussing your work'. This role was also reflected in the comments of some of the academics: 'To give her/him the pleasure (hopefully) of discussing the thesis topic at length with someone who has expertise in the field and has read it [the thesis] carefully' (Professor, Social Policy). So the viva is viewed by some examiners as a reward for (successful) candidates after many years of hard work.

Ritual/rites of passage

In some countries the purpose of the viva is principally ritualistic (see Box 2.4 for an example of a viva in Sweden). Whilst ritual is not necessarily the *primary* purpose in the UK, it can be *a* purpose in some cases. Several academics specifically mentioned that the viva can be a rite of passage that serves as an entry into an academic community:

[The viva acts] as a rite of passage into the guild of academics.

(Professor, Arts and Humanities)

It is a genuine 'rite of passage'.

(Professor, Linguistics)

Perhaps most important, especially in successful cases, as a rite of passage.

(Senior Lecturer, Economic History)

Some candidates also spoke about the viva as a rite of passage, although this was by no means a common response. A few candidates spoke about this in positive terms, for example: 'Mine also felt like a movement of credibility/competence from student to colleague' (PhD student, Sociology). However, other candidates (a small minority) were negative about the rituals sometimes associated with the viva.

[The purpose of the viva is] to subject the candidate to the most unnecessary form of misery and humiliation possible. Then, to check that they really are responsible for the work presented for examination. Finally, to remind the candidate that they have a long way to go before they can achieve the superior knowledge of senior academics. I have never felt more of a failure *and* a fraud than when I passed this examination.

(PhD student, English and American Studies)

From my experience, however, it looks as though the purpose is to harass certain students and encourage some others.

(PhD student, Economics)

Perhaps to make me suffer a bit for induction into the 'Guild of Doctors'.

(PhD student, Computer Science)

Box 2.4   Case study

A SWEDISH DISPUTATION

by Professor Stuart Powell, University of Hertfordshire

I was invited to be an opponent at a disputation at a leading Swedish university. In fact, initial contact was made in the context of 'examining a PhD'. As events unravelled it became clear that I was engaging in a process very different from that in the UK. Of course, the Swedish model of doctoral assessment is much closer to mainstream European practice than is the UK version. I report the experience from a personal perspective – the candidate was male and therefore I use the masculine form wherever appropriate. Universities within Sweden vary slightly in their approach and therefore what is described here is a specific example to indicate a more general trend.

I was invited to be an opponent rather than an examiner. The opponent does not have a formal role in the process of decision making about the success or otherwise of the candidate – an examination team of three academics did this (one internal, one from a different faculty in the university and one from another Swedish university).

- As opponent, I was the only questioner (though any members of the audience, including the formal examination team, could ask questions after my interrogation was completed). I was also charged with summarizing the thesis for the audience before the questioning began.
- The purpose of the questioning was to allow the candidate to demonstrate his knowledge and expertise.
- It was extremely unlikely that the thesis would fail. The work had already been given peer approval (both within the department and, at least partially, by refereed publications). The preliminary information sent prior to the event indicated 'it is very rare for a Swedish thesis to be rejected after formal defence'.
- There was an element of entertainment about the whole procedure. It was made clear to me beforehand that I would need to keep the audience interested by my questions, and it was suggested that I should wear academic dress if possible to 'add to the sense of occasion'.
- The thesis comprised an introductory text and four papers that had been either published or submitted for publication.

As the event unfolded it became clear that there were powerful sub-texts. The sense of occasion and rite of passage was palpable. I contributed to this by being from overseas and by wearing academic robes. The line to be trodden between 'scientific rigour' and not undermining the candidate's thesis was fine but distinct. There was an audible sense of approval at a 'difficult' question (one that at least sounded erudite) and a sense of relaxation at a successful answer; there was an even stronger sense of approval when the opponent acknowledged the accomplishment of the candidate in producing such an answer. The three examiners sat in the audience and asked questions after the interrogation had finished. The examiners' meeting followed the interrogation and was held during lunch; the supervisor attended. Whilst it was clear that the result was not really in question, the meeting was conducted formally and, again, with a distinct sense of occasion.

An earlier version of this case study appeared in a UK Council for Graduate Education newsletter (1999).

2.3 Is the viva always an examination?

Although the viva serves different purposes there should always be an element of examination, even if the thesis is judged by the examiners to be excellent. As a minimum, the viva should serve to examine that the candidate has actually undertaken the work presented in the thesis: that is, it should *authenticate* the thesis.

However, our research revealed practices that call into question the notion that the viva is always an examination. Our questionnaires to candidates revealed that 32 per cent were informed of their examiners' decision at the start of the viva. There were, however, notable discipline differences regarding this practice: 47 per cent of candidates in the arts, humanities or social sciences were informed of the examiners' decision at the start of the viva compared with only 15 per cent in the natural or applied sciences. When candidates are told the examiners' decision at the start of the viva, it is clear that the viva is not then a part of the examination process. There are two main problems with this approach:

- The viva should serve as a site for authenticating the thesis. If the examiners tell the candidate that s/he has passed but then they become doubtful as the viva progresses that the work was actually conducted by the candidate, the examiners would be placed in a very difficult position. For this reason, it is risky for an examiner to declare unreservedly at the start of a viva that a candidate has passed.
- For the reason cited above, some examiners will not release a (provisional) decision at the start of a viva, even if they judge the thesis to be excellent. Variations in practice within and between institutions mean that candidates do not know how to interpret the 'silence' when examiners make no comment about their decision at the start of a viva. See Chapters 11 and 12 for further discussion.

Is the viva usually the key site of decision making?

> Decisions about passing and failing a PhD are largely made on the basis of the examiners' reading of the thesis.
>
> (Lecturer, Art History)

Questionnaires to examiners indicated that the viva was not, in the majority of cases, the site of decision making: 'Normally, a decision could be made without a viva but just occasionally, depending on the thesis, [the viva] can make a difference' (Professor, Social Policy). Forty per cent of examiners (internal and external) said that the decision about the thesis was made before the viva. Furthermore, in 74 per cent of cases the candidate's performance in the viva served merely to confirm the examiners' opinion of the candidate's work.

> I have never known a viva result in an examiner changing his/her mind about the result, in over 50 vivas; nor do I see how it could.
>
> (Professor, Arts and Humanities)

> [The purpose of the viva is] to confirm the judgement made on the basis of reading the thesis.
>
> (Professor, English)

> I have been involved as external in three cases where the PhD was failed. On each occasion the viva *confirmed* clearly that there was fundamental misunderstanding or ignorance of key methodological issues.
>
> (Professor, Economics)

Where the viva did influence the examiners it did not necessarily alter their decision. The exceptions were usually cases where the candidate/thesis was regarded by the examiners as borderline. For example, a professor of arts and humanities told us: 'in one case where the thesis was referred a good performance helped convince the examiners that the candidate was indeed capable of achieving doctorate standard through [thesis] revisions'. In the majority of cases, however, the viva merely serves to confirm a decision made on the basis of reading the thesis.

2.4 Summary

In order to understand PhD vivas one needs to explore their purposes. This chapter has considered the key purposes set out in institutional policy. Such policies vary in terms of the stated purposes of, and criteria for, the viva. We concluded that institutional policies can provide only a limited and partial framework for understanding the purposes that PhD vivas serve in practice. In practice, the views of examiners are most important in shaping the purposes of vivas, and so we explored in detail the range of key purposes outlined by the academics in our sample. In recognition that examiners' intentions about purposes and candidates' 'received' understandings are sometimes at odds, we also mapped out candidates' perspectives. For both examiners and candidates the key purposes fell into three broad categories: examination, development and ritual. We finished the chapter by noting that whilst examination functions are important aspects of (most) vivas, the viva is not usually the key site of decision making about the outcome of the examination process.

This chapter has explored examiners' perspectives about PhD vivas in general. It is clear that an individual examiner's views about purpose will shape the way that s/he approaches a viva. Whilst, in general, examiners see vivas as serving a blend of examination, development and ritual purposes, the purposes that predominate in any individual viva will be determined by: (1) the examiners' assessment of the thesis, (2) the examiners' knowledge expectations, (3) examining styles, (4) examiners' personal/political agendas, and (5) interpersonal dynamics. Each of these factors is explained and explored in the next chapter. That chapter moves to the second stage in our quest to understand the viva by exploring how vivas work.

3

Understanding the Doctoral Viva – How does it work?

Chapter overview

Attempting to understand the PhD viva is a two-stage process. In the previous chapter we considered stage one – understanding the range of purposes that PhD vivas serve. Stage two – which is the focus of this chapter – involves understanding how vivas work. Understanding both the range of purposes of the viva, and how vivas work, is crucial if candidates and examiners are to approach the viva in well-prepared and productive ways.

If you have not yet read Chapter 2 we advise you to do so before proceeding with this chapter.

Students   ☺☺☺   Examiners   ☺☺☺
Supervisors ☺☺☺   Chairs   ☺☺☺

Chapter contents

3.1 Components of a viva

In the previous chapter we explored key purposes of the viva. These purposes were categorized according to whether they related principally to examination, development or ritual. We concluded by saying that the examiners' views about the purposes of the viva are of particular importance in shaping it. Whilst, in general, examiners see vivas as serving a blend of the three purposes (examination, development and ritual), the purposes that predominate in any *specific* case will be determined largely by five factors. These are: (1) the examiners' assessments of the thesis; (2) the examiners' knowledge expectations; (3) examining styles; (4) examiners' personal/political agendas and (5) interpersonal dynamics. A sixth factor that shapes the viva is its structure: the fact that it is an oral examination. These factors are explored in this chapter, as they are crucial to understanding how vivas work.

The six factors shaping vivas are mapped out in Table 3.1. We suggest that these factors, which are cross-cut by the more general viva purposes outlined in Chapter 2 (examination, development, ritual), affect the way that an individual viva works by shaping its key components. These key components are skills, content and conduct.

Table 3.1   Factors shaping the viva components, with cross-cutting key purposes

Factors shaping the components[a]	*Key purposes*			*Viva components*
Structure of the viva – an oral examination				Skills
Examiners' assessments of the thesis – pass, borderline/refer, fail	Examination	Development	Ritual	Content
Examiners' knowledge expectations – what PhD candidates should know				
Examining styles – type of academic exchange the examiners expect PhD candidates to manage				
Examiners' personal/political agendas				Conduct
Interpersonal dynamics in the viva				

Note:
[a] Examiners' views on content and conduct can be informed or regulated by university and/or professional guidelines.

Source: Adapted from Tinkler and Jackson 2002: 89

In identifying common key components of vivas we are not presenting a model of a uniform viva. Far from it. Our model attempts to capture the complexities of individual viva examinations. We believe that if candidates are able to identify the key components of the viva, and recognize the factors that shape them, then they are well placed to work out how to prepare effectively for the oral examination (discussed in Chapters 4, 9 and 10). Candidates need to match their training and preparation to the different viva components, rather like the way in which a triathlete trains for the particular elements of a triathlon. If triathletes do not identify correctly and understand the different elements involved (swimming, cycling and running), they may train inappropriately and so find themselves unprepared for the specific demands on the day. The same applies to the PhD viva. This chapter outlines and discusses the different viva components and the ways in which they are shaped, as a prelude to considering viva preparation in later chapters.

Figure 3.1 Understand the challenges you face – misjudging what is required may leave you ill prepared on the day. © Mario Chin

3.2 Skills

The skills element is determined largely by the structural requirements of the viva and is probably the least variable element of it. By structural requirements, we mean that the viva is always an oral examination. As such, the candidate's verbal skills are explicitly or implicitly crucial to the examiners' assessments of the candidate. The centrality of verbal skills is evident in the frequent reference in university policies to candidates being able to 'defend' their thesis and 'clarify' aspects of their work.

The 'skills' component requires candidates to:

- 'think on their feet' usually without recourse to notes, books or advisors;
- perform/communicate clearly whilst under pressure;
- explain and justify/defend their work, interpretations and ideas during the viva (which also acts to authenticate the thesis).

3.3 Content

The 'content' component of the viva is shaped by (1) the examiners' assessment of the thesis and (2) their knowledge expectations. The 'content' component of the viva usually requires candidates to:

- authenticate the thesis;
- locate the PhD research in the broader context;
- clarify aspects of the thesis;
- develop ideas;
- justify/defend aspects of the thesis;
- reflect critically on their work.

See Chapter 2 for discussion of these.

Examiners' assessments of the thesis

An important factor shaping most, if not all, vivas is the examiners' assessments of the thesis. This shaping factor is explicit in British Psychological Society/Universities and Colleges' Staff Development Unit (BPS/UCoSDA) guidelines on PhDs: the oral examination 'serves different functions for candidates of differing qualities' (1995: 11). In general, candidates are judged, on the basis of reading the thesis, to be either strong/successful students, borderline cases or very weak candidates. The ways that examiners approach vivas are shaped by this assessment. For example, one lecturer in politics wrote that the purpose of the viva:

> Depends.
> 1. If [the] thesis is a clear pass → gives opportunity to discuss issues/ argument and give advice to candidate re. publication.
> 2. If unclear/referral → opportunity for candidate to defend/explain priorities and examiners to make decisions re. pass/fail or nature of referral.

We have identified three basic types of viva depending on the assessment of the thesis – these are summarized in Table 3.2 and discussed below.

Table 3.2 Model of the key purposes of vivas depending upon the examiners' assessments of the thesis

Examiners' assessments of the thesis	Key purposes of the viva
Good thesis	The viva is used to authenticate the thesis, explore the broader context, clarify points, develop ideas and offer advice on publication
Borderline/referred thesis	The viva is used to authenticate the thesis and to: 1. decide whether the candidate has done sufficient research of an appropriate standard to produce a thesis for the award of PhD 2. decide whether the candidate understands and can reflect critically on their research, and the broader context, in ways that are appropriate at PhD level 3. explore ways in which the thesis can be raised to PhD standard
Failed thesis/award of lower degree	The viva is used to confirm the fail and explore why the candidate has failed. The examiners will also determine whether a lower award is appropriate, for example, an MPhil

Good thesis

If the thesis is judged to be good, the viva is frequently used to authenticate the thesis, clarify and develop points, and provide the candidate with advice and guidance. In general, it is used for 'advanced developmental' purposes (see Chapter 2). This set of purposes was identified by a lot of our respondents who said that the viva should provide 'good' candidates with valuable experience and information and provide an opportunity for her/him to discuss and develop ideas with an expert in the field. The viva should also offer an opportunity for such candidates to receive guidance on the publication of their thesis: 'to discuss ideas for further development of the research, including publication' (Senior Lecturer, Government). It should also be a valuable and enjoyable experience for the candidate: 'giving the candidate some stimulating and enjoyable feedback on the work which has probably occupied them for the past three years' (Professor, Social Policy).

Borderline/referred thesis

For a candidate whose thesis is judged to be borderline or in need of further development, the viva is a forum within which examiners can provide constructive feedback and guidance: 'to provide constructive criticism of points regarded as weak' (Lecturer, Social Anthropology). Many of our respondents suggested that the viva allows borderline candidates the opportunity to defend their work.

Failed thesis/award of lower degree

In rare cases where the thesis is failed, the viva acts to confirm this and to explore why this has occurred. The examiners will also determine whether a lower award is appropriate, for example, an MPhil.

A more detailed discussion of the range of viva purposes is provided in Chapter 2.

Examiners' knowledge expectations

Whilst vivas are shaped by the examiners' assessments of the thesis, they are also shaped by the knowledge expectations of the examiners. By this, we mean what examiners expect PhD candidates to know and be able to demonstrate in the viva in order to be worthy of a PhD. In general, examiners' knowledge expectations can be divided into two types according to whether they relate to breadth or depth of knowledge.

Breadth
Alongside knowledge of their thesis, PhD candidates are also expected to display knowledge of the 'broader context'. However, as discussed in Chapter 2, 'broader context' is interpreted in different ways by examiners – discipline background can be influential here. What candidates are expected to know and demonstrate in the viva will depend on how the examiners define broader context, and how they 'test' knowledge of it. So, for example, in Chapter 2 we saw how Bob, a chemistry candidate, was asked to read and summarize a research paper in his viva. Shaun, an electronics candidate, commented on the types of broader knowledge expected in his discipline: 'one they like to do in electronics is [to ask] "how does a transistor work?" – something really basic and fundamental which may have nothing to do with your software project.' Although expectations about the breadth of knowledge required for a PhD may be shaped by discipline, it is also very much shaped by the individual examiners, their interests and their specific ideas about what doctoral graduates should know.

Depth
In addition to different expectations about breadth of knowledge, examiners also have different expectations and practices about the depth of knowledge that they expect candidates to demonstrate in the viva. Some candidates in our research reported 'very deep', 'high-level', 'heavy' questions in the viva, whilst others commented that the questions and discussion were rather superficial (depth of questioning in the viva is likely also to be shaped by the examiners' assessments of the thesis). In cases of the latter, some students felt rather disappointed that the questions were not very challenging and that the discussion was not sufficiently intense. Challenging though, does not

mean aggressive and hostile; there is an important distinction between 'depth' and 'tone'. Many candidates expect deep and engaging discussions about their work, and some are disappointed if they do not get them. No candidates in our research, however, wanted the 'tone' of the viva to be aggressive and hostile. Tone of the viva relates to conduct, and it is to this aspect that we now turn.

3.4 Conduct

> There are considerable variations in the conduct of the viva.
>
> (Phillips and Pugh 2000: 189)

'Conduct' refers to how the examiners behave in the viva and how the group – examiners, candidate and other participants – interact. The conduct of the viva is potentially the most variable aspect; it is also the least regulated. Only a few institutions provide conduct guidelines for vivas, but these are effective only if they are accompanied by mechanisms to ensure that they are adhered to. There are three sets of factors that shape the conduct of the viva: examining styles; examiners' personal/political agendas; and interpersonal dynamics.

Examining styles

Candidates are treated in different ways in the viva depending on the examiners' views of what types of academic exchanges a doctoral graduate should be able to manage (the examining style). Collectively, the styles of the examiners shape the tone of the viva. Examining style can reflect an individual view and/or it may represent assumptions about professional exchange that are specific to particular disciplines or cultures. A harsh examining style is portrayed by Wallace and Marsh (2001: 53–4): 'The viva is an ordeal, a baptism of fire. The external examiner, when challenged by Barbara's supervisor, insists that the candidate must learn to fight and take hard knocks as a preparation for the academic world.' Phillips (1994: 135) quotes an examiner who shares this view: '[the viva] is a *rite de passage* and as such should not be enjoyed but reasonably traumatic, so that one may look back at 50 on how hard a time one was given'. It is this type of style that Delamont *et al.* (1997a: 145) criticize in their guide to supervisors: 'a graduate student's examination is not the right place to practise the academic equivalent of the martial arts'.

Fortunately, it is probably fair to say that most examiners do not subscribe to the view espoused by Phillips' interviewee. Many examiners, whilst wanting to question and examine the candidate, will *not* regard the *raison d'être* of the viva as being to give the candidate a 'hard time' and to deliver 'hard knocks'. Many examiners attempt to make the tone of the viva as non-confrontational as possible, and aim for a relatively relaxed debate and discussion. For example, a professor of policy studies, told us that, 'I like it [the main dialogue in the viva] to be a kind of debate and conversation, not a medieval joust'.

In addition to the tone of the viva being determined largely by the examining style, so too is the pace. Some examiners prefer to work slowly and carefully in the viva, giving the candidate plenty of time to think and respond. Others provide the candidate with a constant barrage of questions and encourage relatively short, prompt responses. Angela, a women's studies candidate, told of the unrelenting nature of the questioning in her viva: 'it's just they [the questions] keep coming and coming and it's endless . . . It's very intense' (see also Chapter 11).

It is clear that examiners have very different examination styles, and that these are extremely influential in shaping the conduct of the viva. In the next chapter we discuss how candidates can equip themselves to handle these different styles. Now, though, we turn to another aspect that shapes the conduct of the viva, namely, the examiners' personal/political agendas.

The examiners' personal/political agendas

As a socially-constructed and contingent activity, the viva is a process of engagement in which multiple agendas are at work and the rules are more implicit than explicit and are only vaguely defined.

(Park 2004)

Candidates' accounts of their viva experiences suggest that the conduct of examiners in a viva is sometimes driven by personal/political agendas. These accounts must be treated with caution because PhD candidates are not privy to the intentions of examiners, and their accounts are often produced from positions of defensiveness and stress. Nevertheless, these candidates' views do reinforce accounts from academics which suggest that some examiners are motivated by non-academic agendas. These agendas, which are discussed in Chapter 5, can include:

- promotion of discriminatory beliefs and/or interests, such as the exclusion of specific social groups from the academy;
- pursuit of grudges against individuals;
- promotion of favourites;
- pleasure in making the relatively powerless PhD candidate suffer;
- jealousy;
- self-promotion and aggrandizement.

Baldacchino (1995: 73) for example, explains how: 'examiners may be more intent to impress, . . . rather than (or in preference to) listening to and engaging with the student. Examiners may feel that their reputation is at stake, unless they somehow prove to be more knowledgeable or to be capable of prising open an argument; hence, an element of critique may be indulged in perfunctorily.' Phillips (1994: 135) quotes one of her interviewees who has similar concerns: 'the problem with some academics is that they use whatever power they've got to demonstrate something about themselves. I'm concerned about the situation where the relationship is tied up with their own ego defence.'

One of our interviewees, Carla, told us that she was given quite explicit guidance by lecturers in her department about the types of personal agendas that may drive some academics, in this case, junior academics:

> . . . don't touch someone who's very young because they're going to want to prove themselves at your expense. So they [lecturers in her department] are like, don't take a junior anything, they'll be like 'this T isn't crossed' and it'll be more about them than you. So they said, 'Try to get someone established, and if you know their personality, great; but stay away from the junior people who are going to want to mess you about, basically.'
>
> (Carla, PhD student, Art History)

Whilst we would not endorse the view that all 'young' people should be avoided as examiners, it is worth bearing in mind that examiners are human beings and that their behaviour in vivas may be motivated, in part, by their own agenda. This agenda, like all other aspects of the content and conduct of the viva, does have implications for interpersonal dynamics.

Interpersonal dynamics

Interpersonal dynamics are constantly being produced by specific verbal and non-verbal communications within the viva, at the same time they provide frameworks within which group members interpret and respond to each other. These dynamics are extremely difficult to predict because they are unique to each group and to the specific and dynamic contexts in which members of the group interact. Carla, in advance of her viva, had worries about how the interpersonal dynamics would work.

> Oh boy, I'm hoping it won't turn into a big political cafuffle, because I guess I'm hoping that two people are professional enough not to get into something with each other. And the reason why I'm bringing that up is because, I think like Gail [the external examiner] is so established and I mean, Alison [the internal examiner] is doing well in the field as well. But she [Alison] is the junior person and I just hope they don't make it about each other and each other's work, do you know what I mean? So I'm worried about that a little bit – the extent to which power taking will come into it. And also Mary [supervisor] and Gail [external examiner], they're colleagues and they respect each other, but I get the sense they don't necessarily like each other. So I mean I don't want to be in the middle of that either. So there's a little bit of that worrying me. But other than that, in terms of my own work, I'm not worried about my

own work, I'm just more worried about whether or not they [the examiners] have the capacity to be fair.

In the event, the viva went very smoothly and the problematic interpersonal dynamics that Carla had feared were not evident. However, this is not always the case, and it is worth candidates being aware of how important interpersonal dynamics can be, and being prepared to handle these complex relations.

In some viva situations the interpersonal dynamics include the candidate's relationship to her/his supervisor (*if* the supervisor is permitted to attend – this varies between institutions – see Chapter 6). The experience recounted by Shaun, an engineering candidate, provides a graphic, if unusual, example of this:

> None of them spotted the one big mistake [in the thesis] in the viva. I pointed that out ... and obviously some discussion occurred ... in which my supervisor actually waded in and caused the most trouble ... He was arguing about the nature of the correction which I had to make on this mistake and I was adamant it was one thing and he was adamant it was another, and I just thought why don't you shut up, it doesn't really matter what you think, you're not examining this anyway.

3.5 Summary

In this chapter we explored the key factors shaping vivas. We grouped these shaping factors according to whether they influence principally the skills, content or conduct components of vivas. We argued that the general purposes of the viva set out in Chapter 2 (examination, development, ritual) will vary in specific cases according to: (1) the examiners' assessments of the thesis; (2) the examiners' knowledge expectations; (3) examining styles; (4) examiners' personal/political agendas; and (5) interpersonal dynamics. The examiners' assessments of the thesis and the examiners' knowledge expectations shape the content of the viva. Examining styles, examiners' personal/political agendas and viva interpersonal dynamics shape the conduct of the viva. The sixth factor, the structure of the viva – that it is an oral examination – shapes the skills component.

This breakdown of the viva into its components and the factors that shape them makes visible those aspects of the viva that candidates and supervisors can influence and prepare for, and those that are more difficult to control and predict. In Chapter 4 we utilize this model to explore and evaluate the ways in which candidates can undertake long-term preparation for the viva.

4

Viva Preparation – Long Term

Students should start preparing for the viva from day *one* of their PhD.

Chapter overview

Many candidates have expectations of the viva that are markedly different from their experience of it. This disjuncture comes about in part because their understanding of and preparations for the viva are inadequate. Many students erroneously believe that viva preparation should occur only after submission of the thesis. However, to be effective, preparation should commence on day *one* of the PhD process.

The previous two chapters were about understanding the viva. In Chapter 2 we explored the purposes of the viva and in Chapter 3 we looked at how vivas work. Candidates need to understand the viva to prepare well for it; they need to be able to identify the key viva components and recognize the factors that shape them. Candidates need to match their training and preparation to the different viva components, just as a triathlete trains for the elements of a triathlon. In this chapter, we utilize the model of the viva discussed in Chapter 3 to explore and evaluate the ways that candidates can undertake long-term preparation for the viva, that is, preparation *throughout* the PhD process. In Chapter 9 we discuss some short-term preparations for candidates, and in Chapter 10 we look at final-stage preparations. However, short-term and final-stage preparations should be undertaken in addition to, not instead of, long-term preparations.

We start this chapter with a brief reminder of the key components of the viva presented in Chapter 3.

Students   ☺☺☺   Supervisors   ☺☺☺

Chapter contents

4.1 Reminder of the key components of the viva

Skills

The 'skills' component of the viva requires candidates to:

- 'think on their feet';
- perform/communicate clearly whilst under pressure;
- explain and justify/defend their work, interpretations and ideas.

Content

The content component of the viva is shaped by (1) the examiners' assessment of the thesis and (2) their knowledge expectations. Broadly, the content component of the viva usually requires candidates to:

- authenticate the thesis;
- locate the research in the broader context;
- clarify aspects of the thesis;
- develop ideas;
- justify/defend aspects of the thesis;
- reflect critically on their work.

Conduct

The 'conduct' component of the viva is shaped by (1) examining styles, (2) examiners' personal/political agendas, and (3) interpersonal dynamics. In general, the conduct component of the viva requires candidates to:

- engage in the types of academic exchanges that the examiners deem appropriate;

- sometimes cope with difficult personal/political agendas;
- deal with interpersonal dynamics.

Overall, the best way to prepare for these three components of the viva is by accessing 'research cultures'. In the next section we outline what we mean by research cultures and discuss some of the general benefits of accessing them. We then discuss in more detail the ways in which access to specific elements of research cultures can help students to prepare for the skills, content and conduct components of the viva. Before moving on to the next section, candidates might find it useful to rate their competences in terms of the components listed above (see Box 4.1).

Box 4.1   Task for students

STAR RATINGS

Identify your strengths and weaknesses in terms of:

- thinking on your feet;
- performing and communicating clearly whilst under pressure;
- explaining, justifying and defending your PhD work with different audiences;
- knowing the 'broader context' of your thesis;
- coping with different styles of academic exchange;
- dealing with complex interpersonal dynamics.

Use the following scale:

4 – I'm very strong on this
3 – I'm quite strong on this
2 – I'm not strong on this
1 – I'm very weak on this

For all areas where you score below 4, plan a strategy for improvement, ideally in consultation with your supervisor.

    You should revisit this activity at different stages of your PhD – at the beginning, middle and towards the end.

4.2 Academic research cultures

Among the tests of a good supervisor is the extent to which he or she helps graduate students to set up professional contacts with other academics working in closely related fields.

(Becher *et al.* 1994: 120–1)

Access to academic research cultures is a key way in which students may prepare for the different components of the viva. On the basis of a study of social science doctoral students at two universities, Deem and Brehony argue that access to academic research cultures is very important for PhD students. According to Deem and Brehony (2000: 158), academic research cultures include 'disciplinary and interdisciplinary ideas and values, particular kinds of expert knowledge and knowledge production, cultural practices and narratives (for instance, how research is done, and how peer review is exercised), departmental sociability, other internal and external intellectual networks and learned societies'.

Access to academic research cultures can enable candidates to acquire discipline-specific proficiencies that may equip them to handle the skills, content and conduct requirements of the viva. For example, through access to academic research cultures, candidates can acquire appropriate ways of speaking, experience of engaging in different types of academic verbal exchanges, and confidence to present and defend their ideas to different groups of established academics. Some of our questionnaire respondents clearly recognized the benefits of this type of preparation for the viva: 'PhD training with presentations at conferences is the best way [to prepare for the viva], to talk to academics in your field as well as outside' (PhD student, Biology).

There are important discipline differences in research cultures and in how research students access them. Natural and applied science students may have greater access to research cultures than their non-science counterparts because of the different ways of working within these disciplines. In laboratory-based science subjects, students are commonly attached to a research team and as such they are thrust into a network of doctoral, postdoctoral and academic staff relationships. Here, there is a 'cascading of research problems and methods from generation to generation' (Delamont *et al.* 1997b: 536). In contrast, most research students in social sciences, arts and humanities work in relative isolation: 'The difference between us and social science is that we tend to do PhDs through team work. Social scientists are loners' (Professor, Physical Geography, quoted in Delamont *et al.* 1997b: 537). It is important to bear in mind discipline differences because (1) students/supervisors may otherwise mistakenly assume that practice across an institution is uniform, and (2) students in some disciplines may need to make deliberate efforts to access research cultures.

In general, building up the 'tacit knowledge' that facilitates access to research cultures is a slow process. Gerholm (1985) signals the slow nature of it in his discussion of the socialization of doctoral students:

Any person entering a new group with the ambition of becoming a full-fledged, competent member has to learn to comply with its fundamental cultural rules. This applies also to academic departments. To function smoothly within the group of teachers, fellow students and secretaries, the student needs a considerable amount of know-how. Most of it will be acquired slowly through the interaction with others and without anyone ever making a deliberate effort to teach the newcomer

the rules of the game. Nonetheless, failure to comply with these implicit rules will undoubtedly affect the student's standing within the group.
(Gerholm 1985, quoted in Becher and Trowler 2001: 49)

Building up department and discipline know-how is important preparation for the PhD viva and for an academic career after it. As discussed in Chapter 2, PhD examiners act as gatekeepers for disciplinary fields, and so it is important that candidates demonstrate that they are competent and have the 'know-how' to become 'full-fledged' members of those fields. Becher and Trowler (2001: 50) argue that 'membership of a disciplinary community in its fullest sense involves "the ability to define the situation correctly and to use the type of discourse required by that very situation" '. Long-term preparation for the viva involves developing the skills of definition and application that Becher and Trowler identify as central, and this is a long process that relies upon engagement with department and discipline research cultures.

Deem and Brehony (2000) suggest that some groups of students have greater difficulty accessing research cultures than other groups. They found that international and part-time students have the most difficulty accessing academic cultures; they tentatively suggest that women encounter difficulties too. Our research suggests that other factors can also be important: access to research cultures is shaped in important ways by language and by social class and, more specifically, whether the student comes from a family with an academic background (Jackson and Tinkler 2001). Candidates in our interview sample whose parents had experience of academia already knew what sorts of activity they should engage in, and so actively sought access to research cultures. In contrast, many students simply do not realize the benefits and importance of being part of academic research cultures. There are many benefits – here we suggest that access is an important part of long-term viva preparation. However, students often need to actively seek out opportunities to access research cultures because, as Becher *et al.* (1994: 121) suggest, usually supervisors leave the establishment of links to 'the ingenuity and enterprise of the students themselves'. This view was expressed strongly by one of our interviewees:

It's like, you'd better go to the conferences by yourself, you'd better talk to the lecturers in the department by yourself because there's not necessarily that forced opportunity . . . So you have to be a pretty independent minded person to actually use the resources of the department or the faculty properly.

The department has been good to me but I looked for the opportunities. I had fellow students who went through at the same time as me and who haven't done as much as I have and don't feel like they are as much a part of the department. But I think that's more on them because it's like they [academics] don't come looking for you necessarily. You kind of have to stick yourself in there and say, 'I'm here, can I do this?'
(Carla, PhD student, Art History)

In the next section we address PhD students directly and map out and evaluate some of the ways in which they can build up department and discipline 'know-how' – we make explicit what is frequently tacit. Our discussion is necessarily limited to the ways in which the selected activities are useful viva preparation.

4.3 A closer look at academic research cultures: activities that are useful long-term viva preparation

> Research students . . . need more help to understand the different ways in which they can maximise the benefits to be derived from supervision, research training, reading groups, seminars and participation in learned societies.
>
> (Deem and Brehony 2000: 163)

In this section we look closely at some of the key activities that make up academic research cultures, and discuss the ways in which these activities are useful long-term preparation for the skills, content and conduct components of the doctoral viva. Whilst research cultures are certainly not reducible to the elements that we discuss in this section, these are the most important aspects in terms of viva preparation. We look in detail at teaching, conference attendance and presentation, oral exams and publishing. We also look briefly at seminar presentations, reading groups, social events, administration, PhD taught courses and learned society membership.

Each of the activities discussed in this section is rated according to how useful it is for each component of the viva – skills, content and conduct. The scale used is as follows.

☆☆☆   Very useful
☆☆   Useful
☆   Quite useful
×   Not useful

Teaching

> Your communication skills should develop as a result of teaching, the point of it is to impart complex information clearly and economically to others, after all.
>
> (Grix 2001: 128)

Skills ☆☆☆
Teaching is generally very good preparation for the skills component of the viva. Teaching develops skills in terms of:

- presenting and explaining ideas clearly;
- thinking on your feet. For example, when responding to student questions or when finding new ways to explain ideas that students are unable to grasp;
- performing under pressure. Students usually expect their tutors to be 'experts' – living up to this expectation can be demanding.

But – different audiences make different demands upon you. You may feel more confident and comfortable presenting ideas to, and working with, undergraduate students than with your peers or seniors. As such, it is important that you also work with audiences of peers and seniors.

Content ☆ or ☆☆

The usefulness of teaching for the content component of the viva will depend upon the area(s) being taught. Clearly, if you are teaching areas that relate directly to your research, then it can be very useful for the content component. It is more likely, however, that the teaching will be only tangentially related to your PhD work – this can then be useful for 'broader context'. Research methods teaching can be very useful.

Conduct ☆☆☆

Teaching is generally very good preparation for the conduct component of the viva. Teaching develops skills in terms of:

- engaging in different types of academic exchange. Some students can be very challenging in their questions and approach. Also, some students have particular personal/political agendas that they wish to promote in classes;
- interpersonal dynamics. Very complex sets of interpersonal dynamics come into play in classes. For example, students can become overtly hostile with each other and may require careful managing by the tutor.

But – a certain amount of power is attached to the position of tutor, although this power may be contested and negotiated in specific situations. In contrast, in the viva, the bulk of the power is situated with the examiners, although again this can be contested and negotiated in certain circumstances.

Overall

Overall, teaching can be a very good way of preparing for the skills and conduct components of the viva, and it can have benefits for the content component too. However, there are a number of points that you should bear in mind.

- Teaching is time consuming. Depending upon the type of teaching conducted and the other demands attached to it (marking, preparation, attending meetings etc.), it has the potential to distract you from your PhD work. It is not advisable to take on too much teaching; research councils usually offer guidance about this to the students that they fund.

For example, the Arts and Humanities Research Board (AHRB) encourages its students to undertake some teaching or demonstrating, but states that the total demand on their time, including contact time and a reasonable allowance for preparation and marking, should not exceed 180 hours per year, or 6 hours per week. The Natural Environment Research Council (NERC) and the Particle Physics and Astronomy Research Council (PPARC) also suggest that the total time per week spent on teaching, preparation and marking should not normally exceed 6 hours. In general, these seem to be sensible guidelines. However, students who do not have research funding sometimes have to devote more than 6 hours per week to teaching and teaching-related activities for financial reasons.

- It is a good idea to undertake training sessions – most, if not all, universities have a series of courses for research students and lecturers who are new to teaching.
- Request a teaching mentor. Teaching can be very challenging. Experienced mentors can help less experienced teachers to develop their skills by discussing difficult situations, observing sessions and so on. Mentors can be a very useful source of support and guidance.

Conference attendance and presentation

> In retrospect, further experience of fielding questions following the oral delivery of a paper would have helped my viva performance.
>
> (PhD student, English and American Studies)

There are many benefits attached to presenting your work at, and attending, conferences – networking, publicity and so on. There is not space here to discuss these different aspects; interested readers might take a look at Blaxter *et al.* (1998) who provide some discussion of them. The discussion in this section is limited to how conferences may be useful long-term viva preparation. The benefits attached to attending *and* presenting at conferences are different from those attached to attending only. As such, the discussion below makes the distinction explicit.

Skills – Presenting ☆☆☆   Attending only ☆
Presenting at a conference is an excellent way to rehearse and develop the types of skills required for the viva. There are a number of different presentation formats at conferences: for example verbal presentation followed by questions from the audience, poster presentations with questions from the audience, roundtable discussions. However, all of the different presentation formats require that you:

- explain and present ideas clearly;
- think on your feet – particularly when responding to questions;

- perform under pressure – presenting to an audience of peers always adds a certain amount of pressure;
- justify and defend your work and ideas verbally.

Conference attendance more generally, though, can be useful for the skills component of the viva. Simply by attending and taking part in the conference as a non-presenter you can:

- be exposed to a range of different presentation styles and consider which are the most effective and why. This reflection is helpful when preparing your own presentations;
- see how a range of people react and respond to questions;
- ask questions at other people's presentations – this in itself can be daunting initially. Working out and asking clear questions takes practice;
- engage in discussions with people about your own and their work. Sometimes, you might need to provide a quick summary of key aspects of your work – clear, succinct responses can be difficult, so again this sort of practice is useful viva preparation;
- justify and defend your work in casual conversation – many of the best discussions at conferences take place in the bar or over coffee.

Content – Presenting ☆☆   Attending only ☆

Presenting your work at a conference can be useful preparation for the content component of the viva. It is interesting and useful to get feedback on work-in-progress and to be prompted to reflect critically on your work by more experienced colleagues. Presenting work and getting feedback on it can also help you to develop your ideas. In terms of preparation for the content component of the viva, then, presenting work at conferences has many advantages. It does, however, also have limitations. The main limitation is that you will only be able to present, and hence be questioned on, a small part of your PhD work at a conference, whereas in the viva the examiners will have access to the whole thesis. Because of this key difference and, of course, the different audiences, you cannot predict the content of the viva on the basis of questions that you are asked at conferences. It can be useful, though, to make a note of the questions that you are asked in conferences, seminars and other presentations and to use some of these in your final-stage preparation (see Chapter 10).

Regardless of whether you present or just attend, being at a conference and listening to other people's papers can be very useful for getting to know the work in your field. It can be a long time before work presented at conferences is published in journals or books, and so conference attendance is the best way of keeping up to date with work that is at the cutting edge. The value of this aspect of conference attendance should not be underestimated – it can be very important in the viva when demonstrating knowledge of your field and locating your work within the broader context.

Conduct – Presenting ☆☆☆   Attending only ☆☆

Presenting a paper at a conference and fielding questions from the audience can be excellent preparation for the conduct component of the viva. Your audience is likely to contain academics (and non-academics) with a wide spectrum of questioning styles, and it is good to get used to these different styles – although it can be daunting. The questions asked at conferences sometimes reflect the questioner's personal/political agendas – these questions are sometimes way beyond the scope of your paper but are asked because they relate to the questioner's pet interest. Getting used to handling these sorts of questions is useful, because PhD examiners can have pet interests that extend beyond the scope of your thesis too (see Chapter 11). There can also be interesting interpersonal dynamics amongst the audience – all good preparation for the viva.

If attending only rather than presenting, you can still observe the different styles of academic conduct in the sessions that you attend, although it is not nearly the same as being on the receiving end of it.

Overall

Overall, presenting your work at conferences is excellent preparation for the viva, particularly the skills and conduct components. However, presenting at conferences can be daunting, and so below are some suggestions to 'break you in gently'.

- Start off by presenting your work in your department, perhaps to other research students. Build up to presenting your work to staff in your department. Sometimes, there are research student conferences attached to main conferences (see Box 4.4), these can be a good venue for first-time presenters.
- Try asking questions at conferences even if you are not presenting a paper. Just getting used to speaking in conference sessions is an important first step.
- If you want to present work at a main conference, but do not want to do it alone, ask your supervisor or another student if you can present together. Presenting part of a paper is less daunting than presenting a whole one. Also, there is then someone else to share the questions with you.
- First-time presenters may find poster presentations less threatening than oral deliveries. Usually, this format involves presenting your work on a poster and being available at a set time to answer questions about it.

Finally, Grix (2001: 123) reminds students not to get too carried away with conferences and networking: 'you need to strike a balance between the perpetual conference-goer who knows and networks with everybody but is not known for his or her work, and someone who never attends, because he or she is too busy working'.

Oral exams – upgrading, progress reports etc.

There should be 'vivas' throughout the course of the PhD.

(PhD student, Chemistry)

Skills ☆☆☆

Undertaking oral examinations throughout the course of your doctoral study is excellent preparation for the skills component of the viva. Pretty much any kind of oral examination that focuses upon your doctoral work enables you to rehearse the skills required in the final viva. Oral examinations undertaken as part of an upgrading/conversion (from MPhil to PhD) are especially useful preparation for the skills element as progression depends upon passing these exams, and so students usually feel under pressure in them. Most students are reluctant to actively seek out pressured and stressful situations in which they have to orally defend their work and ideas. However, experiencing these types of situations is extremely important. In general, the more students 'put themselves through the mill' in this way, the less pressured and stressful such situations come to feel.

Content ☆☆

Oral exams can also be a useful preparation for the content component of the viva, although the timing of them is important. Oral examinations early in the doctoral process can help to clarify and develop ideas and may result in you reshaping your work. Oral examinations towards the end of the process may be less likely to result in major changes to the shape of the research or thesis, but may encourage you to reflect critically on your work, clarify aspects of your writing, defend some of your ideas and locate your work within the broader context – all of which are general purposes of the final viva.

It is essential to bear in mind, however, that the content component of the viva is shaped by the examiners' assessment of the thesis and their knowledge expectations. As such, you must not assume that the content of the final viva and earlier oral examinations will be similar; there might be some overlaps, but then again there might not.

Conduct ☆☆ or ☆☆☆

The conduct of examiners in vivas is highly variable. We have already seen how conduct is shaped by: (1) examining styles, (2) examiners' personal/political agendas and (3) interpersonal dynamics. We are not suggesting, then, that oral examinations during the course of the doctorate will give you access to the types of conduct that you will encounter in the final viva. We are suggesting, however, that if you experience a range of styles of academic conduct throughout the course of your PhD, you are more likely to be able to: (1) engage in the types of academic exchanges that the examiners deem appropriate; (2) cope with an examiner's difficult personal/political agenda; (3) deal with complex interpersonal dynamics in the viva.

Overall
Oral examinations of your work throughout the course of your doctorate
are a good preparation for the viva. In particular, they are an excellent way
of developing and refining the 'skills' required in the viva. Oral exams can
also be good ways of preparing for the conduct component, and can have
benefits for the content aspects too. There are, however, some general
points to bear in mind about undertaking oral examinations during your
PhD:

- Examinations can be daunting – build your confidence in presenting and
  defending your work by presenting it to carefully selected peers before
  your formal assessments.
- Feedback – to maximize the benefits of this type of preparation it is
  essential that it acts as formative (as well as possibly summative) assessment. Always ensure that you ask for feedback on your performances.
  Furthermore, ask for the feedback to be as precise as possible so that
  you can target and develop any areas identified as weak. Some students
  like to audiotape or even videotape their performances; this can be
  very useful for a post-exam analysis either on your own or with your
  supervisor.
- Keep a check on your levels of confidence. Sometimes, oral exams can
  act to reduce rather than build confidence. If this happens to you, reflect
  carefully on why this is the case. It is essential to locate precisely where
  your lack of confidence lies. Think about whether your confidence has
  been knocked in relation to the skills, content or conduct aspects of your
  performance. For example, do you feel that you are not very good at
  explaining your ideas orally (skills)? Have you lost confidence in the
  suitability of your chosen research method for your project (content)?
  Do you feel undermined by aggressive questioning (conduct)? Once you
  have identified the specific problem for you, think about why it is a
  problem. Talk to your peers, supervisor, and possibly the examiners
  about it and plan ways to rebuild and strengthen your confidence. (See
  Box 4.2.)

Box 4.2   Task for candidates

HOW DID YOU FARE?

Following an oral examination of aspects of your PhD work, reproduce
and complete the following table. This will encourage you to reflect
upon what you did well, and also what requires further work. It is
important to get precise feedback about your performance from your
supervisor and/or examiners, and to make a list of action points to
improve the areas in need of development. Of course, in addition to
making a list of action points you also need to act upon them!

Components	Component breakdown	*Your perceptions of what you did well*	*Your perceptions of what you did poorly*	*Feedback from examiners and/or supervisor*	*Action points*
Skills	• Thinking on your feet • Communicating clearly • Explaining and justifying your work				
Content	• Authenticate work • Locate research in broader context • Clarify aspects of your work • Develop ideas • Defend aspects of the work • Reflect critically on your work				
Conduct	• Engage in academic exchange • Cope with personal/political agendas of the examiners • Deal with interpersonal dynamics				

Publishing

Publishing aspects of your work in refereed journals or edited books has many benefits, although in some disciplines it is more commonly undertaken and promoted than in others. Aside from viva preparation, publishing has two main benefits for research students. First, in several universities, one criterion for the award of a PhD is that the work must be of publishable quality – if some of the work is published this criterion has been demonstrated. Second, to secure an academic post in a 'research active' department, candidates will need to demonstrate that, at a minimum, they have publishing 'potential'. If candidates have already published, this will be regarded positively by potential employers. Whilst these benefits of publishing are clearly important, in the remainder of this section we focus on how publishing can equip candidates to handle the different components of the viva.

Skills ✕

Publishing has little value for the skills component of the viva which requires oral rather than written communication. Publishing can be good, however, for developing and refining writing proficiency, which is useful for doctoral work generally.

Content ☆☆

An article submitted for publication in a refereed journal will usually be scrutinized by at least two academics that work broadly in your area. The referees will be asked to provide comments on the submission, which are usually sent to the author. Feedback from people working in your field but who are unconnected to your PhD work can be very valuable for getting an 'outsider's' perspective. Furthermore, referees' comments can help and encourage you to perform many of the tasks that may be required in the viva – reflect critically on your work, clarify aspects of your writing, defend some of the ideas, locate the work within the broader context and so on. In this respect, submitting work for publication can be good preparation for the content component of the viva.

Again, however, there are limitations. First, work submitted for publication will relate only to part of the thesis. As such, you would get feedback on only a small part of your work. Second, for reasons discussed in Chapter 3, the referees may assess your work in very different ways from your examiners.

Conduct ☆☆

Submitting work for publication can provide useful insights into aspects of academic conduct. Written comments from different referees, like verbal comments and questions from examiners, can vary tremendously in tone (see Chapter 3). Some referees are careful to stress positive points about work submitted, even if they then go on to identify major problems. On the other hand, some referees skip the pleasantries and go straight for the jugular! Comments in writing, like comments delivered verbally, can be gentle, harsh or somewhere in between in tone. Furthermore, the comments of referees, like the comments of examiners, may be shaped by their personal/political agendas – let us not forget, of course, that examiners and referees are one and the same group. As such, getting feedback from referees can be useful preparation for the conduct component of the viva.

However, as one would expect, there are limitations here too. Written feedback and face-to-face communications are very different forms of exchange. With referees' comments there is plenty of time for consideration before the author has to respond; the candidate does not have this luxury in the viva. Furthermore, the tone used by the examiners could be very different from that of the referees. However, the more familiar you are with different styles of academic conduct, the more likely you are to be able to handle the style(s) encountered in the viva.

Overall
Submitting work for publication can be very useful preparation for the content and conduct aspects of the viva. There are, however, some general points to consider.

• Writing for publication is time consuming. Whilst publishing can be very useful in a number of ways, you would be ill advised to put too much time into writing for publication at the expense of writing your thesis. Ensure that you strike a sensible balance – discuss this with your supervisor.
• Feedback can sometimes be disheartening. Whilst positive feedback and acceptance of one's submission is great; rejection and negative feedback is less easy to handle. Unfortunately, the latter is part and parcel of the process. We have yet to find an academic, however senior or prestigious, who has not received negative feedback and rejection from a journal. Sometimes negative feedback can be constructively critical, but still disappointing and difficult to manage. Other times, it can feel unconstructive and downright cruel. Overall, the diversity of styles of feedback on articles probably mirrors the diversity of examining styles. On an individual level, it is imperative that you discuss any feedback with your supervisor, particularly negative feedback it is a safe bet that s/he will have also received negative feedback at some point.

Other activities

> The reading group is very useful as it builds confidence . . . The group helps me to get used to the technical language of my subject and learn fresh approaches . . . It is very important to build social networks, essential for new ideas, references, to find out what others are doing and the intellectual bouncing of ideas . . . it is also important as being part-time I often feel very lonely in my work. (Female, home, part-time)
> (Deem and Brehony 2000: 159)

There are other activities that are also useful long-term preparation for the viva. These are summarized in Table 4.1, where we have listed the activity, provided the ratings for the three viva components, and provided some comments.

Table 4.1 Ratings of other activities for long-term viva preparation

Activities	Components and ratings	Comments
Seminar presentations	Skills ☆☆☆ Content ☆ Conduct ☆☆☆	As with conferences As with conferences, but you may get less diversity of styles depending upon the nature and size of the audience
Reading groups	Skills ☆☆ Content ☆+ Conduct ☆☆	You need to explain clearly, think on your feet, respond to comments and so on Depends on the topic of the readings. Always good for broader context issues Varies a little depending upon the participants. A large number of participants is likely to provide a greater mix of styles. Some debates can get rather heated, and there can be interesting interpersonal dynamics
Social events	Skills ☆ Content ×/☆ Conduct ☆	You may have to summarize your PhD in a couple of sentences whilst nibbling crudités – this is always a challenge Not particularly useful in general, although they can be useful for 'broader context' issues depending on whom you speak to You may get to see a whole range of interactions
Administration, e.g. department research student representative	Skills ☆☆ Content ×/☆ Conduct ☆☆	You may have to summarize ideas clearly and concisely in meetings. You may also need to justify and defend your position Very occasionally can be useful for 'broader context' Interpersonal dynamics in departmental meetings can be fascinating and can provide insights into different ways of interacting
PhD taught training courses	Skills ☆+ Content ☆ Conduct ☆	Varies depending on the course and teaching methods. For example, group work with peers usually involves explaining and discussing ideas, responding to comments and so on Depends – can generally be useful for 'broader context' You may encounter different styles amongst peers and teaching staff
Learned society membership	Skills ×+ Content ☆☆ Conduct ×+	This will depend on how actively involved you are. If you take on a specific role within the society and/or attend their events it may be very useful (see Box 4.4) Publications from the society can be very useful for broader context issues Again, not particularly useful unless you take on a specific role within the society, or attend their events

4.4 Ways to access academic research cultures

In this final section, we suggest practical ways for students to access research cultures. We recognize that this may be easier for some groups of students than for others, as discussed earlier in this chapter. However, it is our hope that by making more explicit those aspects of academic life that are usually tacit, all students will be more aware of the range of possibilities. It is then for each student to work out what is possible, perhaps in consultation with their supervisor, and to develop a plan that is likely to work for them. We recognize that some barriers are difficult to overcome, but we encourage students and supervisors to think creatively about how to access academic research cultures. Some ideas for students are mapped out below.

By attending:
- departmental seminars. Make sure that you are included on the mailing lists, not just in your own department, but also in related departments. Contact departmental secretaries to find out what is going on and to ensure that you are included;
- training courses – departmental, faculty, university, learned societies, funding bodies;
- conferences. Funding may sometimes be sought from your department, funding bodies, the conference organizers (via a bursary scheme) – do not be afraid to ask (see Box 4.4);
- department social events.
- specialist events. Some professional bodies have special interest groups – check them out (web pages are usually a good starting point) and ensure that you are on relevant mailing lists;
- department or faculty reading groups – consider setting one up if they do not already exist.

By undertaking:
- conference presentations. Ask your supervisor about conferences at which you might present a paper or poster;
- teaching in the department. Put yourself forward – don't wait to be approached. If teaching by postgraduates is not common in your department, perhaps ask your supervisor if you could be involved in her/his course in some way;
- oral presentations in your department. Ask for opportunities to present your work in the department. If you're unsure about presenting to staff in the department, organize a session where research students can present to each other first.

By publishing:
- speak to your supervisor about whether you should write an article for publication in an academic journal whilst undertaking your PhD (perhaps jointly with your supervisor). Academic publications are particularly desirable if you are planning to stay within academia after your PhD;

- some professional bodies have student pages in their publications. For example, the British Psychological Society has a student page in *The Psychologist.* Check out relevant professional bodies to see if they offer student space in their publications and think about contributing to these. If they don't already have student space, ask for some.

Box 4.3   Task

BREAKING IN

Plan ways in which you/your students can access research cultures.

Box 4.4   Case study

HOW BERA SUPPORTS RESEARCH STUDENTS
by Carol Boulter, BERA Training Consultant

As indicated and discussed in this chapter, a successful viva is the result of many influences and developments that take place throughout the entire PhD process. Many of these developments and influences occur, and are monitored, within the institution where a student is registered, but there is much that is available for students within professional bodies. Becoming part of a professional body is an important aspect of professional induction. Meeting students from other universities, being challenged to present arguments away from the security of one's own institution, and being required to think deeply about methodology can all be very significant milestones in developing the confidence and skills that the viva requires. In order to provide an indication of the types of support offered to research students by professional bodies, this case study flags some of the benefits offered to research students by the British Educational Research Association.

The British Educational Research Association (BERA) has been sustaining and promoting a vital research culture in education since its inception thirty years ago. One of its specific aims is the training and education of educational researchers, their effectiveness, conditions of work and rights. Educational researchers can come into educational research by many routes and BERA sees its task as working towards supporting the ongoing methodological training of all its members from the most experienced to those at the start of their careers. Since the mid 1990s the association has focused effort on recruiting and providing for student members who are in the process of undertaking their postgraduate training for higher degrees in educational research. The proportion of student members in BERA is about 7 per cent, and they represent a large range of experience, age and spread across the UK.

BERA provides support for research students in three main ways: through conferences, resources and workshops; through financial assistance; and through mentoring and networking.

The annual Student Symposium, which precedes the main conference, now draws over 70 student presenters. This allows many students to present their papers for the first time to an academic audience outside their own institution. Time is allowed for discussion of the papers in parallel sessions with an experienced chairperson. Also at the conference, an invited lead speaker deals with an aspect of the process of doing a PhD. The experience of presenting and interacting with others has proved valuable to many new researchers. Furthermore, students new to giving a paper and attending a conference are provided with mentors from amongst BERA's experienced members. Each year BERA provides a number of flat rate bursaries to enable students to attend the conferences (the annual Student Symposium and the main conference). In addition, a Dissertation Award of £500 is awarded annually to an outstanding student thesis published in the previous year.

The Economic and Social Research Council (ESRC) has funded with BERA research training development activities (TDAs) since a programme was launched in 1997. These TDAs provide high-level methodological training within a multidisciplinary framework. They are advertised on the BERA website and in the BERA newsletter *Research Intelligence*. These events are often oversubscribed and BERA is striving to provide more of this type of high-level methodological training. In particular, a series of one-day master classes is being developed on significant aspects of methodology. As a professional body, BERA is committed to making the resources that it develops as accessible as possible to members, and so these master classes, together with presentations of other eminent speakers, are to be digitally recorded and made available to all members.

BERA works closely with the ESRC Teaching and Learning Research Programme Research Capacity Building Network, which also seeks to make methodological resources more accessible. BERA publishes many booklets of guidance on educational research that are sent to members. A new edition of the ethical guidelines is being published in 2003 and there will soon afterwards be guidelines for teachers engaged in educational research.

BERA allows students to access and correspond with each other and to make their views known on the BERA email list. The development recently of special interest groups (SIGs) means that students can be included easily into the association and can attend SIG events and even set up their own student research SIG.

4.5 A flexible conclusion

Earlier in the chapter we quoted Becher and Trowler (2001: 50): 'Membership of a disciplinary community in its fullest sense involves "the ability to define the situation correctly and to use the type of discourse required by that very situation".' It is worth returning to this quote and reflecting on what it means for the PhD viva. It is implicit that being a successful member of a disciplinary community requires a degree of flexibility – to judge what specific situations require and to respond accordingly. The same applies to the viva. It is *very* important that students are flexible in thinking about and approaching the viva. As we have seen, vivas are variable and it is imperative that students recognize this. Our research suggests that candidates that work with a fixed model of the viva are likely to be shocked if it does not adhere to their expectations: such students were ill prepared for, and unhappy about, the ways that the viva proceeded. On the other hand, students who have less fixed notions seem more prepared for the varying demands of the viva. Carlos, an education candidate, provides a graphic example of the difficulties that can arise when there is a mismatch between expectations and experience.

> They asked me questions I did not expect and I will explain what I mean by that. I sent an email to my supervisor and I asked his opinion about what questions the examiners may ask and he sent back some questions. As well I contacted another teacher from the University of X who was aware of my work and he sent me questions and I had altogether close to 25. I prepared these questions and, to be honest with you, they asked one or two of these questions, but one or two only.
>
> *Interviewer: So what was the content of the exam?*
>
> Well, for example, personally I was expecting questions such as: What are the main findings of the study? What do you see as the main contributions of your study? Would you do anything different now? How do you see things five or ten years from now? They did not ask many questions that examined my knowledge. They were interested to find out more about the methodology and procedures . . . I expected something about that, but not for it to be the main content of the viva.

Carlos was very distressed after his viva because it had not gone as he had expected. It is crucial that candidates and supervisors recognize that it is not advantageous to have rigidly held views about the content or conduct of the viva. A flexible approach is best.

4.6 Summary

In this chapter we explored the ways in which students can undertake long-term preparation for the viva. Long-term preparation is essential for developing ways to manage effectively the skills, content and conduct components of the viva discussed in Chapter 3. Access to academic research cultures is key to long-term preparation, and in this chapter we discussed the benefits and limitations of a number of specific (research culture) activities for the three viva components. We also suggested practical ways in which students might gain access to, and engage in, these activities. Finally, we stressed the importance for candidates of a flexible approach to the viva.

5

Selecting Examiners

'My colleague, Brian Clarke, once said "There are three types of interviewer – good, bad and mad" and that is regrettably true' (Higham 1983: 88). The same can be said of PhD examiners.

Chapter overview

Examiners are crucial to the doctoral examination process in a number of different ways. This chapter explores the importance of examiners and it introduces and discusses factors and issues to consider when selecting examiners.

Students ☺☺   Examiners ☺   Supervisors ☺☺☺

Chapter contents

5.1 Why are examiners important?

There are four main reasons why PhD examiners are important to the candidate and their supervisor. First, the award of a PhD depends on the judgement of the examiners. It is therefore essential to select examiners who have appropriate expertise and who are prepared to judge fairly the overall standard of the thesis and the approach that the candidate has adopted. Second, the choice of examiners will shape the candidate's experience of the oral examination. As we saw in Chapter 3, the content and conduct of the viva are shaped by the examiners' assessments of the thesis, their views about what candidates should know, their styles of examining, personal/political agendas and their interpersonal skills. Third, the importance of the examiners extends beyond the decision to award a doctorate. In cases where a doctorate is awarded, examiners can usually be expected to provide guidance on academic career development, to write references and, in relation to academic careers, to provide sponsorship (see Chapter 2). So for those candidates who wish to seek employment in higher education, the selection of examiners is a form of investment. Delamont *et al.* (1997a: 144) make this point by adapting a well-known animal welfare slogan: 'An external isn't just for the examination – he or she can be a patron, referee and gatekeeper for life.' Fourth, the status of a doctoral award, rightly or wrongly, is also frequently judged by the identity of the examiners and the place where the PhD is awarded. The following extract from University of Brighton (2002b: 21) regulations makes this quite explicit: 'The quality of the candidate's examination team is an important indicator of the quality of the resulting degree.' For all these reasons, the choice of examiners is 'strategic': 'you need professional and respected people' (Leonard 2001: 248).

From the perspectives of the institution and discipline, PhD examiners are important because they are a means to promote common academic standards. According to this view, academic standards are upheld if doctoral candidates at one institution are assessed by at least one appropriately qualified representative from the wider academic community. This procedure is also linked to a concern to gain validation and status from the broader academic community for the institution's research degrees and the candidates who are awarded them.

Given the varied ways in which examiners are important in the doctoral examination process their selection is a serious matter. Next we look at procedures for appointing examiners before turning to selection criteria.

5.2 Selection procedures

How many examiners?

Usually there are two examiners, one internal and one external. However, there are several variants on this general practice. If the candidate is a member of staff at the institution where they are registered for their doctorate it is usual for two examiners to be external. Two external examiners can also be appointed at some institutions if there is no suitable internal examiner; in these cases an internal chair is usually appointed (some institutions have independent chairs in all PhD vivas – see Chapter 6). In the case of interdisciplinary or multidisciplinary theses the examining team may include an additional external or internal examiner. At some institutions two internal examiners can be appointed if the preferred internal examiner is deemed too junior or inexperienced to act as the sole internal examiner. Also, in rare cases where a candidate's past or present supervisor has to be appointed as an internal examiner it is usual to appoint an additional examiner. (See Chapter 6 on the roles and responsibilities of viva participants.)

When should examiners be selected?

Institutions usually specify a point when potential examiners must be identified, this is usually a few months before the thesis is submitted. The proposed examiners are then considered and, if appropriate, approved by a research degrees committee or equivalent before they are invited formally to serve as examiners.

There are advantages to supervisors and candidates reflecting on suitable examiners considerably earlier than required by the institution. Potential examiners can be approached informally about their willingness to examine a PhD some time before the thesis is submitted. This practice allows time to find alternative examiners if the preferred choices are unavailable. Another advantage is that the final version of the thesis can be written with the examiners in mind, although candidates should not orient their thesis around the interests of their prospective examiners or use their publications in a gratuitous or ingratiating manner.

Who selects the examiners?

It is usual for supervisors to be centrally involved in deciding which examiners to appoint, although the selection has to be formally approved, usually by a committee responsible for research degrees. At some institutions the supervisor must suggest a list of possible examiners; a graduate research committee then assesses the suggestions and makes the choice without involving the supervisor in the final decision (Becher *et al.* 1994). Whilst the appointment of examiners routinely takes account of the preferences of supervisors, practices and views vary widely concerning the role of the candidate in the selection process.

Should the candidate be involved?
Our questionnaire to candidates revealed that 54 per cent were involved in selecting their external examiner and 41 per cent in selecting their internal

examiner. Academics are divided about whether candidates should be involved in the selection process and practice varies by supervisor, department and institution. Our research revealed a marked variation in practice by discipline: 77 per cent of candidates in the arts, humanities and social sciences reported that they were involved in selecting the external examiner, compared with only 45 per cent in the sciences.

Many supervisors think that it is appropriate to discuss the appointment of examiners with their students for one or more of the following reasons:

- To discover whether there are academic, personal or financial connections between the candidate and prospective examiners that may undermine the independence of the examiners.
- To discover whether the candidate has a personal or academic clash with one of the prospective examiners that may influence (1) how the candidate performs in the viva and/or (2) the examiner's assessment of the candidate's thesis and their treatment of the candidate in the viva.
- To assess whether the candidate's approach would be incompatible with that of the prospective examiners.
- To find out whom the candidate would like to meet and discuss their work with.
- To identify an appropriate future sponsor for the candidate.
- To draw upon the candidate's detailed knowledge of their own work to identify suitable examiners.

Where candidates are involved, the extent of their involvement varies and ranges from the candidate suggesting possible examiners for the supervisor to consider, to the candidate merely checking that the supervisor's preferred examiners are unproblematical.

Some supervisors and departments are against any form of student involvement in the selection of examiners. Becher *et al.* (1994: 138) discovered that science students at some institutions 'had not only not been consulted about their examiners but also had no idea who they were'. The principal reasons for this are twofold. First, that doctoral students should not be allowed to specify the conditions of their examination. Second, that the supervisor is judged able to identify appropriate examiners without the student's input.

Even where it is not formal policy to attend to the views of the candidate about their examiners, it is generally accepted that it is not advisable to appoint academics that a candidate is strongly opposed to. If a candidate is strongly opposed to the appointment of a particular examiner we advise that they discuss the matter with their supervisor(s) and/or the person responsible for postgraduate matters in their department.

5.3 Factors to consider when selecting examiners

In this section we map out key factors and issues relating to the choice of examiners. Before doing this, we introduce the institutional regulations that provide a framework within which supervisors and/or research degree committees make their decisions.

Institutional frameworks

The selection of examiners is regulated by the appointing institution, although at many institutions, especially old universities, the guidelines are sparse and vague (Tinkler and Jackson 2000) – see Box 5.1. Institutional criteria for the selection of examiners usually relate to (1) academic credentials and experience, and (2) 'independence'.

Box 5.1   Task for supervisors

INSTITUTIONAL FRAMEWORKS

Check whether your institution has specific regulations governing the appointment of PhD examiners, although many do have rules, there are some that do not.

Ensure that you abide by these rules where they exist, but also consider the factors and issues in the following section of the text.

---

1. *Academic credentials and experience.* Many universities provide no guidance about academic credentials and experience. Among institutions that do provide guidance on these matters, there is considerable variety as the following examples demonstrate.

   > Examiners shall be experienced in research in the general area of the candidate's thesis and, where practicable, have experience as a specialist in the topic(s) to be examined . . . At least one external examiner shall have substantial experience of successful supervision and examination of research degree candidates, and/or evidence of a consistent, recent and extensive record of publication in refereed journals or other appropriate media.
   > (Nottingham Trent University 1998: 15–16)

   > External Examiners shall normally be at least a Senior Lecturer from a pre 1992 University or a Principal Lecturer from a post 1992 University.
   > (Loughborough University 2003: 19)

2. *Independence.* Independence of the external examiner is a selection criterion that has high profile in the documentation of most universities. Independence is typically promoted in one or more of the following three ways:

- by rules regarding the period that must have elapsed since the external examiner had any formal attachment to the university – employment clause;
- by regulations that stipulate how frequently individuals can be allowed to examine at an institution – frequency clause;
- by rules which govern whether, and under what conditions, a candidate's supervisor can act as an examiner – supervision clause.

Arguably, these regulations attempt to safeguard or promote an examiner's objectivity and impartiality. This is made explicit in the policy of most new universities: the 'same external examiner is not approved so frequently that her/his familiarity with the department might prejudice *objective judgement*' (University of Glamorgan 1998: 22, our emphasis). Whilst this statement clearly concerns familiarity at the level of the *department,* in the case of other universities familiarity with the *university* is seen to endanger objectivity. Whilst the aims of 'independence' and 'objectivity' appear to be common amongst universities, the ways in which institutions operationalize the three clauses highlight the relative and slippery nature of the two concepts (see Tinkler and Jackson 2000; Jackson and Tinkler 2001).

- *Employment clause.* Although institutions usually state that external examiners must be 'independent' of the institutions at which they examine, few old universities provide clarification to the extent that most new universities do. Institutions that provide detail usually state that the external examiner must not have been employed by the university during the past three years, although this can be as long as six years in some cases.
- *Frequency clause.* Conceptions of how much examining leads to familiarity with a department or university are, not surprisingly, variable. Institutions offer very different specifications about how frequently a person can examine; these range from twice in five years, to once or twice a year.
- *Supervision clause.* Few institutions unambiguously state that the supervisor cannot act as an examiner, more usually policy states that supervisors cannot 'normally' be appointed as an examiner and in most cases guidance is provided about exceptions to this rule. In rare cases where it is deemed necessary to appoint the supervisor as an examiner, an additional examiner usually has to be appointed.

Although these clauses are designed to ensure that an academic's loyalties or grudges do not impair her/his judgement, it is highly contentious as to whether independent judgement can ever be attained (see feminist critiques of this positivist feature, for example Stanley and Wise 1993). Academic interests are not bound only by department or institutional loyalties but by inter-institutional and interdepartmental relations (Becher 1989; Delamont 1997b,c). Some institutions do attempt to regulate these relationships: we discuss this in the section on personal/political agendas.

Other factors and issues

The choice of examiners is strategic.

(Leonard 2001: 248)

The factors that supervisors need to address when selecting examiners extend beyond the criteria stipulated in institutional policy. In this section we consider these factors (unless otherwise stated, the comments refer to both external and internal examiners). Before proceeding with this discussion it is useful to reflect on the reasons why academics choose to examine (see Chapter 7 for a fuller discussion).

Reasons to serve as an external examiner of a PhD are varied, although most academics agree that money is not a factor. Key motivations include career development and academic recognition, intellectual interest and service to the academic and/or discipline community. Less important reasons include the opportunity to visit colleagues, friends and family and, in some cases, the hope that the candidate's supervisor may, at a future date, be persuaded to examine their PhD students. Some of the reasons that internal examiners agree to examine are similar to those of external examiners: career development, interest, service to the academic community, and a need to secure, from amongst their colleagues, internal examiners for their own PhD students. Internal examiners can, however, feel less able to decline a request to examine than their external counterparts because of obligations to their department and colleagues. The reasons that people agree to serve as internal or external examiners can have far-reaching consequences for the way in which they assess a thesis and conduct a viva.

The selection of examiners involves consideration of academic and also personal factors. These factors have implications for the assessment of the candidate's thesis, the content and conduct of the viva and, also, for the support that is made available to a successful candidate following the examination. The significance of different selection criteria for doctoral assessment is as follows:

- Assessment of the thesis – shaped by examiner's expertise, academic approach (including willingness to accept alternative approaches) and personal/political agenda.
- Content and conduct of the viva – shaped by examiner's assessment of the thesis (factors cited above), examiner's expectations of the candidate's knowledge, examining style and interpersonal dynamics in the viva.

Each of the selection criteria will be considered in turn.

Expertise

It is accepted that the external examiner should have expertise in the area of the thesis; this is less necessary, or even possible, in the case of the internal examiner. However, it is often difficult to match precisely the area covered in a thesis and the area of an external examiner's expertise; this is particularly so with interdisciplinary research. Some institutions actually specify that the examiner must be in the same discipline as the candidate (Phillips 1994: 134); this 'fit' may be assessed using the academic's qualifications or their department. In many cases the external examiner is not an expert in the candidate's specific field of study but

- an authority on an aspect of the candidate's field of research;
- an authority on the broad area within which the candidate's research falls;
- experienced at tackling similar problems to those addressed by the candidate;
- experienced at using a similar methodology.

The important point is that the examiner is able to assess the research presented in the thesis *and* the candidate's performance in the viva. These are also necessary requirements when selecting an internal examiner.

Academic approach – open or closed

Expertise is not enough to ensure that someone is an appropriate examiner of a particular thesis. Grix (2001: 106–7) cautions students against choosing 'the biggest celebrity in your field': 'living legends', he argues, 'may have a particular approach to your topic and may not be sympathetic to your "innovative" approach'. Although a 'celebrity' academic can be an extremely good sponsor of a PhD candidate whose approach they approve of, 'it is far better to have passed your viva than to have failed with a well known examiner' (Grix 2001: 107). In selecting both an external and internal examiner it is, therefore, important to consider the academic's approach to knowledge and research and whether they are prepared to accept alternatives to their own ways of working.

Some academics have fixed views about how specific research problems and/or topics should be tackled and are unable, or unwilling, to accept research that uses a different approach. These examiners approach the thesis and also the viva in ways that do not do credit to the work of the candidate. Some types of doctoral work are particularly vulnerable to the effects of blinkered examiners for instance interdisciplinary work and theses which employ methods or styles of presentation that are innovative within their discipline. The examination of feminist PhD work by non-feminist examiners can also generate problems (Delamont *et al.* 1997a; Morley *et al.* 2002), although it can sometimes be difficult to distinguish between an unsympathetic academic approach and personal/political antagonism. Delamont *et al.* (1997a: 146–7) describe the case of a student who submitted a socialist-feminist analysis of the role of women in Brazilian trade unions. The examiner turned out to be an 'old-fashioned Marxist who believed passionately that men built revolutions and women should be barefoot, pregnant and ignored by social science'. Not surprisingly, the external 'hated' the submission, 'he loathed the whole idea of the thesis', and the thesis was referred. However expert they are, academics who are wedded to a particular approach are best avoided as examiners unless, of course, the candidate's work falls neatly within the academic's preferred approach. Delamont *et al.* (1997a: 146) offer sound advice on this matter: 'The good examiner needs either to be a user of the same broad theory and methods of data collection and analysis as the candidate, and have an interest in the empirical subject matter, *or* to be broadminded enough to appreciate the merits of approaches other than his or her own.'

Knowledge expectations

The content of the viva is shaped by examiners' views about the kinds of knowledge that a PhD candidate should possess and be able to demonstrate (see Chapter 3 for discussion of this). These views are particularly important when examiners assess the candidate's knowledge of the 'broader context' and when they ask the candidate to articulate the way(s) in which their thesis contributes to knowledge.

Examining styles

Styles of viva examining are shaped, in part, by the examiners' views about the kinds of academic engagement a PhD candidate should be able to handle. As we saw in Chapters 2 and 3, some academics believe that PhD candidates should be able to withstand, and indeed rebuff, aggressive and pointed attacks during the oral examination. In selecting an examiner it is usually best to avoid an academic who has a reputation for an aggressive style of examining as this style can undermine the candidate's ability to perform well in the viva. Our research also suggests that, irrespective of outcome, candidates are very unhappy about the way this type of academic exchange makes them feel during and after the viva (see Chapter 13).

Other styles of examining may not be confrontational but they can still be undesirable in a PhD viva, for example, the 'proof-reader, who spends the viva going through the thesis making detailed corrections of spelling, punctuation and grammar', and the 'committee man, who takes up points page by page, in the order they occur in the thesis rather than synthesizing them into key questions' (Brown and Atkins 1988, cited in Leonard 2001: 251). Examining styles can be culturally variable and academics from outside Britain may be used to different assessment standards and examining styles from those of their British counterparts – see Boxes 5.2 below and 2.4 in Chapter 2.

Box 5.2   Case study

EXAMINING A FRENCH PHD THESIS IN SOCIOLOGY AND RELATED
DISCIPLINES

by Rod Watson, Reader in Sociology, University of Manchester

It cannot be assumed that the examination of PhDs in Britain can work
as an experiential precedent for examining PhDs in France or vice
versa. For a start, the academic standard of French PhDs is, typically,
considerably higher than that in Britain and the requirements are,
accordingly, more elevated. Traditional academic values prevail far
more than in contemporary Britain. The French have no truck with
transferable, commercially relevant skills or the 'applied' pertinence of
the thesis to the economy or business world: theses are adjudged on
purely academic grounds. The whole examining process in France is
also more complex and onerous. In addition, the viva voce is more
ceremonial than is usually the case outside Oxbridge in Britain. It is
also a 'public witnessing', much in the nature of a traditional marriage
in Britain.

The viva voce is a lively affair – the following offers an account of
common practices. The examining committee (or 'jury') has from four
to six members plus a chairperson (or 'president') who may also act as
an examiner. More than one jury member may be an external examiner. The viva is also open to the public and any number from a dozen
to hundreds of people may attend. Typically the viva begins with
the president introducing the candidate and then the jury members.
Then the president invites the candidate to present a fairly extensive
résumé of the thesis to the jury and audience. This presentation may
last from 20 to 30 minutes. The public/audience will then be invited
to offer comments, criticisms or questions. Few members of the
public respond, but those who do can produce questions from way out
on 'left field'. The president then calls on each jury member in turn
and, typically, the member will produce a critical review lasting anything from 15 to 30 minutes. The review usually comprises a summary
of the thesis, a review of what the jury member considers to be the
positive and negative aspects of the work and a set of questions for the
candidate to answer. Normally, these will be presented in a single
block of talk from the jury member rather than being organized
around the question–answer–question–answer pattern of British
defences. The candidate will then reply, again in a single 'block' of talk,
though the jury member may occasionally put 'pursuit questions' or
other responses. The president then asks the jury member if s/he is
satisfied: there is a normative preference for an affirmative answer but,
nonetheless, this is the place for the jury member to make a case to
counter the candidate's response should s/he deem it necessary, and

to request a further reply from the candidate. This procedure is repeated for each jury member, so the viva can last anything from two-and-a-half to four hours. Given its public, and often highly formal and ceremonial, nature, it can be almost as much of an ordeal for the jury member as for the candidate.

After the defence, the jury retires for discussions. These do not just concern whether the candidate has passed – a mere pass is virtually worthless, at least if the candidate wishes to enter academic life. French PhDs are stratified into a series of classes or 'mentions', much like British undergraduate degrees. Only the top mention ('mention très honorable avec les felicitations du jury') or, perhaps, the second best one ('mention très honorable') will be of a sufficient level to enable the candidate to credibly apply for an academic post. The jury then files out and the president announces the level of mention to the candidate and audience. It is certainly not unknown for a candidate to break down and weep on the spot if s/he has passed but has not attained the requisite mention. This is not much fun, especially as the candidate's family and friends are usually in the audience. The jury members then sign the appropriate formal documentation.

The viva voce is, though, only one stage in quite an extensive series. The jury member will receive a thesis which can be approximately twice as long as the British equivalent. S/he may then have to submit an extensive pre-report to the president: sometimes all jury members have to do this but often it is just the designated 'specialists' amongst the jury who are asked to do this. The report can be up to five A4 sides of closely argued critical review – perhaps even more. All pre-reports will be made available to other jury members just before the viva. After the viva the jury member will have to submit another report, a final one that includes comments on the candidate's oral defence. Along with one's presentation notes for the viva voce, this involves much more work and a much longer timescale than for the examining of a British PhD: and jury members usually receive only expenses – no fee. Throughout the whole process, the PhD candidate plays a much more responsible and proactive role than is typically the case in Britain. Indeed, it may well be the candidate who approaches you to be a jury member in the first place.

Personal/political agendas

So far we have considered the importance of academic factors for selecting examiners. Personal/political agendas are also important because they can prejudice the examiner's assessment of the thesis and shape the content and conduct of the viva. These agendas can include:

- the promotion of discriminatory beliefs and/or interests, such as the exclusion of specific social groups from the academy and/or the

suppression of particular political, academic, religious perspectives (see Box 13.1 in Chapter 13 for an example);
- the pursuit of grudges against individuals;
- the promotion of favourites;
- pleasure in making the relatively powerless PhD candidate suffer for their aspirations;
- jealousy;
- academic self-promotion and aggrandizement including the 'drawbridge' mentality: 'the examiner, having achieved a higher degree, believes that he or she should be the last person to enter the ivory tower before the drawbridge is raised and unworthy unwashed multitudes lay siege to the castle' (Delamont *et al.* 1997a: 146).

At one extreme, personal/political agendas may not be specific to any particular thesis and/or candidate. At the other, they may appear only in relation to the examination of a particular candidate and/or thesis. An academic's reputation is usually a good indicator of whether they are likely to pursue problematic agendas whilst serving as a PhD examiner. However, these types of agenda are not always apparent in advance, as is clear in the following account.

> The external examiner left the student in tears after the viva. He gave no indication that there was anything wrong with the thesis to me beforehand or to the student or to the internal examiner. They [the examiners] had a very amicable lunch to discuss things and so on, then he came in and he basically took the student apart. It turned out that he [the external examiner] was very bitter about the research group that I was part of, that we had got money to do research and he hadn't. So I think, he never said it, but I think he was getting his own back, not at the student but using the student to get his own back, not at me, but at the group I belonged to. The student had to do some rewriting, she didn't have another viva, she just had to rewrite it and resubmit . . . And when I talked to people afterwards there were a number of people who said, 'Well, I could have told you he was a difficult person', but nobody ever said that beforehand.
>
> (Professor, Management Studies)

Although some colleagues admitted after the examination that this examiner was 'difficult' it is unlikely that the supervisor could have predicted accurately the examiner's behaviour in the viva and his unsuitability for the job of examining this candidate/thesis.

Relationships between academics (and occasionally between academics and candidates) are sometimes a source of unproductive personal/political agendas. There are several types of relationship that are not usually regulated formally, such as the relationship between ex-supervisor and PhD student and between academics who regularly write together or who have recently worked on a joint research programme. There is also a range of personal, often intimate, relationships that cross-cut institutions including those of close friend or sexual partner. Morley *et al.* (2002: 270) offer the example of 'two professors, married to each other but working in different institutions, [who] regularly examine (and pass) each other's doctoral students'.

The potential significance of academic and personal relationships between individuals involved in the doctoral examination has prompted several universities to introduce regulations to monitor them. One way this is done is by asking academics to declare their academic and personal interests in relation to other examination participants, so that these are overt when examiners are considered. Even if an institution does not formally monitor relationships, those who select examiners can request that potential examiners declare their personal and academic relationships with the co-examiner(s), supervisor(s) and the candidate.

To know or not to know – issues relating to the selection of 'known' and 'unknown' external examiners

In most academic fields the supervisor and examiner will be part of a common academic community and therefore know each other's work, if not each other personally (see Box 5.3 for discussion of gender issues). In our questionnaire survey, only 6 per cent of supervisors and external examiners reported that they did not know one another at all. Many supervisors deliberately select an examiner that they 'know' quite well in professional and/or social terms. For example, when asked about his examiners, one PhD candidate told us:

> I know who they are. Harry is one and I know him from the pub casually. I've never worked with him but I've met him down the pub so I've got to know him. The other one is a guy called Leon, I know him as well actually but only through attending conferences and research workshops. The . . . research community is quite a small group in the UK actually, so I've met him at conferences and he was a PhD student of my supervisor many years ago, so we have the same kind of attitude to science.
>
> (Douglas, PhD Student, Sociology)

Another candidate told us that her supervisor warned her of the dangers of selecting an examiner whose academic agenda is unknown:

> I came up with a few names of people that Mary [her supervisor] didn't know and she was kind of like OK it could be dangerous when you don't know them at all. So in the end I was reading a lot of Gail anyway and she knows Gail and they have a lot of respect for each other's work.
>
> (Carla, PhD student, Art History)

There are various reasons for selecting an external examiner that supervisors know quite well, including:

- to enable the supervisor to have a broad idea about the likely content of the viva (although this cannot be guaranteed);
- to ensure the appointment of a 'sympathetic' examiner – someone who will appreciate the candidate's approach;
- to protect against a rogue examiner – someone who does not play fair with the candidate and, in some cases, also with the co-examiner. One could argue that this is a sensible strategy in the context of an examination that hinges usually on only two examiners;
- because it is known that they will be interested in the thesis and a good future publicist for the work and the candidate;
- because the examiner is known to be a 'nice' person, someone who will conduct the viva in a pleasant manner.

Whilst there are intellectual, strategic and practical reasons why supervisors select examiners that they know, this practice is often underpinned by problematic assumptions which can lead to difficulties. For example, selecting known examiners is often assumed to guarantee the content, or even conduct, of the examination; it does not (see Chapter 3). For example, both Carla and Douglas had examiners that were 'known' quite well by their respective supervisors. However, after her viva, Carla's supervisor commented that the examiners had been unexpectedly 'hard' on her: 'so she called me that night not knowing if I'd passed ... and she was excited because she said, "I wasn't sure if they weren't going to refer you from the tone of the questioning".' Similarly, Douglas noted in his post-viva interview that his supervisor 'was quite surprised I got them [questions] really. And some of the questions I just didn't understand. It wasn't unpleasant, but it wasn't how I expected it to be, given how well I know these people.' Douglas's supervisor may have been particularly surprised by the examiner's approach given that he had supervised the external examiner's PhD. One possible explanation for the external examiner's behaviour may relate to interpersonal dynamics and the external examiner's need to demonstrate his intellectual competence and independence to both his ex-supervisor, who attended the viva, and the candidate.

The selection of 'known' examiners can sometimes generate problems for the examiner and lead to an uncomfortable compromise of their intellectual 'independence' (issues for examiners are discussed in more detail in Chapter 7). This can arise in situations where the examiner's relationship with the candidate's supervisor, her/his co-examiner or the candidate leads to a sense of obligation to pass the candidate. An example of this is where a relatively senior supervisor invites a more junior academic, perhaps an ex-student, to examine their supervisee. Mutual examining arrangements – the 'I'll examine yours, if you examine mine' practice – can also cause problems as examiners may feel obliged to pass each other's students. A further, but related problem, concerns the compromise of academic standards that may result from an examiner being unable, or unwilling, to sustain an independent assessment of the candidate. This has implications for the examiner's reputation as well as that of the institution that awards the degree.

Unknown examiner, but not an unknown quantity

Although there are issues to consider in appointing known examiners, it is not advisable to appoint an external examiner that is an unknown quantity. Those responsible for selecting examiners need to know that the potential examiner can be relied upon to be fair and professional in their dealings with the candidate, co-examiner(s) and university administrators.

The following questions provide a guide to assessing the merits of appointing a particular academic as an examiner:

- What is their perspective and are they receptive to different approaches?
- Does s/he have a reputation for exercising realistic standards at PhD level?
- Does s/he have a reputation for a particular style of examining in the PhD viva?
- Is the person known to be reliable in terms of: committing themselves to a date for the viva; liaising with their co-examiner and university administrators; producing appropriate documentation?
- Is s/he known to have personal/political agendas that may lead to unfairness in assessing the candidate's thesis and viva performance?
- Is s/he known to have close academic, personal or financial links with the candidate, supervisor or prospective co-examiner that might compromise their interests when examining?

There are several ways of finding out whether an academic would be an appropriate PhD examiner, these include checking the following:

- the academic's published works;
- reviews that they have written of other studies;
- their conference presentation style;
- their manner of responding to, or asking questions at conferences, and the content of these questions;
- their reputation as PhD examiners;
- the type and standard of PhDs they have previously examined;
- the academic's declaration of their academic, personal and financial relationships with the candidate, co-examiner, supervisor etc.

It is essential to remember that whilst an academic may be an ideal examiner for one candidate they may not be for another – this is a matter not just of expertise but also of academic approach and personal factors.

Box 5.3   Issue in focus

THE GENDER POLITICS OF SELECTION

Questionnaire responses concerning the gendering of roles within the PhD examination (the most recent examination in which the respondent was involved) revealed that women were marginal in the roles of examiner (internal and external) and supervisor, even though 47 per cent of the candidates were female. Indeed, 76 per cent of external examiners, 79 per cent of internal examiners and 82 per cent of supervisors were male. The lower proportion of women relative to men serving as external examiners was, however, consistent with the preponderance of men in senior academic posts, that is senior lecturer/ researcher and above. Higher Education Statistics Agency figures reveal that of the 31,003 men and women holding senior academic grades (full and part time) in 1997/98, approximately 17 per cent were women. These findings show that men are the principal gatekeepers in doctoral examinations as they are in other areas of academic life (Ramazanuglu 1987; Brookes 1997).

Whilst the proportion of male and female examiners and supervisors is consistent with the gender composition and hierarchy of academia, the gender relationships between examiners, supervisors and candidates cannot be explained solely with reference to this. Our data are suggestive of more complex gender dynamics operating in the context of the PhD examination. Our questionnaire data, which related to 222 PhD examinations across Britain, revealed the following:

- that men were more likely than women to serve as external examiners of male or female PhD candidates;
- that women were more likely to act as external examiners for female than male candidates; 40 per cent of female candidates were examined by women compared with only 10 per cent of male candidates.
- a relationship between the gender of the supervisor and that of the external examiner – 44 per cent of women supervisors selected female external examiners compared with 19 per cent of male supervisors.

Implications
These data suggest that supervisors utilize networks in gender-specific ways to select examiners, and/or that they draw upon gendered networks. The importance of networks to the selection of examiners is evident from data revealing that in 75 per cent of cases the supervisor knew the external examiner personally.

Points for supervisors to consider

- Are you more likely to select female external examiners for female than male PhD students?
- Do you tend to select external examiners of the same gender as yourself?

For further discussion of gender dimensions of PhD examinations see Jackson *et al.* (2002).

Source: Adapted from Jackson and Tinkler 2001

5.4 Summary

Selecting examiners is an important matter, it therefore requires careful consideration by supervisors and candidates well in advance of submitting the thesis. In this chapter we have outlined appointment procedures. We have also looked closely at the range of factors that supervisors and candidates should consider when selecting external and internal examiners. Of course, when a person is invited to serve as an examiner they have a different set of factors to consider before they can accept or reject the appointment – these are discussed in Chapter 7.

6

Who Attends the Viva? Roles and Obligations

Chapter overview

The British viva is frequently portrayed as secret, private, confidential and occurring behind closed doors. This model is often juxtaposed with the open and public systems of vivas in many other countries. Aside from the examiners and candidate, there is no common rule in British higher education about who should or can attend a viva. This chapter introduces the key models used by institutions, outlining who can attend and in what capacities.

Students   ☺☺☺   Examiners   ☺☺☺
Supervisors   ☺☺☺   Chairs   ☺☺☺

Chapter contents

6.1 Viva attendance

The British PhD viva is usually a relatively private affair in comparison to the public vivas conducted in other parts of the world (see Boxes 2.4 and 5.3 for discussions of vivas in Sweden and France, respectively). However, blanket statements describing the British viva as 'private' obscure the diversity of forms that it takes. Indeed, a 'private' examination is not universal policy in British universities.

Who may attend the viva?

It depends – there are a number of permutations that are determined by the regulations of the institution where the examination takes place. The possible permutations are as follows:

- *Candidate and examiners only.* It is not particularly common for university policy to state that the viva must be attended by the examiners and the candidate only – 4 institutions out of 20 in our sample specified this.
- *Candidate, examiners and supervisor.* At a small number of institutions, policy states that the supervisor *must* attend the viva. More usually, institutions specify that the supervisor *may* attend subject to the consent of the candidate *or* the examiners *or* both the candidate and examiners. If you are at an institution where the supervisor may attend you are advised to think carefully about the advantages and disadvantages of the options available – we map out and discuss these later in this chapter.
- *Candidate, examiners, independent chair or university official (and possibly supervisor).* In some cases the viva can or must be attended by an independent chairperson or a university official. The roles of these various people are discussed later in this chapter.
- *'Public' vivas.* In at least two British universities the oral examination is 'public', although not just anyone may attend (see Box 6.1).

Reminder – how many examiners are there?

PhD examinations commonly involve two examiners, one external to the institution and one internal. There are exceptions to this. For example, if the candidate is a member of staff at the university where s/he is being examined there are usually two external examiners. In some cases, two external examiners will be involved if there is no suitable internal examiner. Also, if the PhD is interdisciplinary there may be an additional external or internal examiner. See Chapter 5 for more detail and discussion.

Box 6.1   Case studies

UNIVERSITIES WITH 'PUBLIC' VIVAS

At the Universities of Oxford and Manchester the viva is 'public'. Public is, however, interpreted in a very particular way to include members of specific academic communities.

University of Oxford

Policy states that 'the examination may be attended by any member of the University in academic dress. Non-members of the University may attend it only with the consent of both examiners'
(University of Oxford 1998: 3).

University of Manchester

Policy states that 'the PhD oral examination may be attended by academic supervisors, all academic staff at the University and all candidates for the degree of PhD. Observers are not allowed to participate in the viva discussion, must withdraw from the examination room during the final deliberations of the examiners or just before if the examiners want to speak to the candidate alone, and observers should have no part in the formulation of the examiners' recommendations. Furthermore, the examiners and all observers must sign an undertaking of confidentiality before the examination commences'
(University of Manchester 2000).

6.2 Roles and obligations of attendees

Although there can be more than one external and internal examiner, and more than one supervisor, for ease of communication we use the singular in this chapter.

External and internal examiners

The roles of external and internal examiners are institutionally variable. In this section we map out roles of examiners that are core to most/all PhD vivas, and then outline ones that vary according to the institution.

Core roles

- To attend the viva voce.
- To read and assess the thesis prior to the oral examination.
- In cases where there are materials to be examined in addition to a written thesis – for example, a performance or an exhibition – the examiners must spend time examining this work before the oral examination.
- To meet with the co-examiner(s) (and sometimes a chair) immediately before the oral examination to agree the issues to be discussed in the viva and to set an agenda for it.
- To examine the candidate orally.
- To detect and assess any extenuating circumstances that may have affected the quality of the candidate's work (see Chapter 12).
- To make a recommendation to the university about the outcome of the examination.
- If necessary, to re-examine the candidate and/or their work.

Roles that vary according to institutional regulations and/or the particular viva

- Lead role and/or chair of the viva. In some institutions the external examiner is expected to lead and/or chair the viva, whereas in other institutions the internal examiner is expected to chair it (see Box 6.2 for examples of procedural diversity). In some institutions there is an independent chair (see later in this section).
- In most cases the external examiner has greater expertise in the area of the candidate's topic than the internal examiner. This sometimes, although not always, means that the external examiner will ask more questions than the internal, and sometimes these can be more probing. This matches one candidate's experience: 'the lead was all from the external which was what my supervisor had led me to believe. He said that it was up to the external to take the lead and set the tone and the internal examiner in some ways is there as prisoner's friend' (Kali, PhD student, English). Another student also suggested that the external examiner was more challenging:

> It felt very much like a double act, my internal examiner was very kind and didn't really criticize my work very much and praised me quite a lot. Whereas the external was kind of much more harsh, really to the front and picking up faults a lot more. I think they possibly set that up . . . it really was good cop bad cop.
>
> (Alice, PhD student, Geography)

However, this is not always the case. Kate, a psychologist, suggested that her internal and external examiners played an equal role in her viva and 'basically took it in turns to ask me a series of questions about the work'. Other candidates have suggested that the internal examiner asked most of the questions, which, in some cases, were more challenging than those of the external examiner. Dan, a chemistry candidate, told us that in the viva 'the internal did about 95 per cent [of the questioning], the external just left it to him'.

- In many cases the internal examiner is expected to set up the viva, this may involve: liaising with the viva participants to set a date and time; organizing a venue; informing appropriate university officials about the arrangements; and generally acting as a contact person for the external examiner. The internal examiner is also frequently responsible for 'looking after' the external examiner, which may involve sending them information about travel, booking accommodation, arranging lunch, and so on. Sometimes, administrators undertake some of these roles, but again this will vary by department and institution.

Supervisor

If the supervisor is allowed to attend the viva, her/his role within it varies according to institutional policy. The different roles are:

- Silent observer – the supervisor is an observer who must remain silent unless explicitly invited to comment on a particular point by the examiners.
- Participant on invitation – the supervisor is allowed to participate in the viva on invitation from the examiners.
- Participant without invitation – the supervisor is actively encouraged to take part and the examiners are prohibited from denying this participation (see Box 6.2).
- Candidate's friend – some institutions expect the supervisor to be a 'friend' to the candidate: 'The supervisor may be present for all or part of the oral examination: this would be to give friendly support to the candidate, but not to take part in the examination' (University of York 1997: 6). What it means to be a 'candidate's friend' and give 'friendly support' is not clear. People's interpretations of what this means and how it can be translated into action will vary considerably. (See also Box 6.2.)

In most institutions where supervisors may attend the viva they must withdraw from the examination room before the examiners commence discussion about the outcome.

Box 6.2   Case studies

ROLES AND OBLIGATIONS OF ATTENDEES AT TWO INSTITUTIONS

To illustrate how the roles and responsibilities of viva participants vary between institutions we have included extracts from policy at two institutions. There are some important differences, so it is imperative that examiners and candidates check the institution's regulations where they will examine/be examined so that they do not get any unpleasant surprises on the day.

University of Hertfordshire

> It is the view of the University that all the appointed examiners have an equal status and role. Nevertheless, it is customary for the External Examiner(s) to lead the oral examination, but in doing so, the External Examiner has the responsibility to ensure that each examiner plays a full role.
>
> The University's regulations allow one supervisor to attend the oral examination with the agreement of the candidate. Where the supervisor attends the viva, s/he acts as the 'candidate's friend'. The supervisor's role is thus complementary to that of the examiners and hence the supervisor should not lead the discussion but rather ensure that the candidate fully understands the tack being taken by the examiners. Examiners do not have the right to deny the supervisor this role.
>
> (University of Hertfordshire 2002: 4)

University of Brighton

> The internal examiner or advisor is responsible for: chairing the examination; ensuring, with the examination team, prior to the viva, agreement on the issues to be discussed; ensuring that the questioning by examiners during the examination is appropriate and fair and that the student is given every opportunity to respond to questioning; ensuring that the viva proceeds in an orderly manner and is completed in good time; advising the examiners on the interpretation of the university's regulations; informing the candidate of the recommendations of the panel and ensuring that the candidate is informed of actions required of them; ensuring that actions resulting from the examination are understood by all; forwarding notification of the outcome to the Academic Registry for transmission to the Research Degrees Committee for approval.
>
> A representative of the supervisory team, subject to the consent of the candidate, may attend the oral examination. He/she may participate in the discussion only if addressed directly by the examiners, and shall be required to withdraw prior to the deliberation of the examiners on the outcome of the examination.
>
> (University of Brighton 2002b: 8, 9)

Independent chairperson

A minority of institutions arrange for an independent chairperson to be present at all vivas. Chairs are usually present to ensure that the viva proceeds fairly and in accordance with the institution's regulations. Ideally, the chair should be a senior academic who has substantial experience of examining PhDs and who has undergone some training for the role. The roles of an independent chair vary between institutions, but the following would be amongst the roles of a good chair:

- The chair should meet the examiners prior to the viva to agree an agenda for the viva.
- The chair should introduce the examiners and candidate at the start of the viva and outline to the candidate the procedure for the viva and the key purposes of it.
- In most cases the chair will not have read the thesis so will not be able to judge the content of the questions, but s/he should be able to judge the style of questioning and 'should intervene in favour of the candidate in cases where, for instance, the questioning of an examiner appears to be unduly aggressive or confrontational, or otherwise inappropriate' (BPS/ UCoSDA 1995: 13–14).
- The chair should ensure that the candidate has the opportunity to respond to all questions posed by the examiners.
- The chair may wish to rephrase a question where it appears that the candidate has not understood it fully (BPS/UCoSDA 1995: 14).
- The chair should ensure that if the viva extends beyond two hours, the candidate is offered a break and refreshments.
- The chair must know the PhD examination regulations of the institution and (1) be able to advise the examiners and candidate of these regulations and (2) ensure that the examiners adhere to them.
- At the end of the examination the chair should ensure that the candidate knows the recommendation of the examiners (or otherwise when the recommendation will be released – see Chapter 11). S/he should also ensure that the candidate is informed of any actions required of her/him and the time limit for such actions.
- The chair should ensure that any actions resulting from the examination are clear and understood by all parties.

In some cases, universities that do not have chairs as a matter of course will introduce one if the need arises. For example, on occasions where there are two external examiners and no internal examiner, a chair may be present at the viva to ensure that the examiners know and adhere to the university regulations. In cases where the internal examiner is junior and/or inexperienced, an independent chair may be appointed to ensure that an experienced person, who knows the university regulations, is on hand in case of difficulties. In the latter case, the internal examiner is then able to concentrate on examining without having the distraction of other roles.

In addition to ensuring that the viva proceeds fairly and smoothly, an experienced chair can also be involved at a developmental level. For example, the chair could provide feedback to an inexperienced internal examiner about her/his performance, the ways s/he handled interactions in the viva, and points for them to consider in future vivas.

City University provides a fairly detailed checklist for viva chairs (reproduced in Box 6.3). This type of checklist can be useful for chairs to ensure that they have covered key roles required of them. It may also be a useful starting point for individuals or universities who want to devise their own checklists for viva chairs.

University official

In some institutions a university official/administrator attends some or all of the oral examination. This is still relatively rare, but where it does happen the role of the administrator is likely to include the following:

- S/he will know the PhD examination regulations of the institution and (1) be able to advise the examiners of these regulations and (2) ensure that the examiners adhere to them.
- S/he may minute some or all of the proceedings.

Box 6.3   Case study

FORM FOR CHAIRS AT CITY UNIVERSITY

Research Student Oral Examinations – Checklist for Chair

NB A senior academic with previous experience of examining and supervising research degree students should fill the role of Chair.

Name of Candidate	Surname:	
	First name:	
Department/School		
Name(s) of Supervisor(s)		
Name of External Examiner Note: Staff candidates require 2 External Examiners.		
Name of Internal Examiner		
Present Degree	MPhil / LLM / MMA / PhD / DMA / DHealth / DPsych	
Date of Viva Voce		

Please tick the boxes once each stage has been completed.

INTRODUCTION AT THE START OF THE EXAMINATION

Introduce the examiners, supervisor(s), candidate and yourself. ☐

Ensure that the candidate has received a copy of the Research Studies handbook and that they have read sections 4.7, 8.4 and 9.11. If the candidate has not read these sections please ensure that they do so before the examination continues. (Some Chairs prefer to go over the regulations with a Candidate a couple of days before the examination. This is acceptable.) ☐

Explain that the examiners have been appointed in accordance with the regulations and procedures contained within the Research Studies Handbook and that the examiners have been given a copy of it to ensure that all parties have had the same information on rules, regulations and procedure. Explain that only the examiners make the assessment. ☐

Explain that the role of the Chair is to ensure that the assessment processes are operated rigorously, fairly, reliably and consistently. Explain that the Chair has a neutral role in the assessment process and takes no part in the actual assessment of the research. He/she should not be called upon for specialist discipline knowledge, but for knowledge of regulations, procedures, policy and practice. ☐

REPORTS AND FORMAL COMMUNICATION OF RESULTS

Explain that the Examiners will produce a written report of the outcome of the examination and that they may make notes during the examination. They are also invited to make general comments about the University's research study provision in a separate report. ☐

Explain that a letter will be sent to the candidate giving formal notification of the outcome of the examination and giving information on what to do next (letter of award with details of graduation, information about minor amendments or resubmission, or – very seldom – failure and appeal procedures). Explain that University has an equal opportunities policy for students and that only matters relating to the research study will be considered in the assessment. ☐

THE EXAMINATION

Hand over to the Examiners to lead the examination.

The Chair can interject:

- To resolve any conflicts.*
- To provide advice on regulations, procedures, policy and practice.
- Where there is any activity that is not 'rigorous, fair, reliable or consistent'.
- Where there is any activity which contravenes the equal opportunities policy. ☐

When the Examiners have finished their discussion with the candidate, ensure that there are no more queries and ask the candidate whether he/she has anything more he/she would like to add or ask. ☐

Draw the proceedings together and outline the next steps (probably that the candidate should leave the room and be outside the door at an agreed time to be invited in to hear the outcome).

RESULT

Where the Examiners have a discussion about the result, interject as before:

- To resolve any conflicts.*
- Provide advice on regulations, procedures, policy and practice.
- Where there is any activity which is not 'rigorous, fair, reliable or consistent'.
- Where there is any activity which contravenes the equal opportunities policy.

In exceptional cases where the result is not given at the viva, explain to the candidate why this is the case and what will happen to inform them of the result. ☐

Lead the Examiners and candidate in following the agreed process for telling him/her the results. ☐

REPORT

Ensure that the Examiners complete their report form and expenses forms where appropriate and that they know where to send them (send them to the Academic Registrar's Office on their behalf yourself if appropriate). ☐

Ensure that you have completed all sections of this checklist and send it to the Academic Registrar's Office (Research Degrees Committee secretariat). ☐

COMMENTS

Please make any comments overleaf on the examination process or note any incidents of good or bad practice here:

Chair's Comments

Chair's Name _____   Chair's Signature _____

Date _____/_____/20____

(please print clearly)

* Note Research Studies Handbook statement on precedence of judgement – External
Examiner takes precedence where s/he is of the view that the work does not reach the
required standard. However, where there is other disagreement but it is agreed that there
is genuine doubt or where two or more External Examiners disagree, the matter should
be referred to Research Degrees Committee for further scrutiny of the work to be
arranged.

Source: City University 2003

Box 6.4   Task for students, supervisors and examiners

POLICY CHECK

Check the guidelines produced by the institution where the viva
examination will take place. What do they say about who may/must
attend the viva? What are the roles of the attendees? Candidates: if
your regulations pose difficulties for you, speak to your supervisor or
postgraduate tutor about them.

6.3 Should the supervisor attend the viva?

If institutional policy permits supervisors to attend the viva then careful consideration needs to be given to the pros and cons of their doing so. There are
important factors to consider for candidates, supervisors and examiners
(depending on what the university regulations allow). We outline below the
pros and cons of a supervisor's presence at a viva from the perspectives of
candidates, supervisors and examiners.

Candidates' perspectives

As discussed earlier, if supervisors are allowed to attend the vivas of
their students, the roles that they can adopt vary from institution to

institution. With this in mind, we have drawn together some of the key reasons why some candidates want their supervisor to attend, and why others do not.

Reasons why some candidates want their supervisor to attend

- A supervisor can provide feedback on viva performance. This type of post-viva 'debriefing' can be very important for many candidates who do not feel able to judge their performance. One candidate told us that the debriefing provided by her supervisor was useful because 'it's a bit like having a wedding or something, you never remember the day' (Jan, Religious Studies).
- A supervisor can make notes about corrections. Whilst candidates should receive written notification of corrections required by examiners, it can be very useful for supervisors to be present when these are discussed in the viva.
- A supervisor can make notes on any advice provided by examiners about publication and/or developing the research further in post-doctoral work.
- A supervisor can offer moral support. Depending upon the university regulations, this may be as a silent supporter or in some cases as an active participant.

Reasons why some candidates do not want their supervisor to attend

- Candidates sometimes want to 'stand on their own feet' and to feel that they are able to 'go it alone'.
- Candidates may sometimes be tempted to involve their supervisor and look to them for help, which is not allowed in some universities. Bob (Chemistry) told us: 'if he was there, there's . . . the possibility that I could turn to him and look at him and he could become involved which he can't do and that could make it a bit awkward'.
- The supervisor may feel to the candidate like another examiner. 'It's enough that there's two people examining you without other people listening and silently examining you' (Carla, Art History).
- Fear of showing oneself up. 'It's a kind of paranoia and anxiety about just making a total idiot of myself and not wanting my supervisors to witness me stammering and blubbering and saying something very stupid' (Leila, Sociology).
- Supervisor may speak out of turn. As Shaun (Engineering) told us: 'he [the supervisor] caused more trouble than either the internal or external put together'. And in response to the question, 'So how did you feel during the viva?', Shaun replied, 'Pretty relaxed until my supervisor started to argue with me.'
- Fear of embarrassing the supervisor. 'It would be unfair on her really, she [my supervisor] would probably be squirming' (Andrew, Physiotherapy).
- Relationship breakdown. In some cases the relationship between supervisor and student breaks down before the viva. In these cases the presence of the supervisor may make the candidate uncomfortable.

- Academic disagreements. In some cases the supervisor and candidate may have disagreed about an aspect of the PhD; it may be more difficult for the candidate to convey and discuss this disagreement if the supervisor is present.
- Discussion about supervision. The candidate may want to talk to the examiners about aspects of their supervision; this may be awkward if the supervisor attends.

It is not always possible for candidates to have input into decisions about whether the supervisor should attend the viva, but where it is possible candidates need to think carefully about the pros and cons. It is worth noting that most students in our research were pleased when their supervisor had attended their viva even if they were unsure about it prior to the examination. For example, Carla (Art History) told us after her viva that:

> Originally, it was really weird because I was really thinking that I didn't know if I wanted them [her supervisors] there because I thought having an audience would make me more nervous. So we talked it through and then in the end I thought, well I'm just going to take them for what they are, which is two people who want me to do well, and in the end I was happy that they were there . . . So anyway, I had them both there, and Mary had to sneak out, but I think I did the right thing because I actually felt supported by them.

We endorse Carla's approach of talking to her supervisors about her anxieties, and thinking carefully about the pros and cons of her supervisors attending (see Box 6.5). If, however, a student does not get on with their supervisor, or they think that their supervisor behaves towards them in an unhelpful manner, it may be best that s/he does not attend the viva. As always, it will depend on what the regulations state at your university. However, if the regulations do not insist that the supervisor is present in the viva and candidates do not want her/him to attend, they should:

- try to dissuade her or him;
- consult the department postgraduate tutor or possibly their internal examiner if they are adamant that they do not want their supervisor to attend the viva but the supervisor insists on doing so.

Box 6.5   Task for students

DECISION TIME — DO YOU WANT YOUR SUPERVISOR TO ATTEND YOUR VIVA?

Make a list of pros and cons of the attendance of your supervisor(s) at the viva (if your institutional regulations allow your supervisor(s) to attend and you can influence the decision).

Supervisors' perspectives

If supervisors are allowed to attend the vivas of their students, the roles that they are allowed to adopt vary from institution to institution. With this in mind, we have drawn together some of the key reasons why some supervisors may want to attend, and why others may not.

Supervisors' reasons for attending their student's viva

- To provide feedback on viva performance.
- To make notes about necessary corrections.
- To offer moral support silently or in some cases verbal support (see section above on the roles of the supervisor).
- To be involved in all stages of the PhD and to see the process through to the end.
- To gain insight into different styles of examining.
- To get feedback on the effectiveness of their supervision.

Supervisors' reasons for not attending their student's viva

- The supervisor may feel that their presence will inhibit the candidate's responses.
- S/he may think that it is appropriate for the student to tackle the viva on their own, to reinforce their independence. One supervisor (Politics) told us: 'the student should be capable of an independent defence of their work'.
- The supervisor may feel uncomfortable being a passive observer.
- S/he may feel that her/his presence will inhibit the examiners.

Examiners' perspectives

In some institutions the supervisor is permitted to attend the viva only with the consent of the examiners. In such cases, examiners need to consider carefully the pros and cons of the supervisor's presence. Key issues for consideration are listed below.

Reasons why some examiners welcome the presence of the candidate's supervisor

- The examiners may be able to invite comments from the supervisor that may be beneficial to discussions in the viva (depending on institutional regulations).
- The supervisor may comment (depending on institutional regulations) on 'any practical or administrative difficulties in pursuit of the research which the candidate may raise' (BPS/UCoSDA 1995: 14).
- The examiners may be able to determine whether the candidate has been poorly or badly advised by the supervisor (see Chapter 12, Box 12.2, for an

example of an examiner who regretted not being able to check on this because the supervisor was absent from the viva).

- The presence of the supervisor may make the candidate more comfortable and relaxed.

Reasons why some examiners do not welcome the presence of the candidate's supervisor

- The supervisor may inhibit the examiners asking questions about, or discussing, the quality and amount of supervision.
- The examiner may be concerned that the candidate will be inhibited by the presence of their supervisor.
- The examiner may feel intimidated if the supervisor is senior to them academically.
- The supervisor may be disruptive and/or may challenge the examiners. The extent to which this is likely will depend upon the institutional regulations and whether there are mechanisms in place to enforce the regulations. For example, an independent chair should stop a supervisor speaking if the regulations prohibit the supervisor contributing to the viva.

6.4 Summary

Who may attend the viva and what they may do in it varies between institutions. It is crucial that all viva participants are familiar with the regulations where they are examining or being examined. It is never too soon for students to check this out. Students also need to think carefully about whether they want their supervisor(s) to be at their viva, although this may depend on the university regulations. Supervisors and examiners also need to reflect on potential consequences of the supervisor's presence for the conduct of the viva.

7

Examiners – Should You Examine?

Chapter overview

This chapter is aimed at academics who are invited to examine a PhD thesis. The decision about whether to serve as an examiner is always context dependent. In this chapter we discuss the various issues that academics should reflect on before accepting an appointment as an internal or external examiner and highlight considerations that will be specific to each doctoral thesis/candidate. Occasionally, academics are asked to serve as replacements for one of the original examiners, or to supplement the original examining team. The issues that these requests raise are also discussed.

Examiners ☺☺☺   Supervisors ☺

Chapter contents

When considering whether to accept an invitation to examine a British PhD, you need to be clear about what the job entails. In what follows we map out the key components of the job and then explore issues that you need to consider *before* agreeing to serve as either an external or internal examiner.

For ease of communication we use a model of two examiners for each PhD examination, one external and one internal, although we recognize that an additional internal or external examiner is sometimes appointed (see Chapters 5 and 6).

7.1 What the job entails

Examining a PhD takes roughly five days although, in the case of re-examination of the thesis and possibly a second viva, the process can take several days more. The job of examining a PhD involves several elements, as follows:

- Practical arrangements. Internal examiners are sometimes responsible for the organization of the viva and arrangements for the external examiner's travel, accommodation and entertainment. More details on the roles and responsibilities of internal examiners can be found in Chapter 6.
- Reading and evaluating the candidate's thesis.
- Writing a pre-viva report on the thesis. Institutions vary as to whether they expect this report to be official and submitted prior to the viva or merely made available to the co-examiner(s) before the viva.
- Conducting the viva. In the case of practice-based PhDs, examiners may also need to attend an exhibition or performance on the day of the viva or the day before.
- Making a recommendation of award.
- Completing a post-viva report and, if appropriate, outlining corrections.
- Post-viva checks or re-examining. The internal examiner will usually have responsibility for checking and approving minor corrections. Where more substantial changes to the thesis are required, both examiners are usually expected to approve them and then to complete appropriate paperwork. In some cases a candidate may require a second viva (see Chapter 13).

Given the demands of examining, why should you accept an appointment? The answer is always context dependent and the question you should always ask yourself is, 'Should I agree to examine *this* PhD?' Next we look at the issues you need to consider before agreeing to serve as an external examiner, then we address issues relating to service as an internal examiner.

7.2 Should you serve as an external examiner?

External examiners are paid a small fee for examining a PhD; they also receive reimbursement for travel and subsistence costs. Although some academics argue that examining takes place during working time and the fee is, therefore, a bonus, most argue that external examining is an addition to an academic's usual workload and is very poorly remunerated. 'Serving as an external examiner is currently badly paid . . . If examinations are to be conducted properly and in a timely manner, then examiners should be paid adequately for the time spent, which is never likely to be less than three working days in total, even in the most straightforward of cases' (BPS/UCoSDA 1995: 20). Most academics agree that money is not the primary reason for agreeing to examine externally at PhD level. So why should you choose to examine a particular thesis?

Potential benefits of agreeing to examine a PhD

There are three main benefits to examining at PhD level, subject to certain conditions (these are discussed later). The three benefits are:

- career development and academic recognition;
- intellectual interest;
- service to academic and/or discipline communities.

There are also practical considerations. We now look at each of these benefits in turn.

Career development and academic recognition
An invitation to serve as an external examiner represents recognition of expertise and conferment of academic status; it is a mark of belonging to the academic, or more usually, discipline-specific, community. Being in high demand as an external examiner is a clear sign that one is recognized as a leading figure within a discipline or, more usually, a specific area within a discipline. Academics who are in very high demand often have to refuse requests to examine. Whereas established academics may not feel the need to assert themselves within their particular academic community, 'new' academics have much to gain from the recognition bestowed by an invitation to serve as an external examiner. Linked to this, evidence of external examining is often requested when 'new' academics seek promotion.

Intellectual interest
For established academics, as well as their less-established peers, a principal reason to accept examining is to keep abreast of developments in the field. Interest is also a key factor.

As examiners we have further access to new ideas and approaches . . . It is exciting to be in on the final stages of a research project and to find candidates in control of their work and proud of their achievements.

(Denicolo *et al.* 2000: 5)

There are probably two really good things about examining PhD theses. The first involves reading new research on a topic that is close to my own research interests, or alternatively, if the topic is miles away from what I work on, reading research that uses theories and methods of relevance to my own work. A second benefit is meeting the researcher and having the opportunity to discuss with them what they've done and what they've made of it. This is very different from the more impersonal process of undergraduate and even MA examining, where it is unusual to meet candidates.

(Professor, History)

Service to academic and/or discipline communities
Examining is a means by which academics participate in discipline communities. This participation involves promoting good scholarship, encouraging promising scholars, maintaining standards, and gatekeeping. Mullins and Kiley (2002: 375) discovered that 'duty', and more specifically the maintenance of standards within a discipline, was a major reason why academics agreed to examine Australian PhDs: 'You are asked to maintain the standards because of your own professional expertise.' The notion of an external examiner as an arbiter of standards across institutions does raise some interesting issues, especially in the light of evidence of considerable diversity in the judgements of academics (Johnston 1997).

Practicalities
Location, and the scheduling of the viva, are sometimes considerations. Examining within easy travelling distance can be convenient and attractive for some academics, particularly those with domestic responsibilities. Others may be attracted by the opportunity to meet up with colleagues, friends and family. Examining a PhD on a Friday in an area of 'outstanding beauty' opens up the possibility of a weekend away. Additionally, in the context of too many work demands, the decision to examine a thesis may be influenced by the willingness of the candidate's supervisor to examine your students.

Important considerations when deciding whether to examine a PhD

Although there are some attractions to PhD examining, there are three main questions that you need to address *before* you accept an invitation.

1. Are you the right person for this particular job?

   • Do you meet the criteria stipulated by the appointing institution?

- Are your interests too closely tied to those of the candidate, their supervisor or the co-examiner in academic, personal or financial terms?
- Is this really your area of expertise?
- Are you prepared to be fair?

2. Do you have enough time?

- Are you already doing too much examining?
- Are you overburdened with other commitments?

3. Are you prepared to examine this thesis in the manner specified by the appointing institution?

We now look at each of these questions in turn.

Are you the right person for this particular job?
Four main factors need to be considered in relation to this question: (1) institutional requirements; (2) personal, academic and financial relationships; (3) area of expertise; (4) fairness.

First, institutions normally stipulate certain qualifications and experiences that an external examiner should have. They also regulate the type of relationship that an external examiner may have to the appointing institution and/or department, and exclude academics from serving as external examiner to a student that they have supervised (discussed further in Chapter 5).

Second, an increasing number of institutions also stipulate that examiners should not be closely involved with other examination participants in academic, personal or financial terms. Some institutions identify the types of relationships that are considered unsuitable, others ask potential examiners to declare their interests and/or involvement (see Chapter 5). In order to decide whether or not you are an appropriate examiner, you must read the institution's regulations carefully.

Even where institutions do not regulate academic, personal and financial relationships between examination participants, it is wise to consider whether agreeing to examine could lead to problems. Relationships that may be problematical, and which you should think about carefully before agreeing to examine, include situations in which

- you are involved with the candidate, the supervisor or co-examiner on a personal or financial basis;
- you are a recent ex-student of the supervisor or co-examiner;
- you are working closely with the supervisor, co-examiner or candidate;
- the candidate's supervisor has recently examined and passed your PhD student – are you confident that the tit-for-tat principle of agreeing to serve as examiner does not extend to agreeing to pass the candidate?

Disagreeing with people is often uncomfortable, and upholding a position when others disagree can be difficult (see Box 12.5), but both can be much more difficult when you are working with people with whom you are closely involved or to whom you feel you owe a debt (for example, they recently examined and passed your PhD student). The question you need to ask yourself, and to answer truthfully, before accepting an invitation to examine is, 'If necessary, could I refer, or even fail, this candidate?' If the answer is no then this is an invitation you should *not* accept.

Third, external examiners are usually required to be 'experts'; this is often equated with having published in the area of the candidate's thesis. Whilst some academics subscribe to the view that the candidate's thesis should fall directly within the area of the examiner's work, others are happy with a looser correspondence between the work of the examiner and candidate.

In our view the external examiner must be able to:

- understand the theories and approaches employed by the candidate;
- assess the candidate's understanding and application of these theories and approaches;
- know the broader context(s) and locate the thesis within it;
- judge whether the thesis meets the minimum requirements for a PhD in the appointing institution and particular discipline area, for example the requirement that a thesis be 'original' and constitute a 'contribution to knowledge';
- conduct a rigorous, but fair, verbal examination about the thesis and, if required, about the broader context;
- where appropriate, identify ways of revising a thesis for the award of PhD;
- where appropriate, offer guidance on the future development of the research and on publication possibilities.

To help academics decide whether they have sufficient expertise to examine a particular thesis, BPS/UCoSDA (1995: 6) recommend that, 'before formal appointment, all proposed examiners should receive a brief abstract of the research, prepared by the candidate . . . This should outline the topic, the contents, and the theoretical and methodological approaches adopted.' This is a good suggestion, although the success of this practice hinges on the clarity and accuracy of the candidate's abstract. If an abstract is not supplied, you should request to see one before you agree to examine. Even after formal appointment BPS/UCoSDA (1995: 9) recommend that you should return the thesis and resign the appointment if you think that you are 'not competent to pass judgement on the written submission'. On occasions, you may not be 'expert' in all aspects of the thesis: this is particularly likely with interdisciplinary or multidisciplinary work. In these instances it may be appropriate to suggest the appointment of an additional examiner with expertise in the areas outside your competences.

With the growth in practice-based PhDs in areas such as creative and performing arts and design, academics who have examined only written PhD theses may be asked to examine 'practice'. Lack of experience of examining practice may suggest that your best response is to decline the invitation. However, it is worth considering the request carefully before responding, particularly if you are already experienced at PhD examining – someone obviously thinks that your interests and experiences make you a suitable examiner.

Fourth, our research and other sources (see Chapter 3) suggest that some people examine in ways that are unfair to the candidate. Typically the examination seems to be used as an opportunity to block certain academic developments and/or to work out a grudge against the candidate, their supervisor or the department. To examine fairly you must be prepared to engage with the candidate's work on its own terms. If you feel that you cannot, or are not willing to do this, then you should decline the invitation.

Do you have enough time?
Our academic interviewees reported a few occasions when their co-examiner had quite clearly not read the thesis properly (see also Phillips 1994: 134). This is not fair to the candidate, their supervisor or the co-examiner(s). It is also a breach of the contract that an examiner makes with an institution when they agree to examine. If you are unlikely to have, or to make, sufficient time to read the thesis carefully and fully then you should decline the invitation to examine.

Another reason for deciding not to examine is that you have already committed yourself to examine other PhD theses. An academic who is in high demand as an examiner can easily become overburdened unless they refuse requests. Some academics set themselves a limit to the number of theses they examine in a year. How examiners decide which requests to accept and which to refuse will probably depend on the factors discussed above.

Are you prepared to examine in the manner specified by the appointing institution?
Many academics assume that the regulations for examining a PhD are fairly standardized, but they are not (see Tinkler and Jackson 2000). Some universities have procedures that you may feel uncomfortable with (for example, rules against the release of a decision at the start of the viva, or rules that stipulate that the pre-viva examiners' meeting must be minuted by an administrator). It is wise to ask to see the guidance for examiners before you agree to examine – ensure that you know what you are letting yourself in for when you say yes.

7.3 Should you serve as an internal examiner?

Whereas external examining carries some kudos, internal examining is of much lower status and is unpaid, although examiners often get a free lunch. Why, then, agree to serve as an internal examiner?

Reasons to examine a PhD

- Internal examining is a way in which academics acquire the skills, experience and confidence to undertake external examining, it therefore contributes to career development.

- Internal examining, like external examining, is also a service to the wider academic community and is a useful way of getting to know colleagues in your own, or related, areas.
- Internal examining is part of an academic's job. It is a responsibility we have within our own institutions to the postgraduate student community and our colleagues who supervise PhDs.
- Internal examining can be academically interesting and provide opportunities to keep abreast of new developments.

For all these positive reasons to examine there are also several important considerations that you need to address before making a decision.

Important considerations when deciding whether to examine a PhD

Whilst some of the considerations discussed in relation to external examining may be pertinent to internal examining, the issues for internal and for external examiners are slightly different. When asked to serve as an internal examiner you are advised to consider carefully the following four questions:

1. In academic terms, can you examine this thesis?
2. Are you doing too much PhD examining?
3. Can you examine this PhD thesis fairly?
4. Do you have experience of examining a PhD?

We now discuss each of these considerations in turn.

In academic terms, can you examine this thesis?
One of the downsides of being invited to serve as an internal examiner is that it is not always, or even usually, the case that the thesis is directly in your area of expertise. This does not mean that you should not examine the thesis; in most cases it is unlikely that there will be another academic, aside from the supervisor, who will be working in the same area as the candidate. The important considerations are (1) whether it is in an area that you understand and have general knowledge of, and (2) whether you find the thesis, or aspects of it (topic, theory, methodology), interesting.

Are you doing too much PhD examining?
Some people are in greater demand as internal examiners than others because of their areas of interest, their reputation as a good examiner, their availability, and so on. Bearing in mind that internal examining takes almost as much time as external examining, it is sensible to work out a feasible annual limit and to stick to it. It makes sense that academics who do a lot of external examining may be disinclined to take on internal examining as well. However, internal examining does provide a means of keeping in touch with

standards within your own institution and it is a service that is fundamental to PhD provision within it.

Can you examine this PhD thesis fairly?
Internal examiners frequently know the supervisor, and even the candidate, quite well. Whilst this is unavoidable, you still need to reflect on the implications of agreeing to examine and whether you may be compromised by your relationship with the supervisor and/or candidate. The pressure on internal examiners to pass a thesis against their better judgement is often heavier than that on external examiners, particularly where the internal examiner is junior to the candidate's supervisor, or the supervisor is head of department. In these instances, the internal examiner may feel under pressure to pass a weak thesis in order to protect their current and future position in the department.

> Junior, internal examiners especially are locked into academic, social, political and economic relationships which have the potential to put a strain on the independent exercise of their judgement and integrity. Their career, promotion, friendships and entire future could be on the line if they want to demur from a favourable view taken by the student's supervisor/s and the other examiner.
>
> Typically: senior academic and principal supervisor (possibly head of department) engages guru at University of Wessex with whom he (sic) has worked for many years – and who owes him a favour – to act as external examiner. He then approaches some malleable departmental colleague in the department inviting her (sic) to act as internal. She feels privileged, obliged to accept (for what grounds are there for refusal?) or merely that this is an important opportunity in her professional development. She finds thesis of poor standard, but is then called by the external saying 'there's no problem here is there?' etc. etc. etc. But, if not a guru, it could be your best friend, the editor of your professional journal or fellow member of the AUT executive.
>
> (Professor, Social Science)

The question you need to consider when invited to examine is the same one you should consider when approached to be an external examiner: if necessary, could you refer, or even fail, this candidate? Novice examiners or junior members of a department are advised to check out the candidate and supervisor before agreeing to serve as an internal. It is not a good idea to be involved in examining a weak student if the supervisor is senior to you and known to be difficult; a more senior or experienced colleague would be better placed to serve as an internal examiner in this situation.

Do you have experience of examining a PhD?
Internal examining is usually the first stage in developing experience as a PhD examiner. If you have no experience as a PhD examiner and you are invited to serve as an internal examiner, it is a good idea to check what

support is available to you. For instance, some institutions provide a mentor (possibly a co-internal examiner) to see novice internal examiners through the whole examination procedure. Alternatively, they appoint a chair for the viva to relieve the internal examiner of responsibility for the administration and conduct of the exam. Staff development courses may provide a means of gaining knowledge about procedures and practices at your institution. Attending various types of mock viva can also be valuable (see Chapter 9).

7.4 Unusual examining appointments

Occasionally, you may be asked to replace one of the original examiners or to supplement the original examining team. This request is usually prompted by one of three scenarios:

1. The original examiners cannot agree a recommendation and an additional external examiner is therefore appointed.
2. A PhD thesis needs to be examined again by a new set of examiners. This situation can arise if the candidate has appealed successfully against the outcome of the original examination on the grounds that there were procedural irregularities in the examination process and or that there was evidence of prejudice, bias, unfair or inadequate assessment in the examination process (see Chapter 13).
3. One or both of the original examiners is not available to examine a resubmitted thesis because of illness, death, absence, retirement or resignation of appointment.

Institutional policy does not usually provide guidance about scenario three and so it seems likely that these situations are handled largely on a case-by-case basis. If you are approached to serve as an additional examiner (scenario one) you will probably be notified that there is a difference of opinion between the original examiners, but the institution may prohibit the release of information about the identities of the original examiners and their specific recommendations. However, as with most areas of institutional life, you may be offered information 'off the record'. Where a new set of examiners is appointed to examine a thesis following appeal (scenario two), it is not clear from policy whether you will be informed of the background to the examination, although you may be informed unofficially of this history.

Agreeing to examine a PhD thesis in the above three circumstances can be even more demanding in academic terms than usual and it can also be fraught with interpersonal issues, particularly in scenario three as illustrated by Robert's predicament in Box 7.1. There is no simple advice on how to assess these different situations because they are idiosyncratic and because you may not be informed of the history of the case. However, it is not a good idea for someone who has little or no experience of examining to accept an appointment under these conditions. Even experienced examiners need to think carefully about these types of request and to recognize that the job may require more time and sensitivity than usual.

It is debatable whether specific case information is helpful in deciding whether to serve as an examiner in the first two scenarios, although you should still make the normal checks outlined earlier in this chapter. However, it is unlikely that 'ignorance is bliss' when it comes to scenario three. In this case it is advisable to find out as much as possible about the examinations before accepting the appointment and to consider carefully the possible implications of your appointment. It is not helpful to discover complex interpersonal relations and/or a conflict of interests once you have been appointed and are already enmeshed in the dynamics between past and present examination participants. Robert's predicament was characterized potentially by both these types of complexity, and if you were asked to examine in this situation you would need to look carefully and honestly at your relationship to the head of department/supervisor before accepting the appointment.

Questions that you may want to ask include the following:

- Why is a new examiner required?
- What happened in the original examination?
- What were the relationships, if any, between the candidate, supervisor and original examiners and were these of any consequence for the original examination or this second one?
- Would you, as a newly appointed examiner, have interests that are closely tied to those of the candidate, supervisor, original examiners and, possibly, another newly appointed examiner?

Box 7.1   Case study

ROBERT'S PREDICAMENT

by Professor John Wakeford, Head of the Missenden Centre for the Development of Higher Education

I received a letter from the head of department at the University of L, outlining the situation where a thesis had been 'referred' (an interesting euphemism, I feel) but with the recommendation that the candidate be allowed to resubmit for a PhD. Following the viva the original external examiner had fallen ill and was not able to serve for the resubmission, though the original internal examiner was still in place. The head of department was someone I knew quite well and had worked with in the past. He did not actually name the original external examiner, but supplied enough information for me to infer who it must be – an extremely eminent lady from one of the ancient institutions, famous for her more than exacting standards. He also explained that the original viva had been an extremely bloody and protracted affair, and that under the University of L's regulations it was not actually necessary to hold a second if both examiners agreed to waive it.

I did have one qualm, on which I sought the head of department's reassurance. I realized that the situation might hypothetically be very fraught if there had been any significant division of opinion between the two original examiners. If there had been a major difference of views between the internal (whom I also know, and know to be embittered by lack of promotion) and the external, my appointment as a second external might – depending on how I saw the case – just constitute a reflection on the internal's judgement, as much as on the candidate's thesis. I was assured there were no significant differences between the original examiners, and with that reassurance I agreed to serve. Only with hindsight did I realize that there were *other* reassurances I should probably have sought as well.

I duly received the thesis, and read it with growing relief: there seemed to me no reasonable doubt that it warranted a PhD. This is particularly important in such cases, because the regulations (which in my experience are the same everywhere in this regard) meant that a further resubmission was out of the question. We could either recommend the award of a PhD, or of a master's degree instead, or fail it. The only leeway we had at all was to allow for minor typos etc. to be corrected.

Having reached the conclusion (that it was of PhD standard), and written my report to that effect, I contacted the internal examiner by email to say that I was broadly satisfied with the thesis, and that in the circumstances I could see little point in conducting a second viva. The reply from the internal examiner agreed that the thesis probably passed, and that a second viva was not necessary, but did so with singular ill grace. The venom of the piece was directed not at the candidate, but at the candidate's supervisor who (and this was where hindsight came into very sharp focus) was also the head of department. This was not exactly news to me, though it had never been openly stated before, because the thesis was very much written around a recent book by the head of department – applying its approach to areas of the discipline that he had not covered in any detail. The main weakness of the thesis was really that it had done this somewhat mechanically and repetitively, showing originality and initiative only in limited and controlled circumstances, . . . a clear pass. The internal examiner in effect conceded this, but proceeded to disparage the original book in question and to imply that the resubmitted thesis had only reached its present standard because the candidate had been so heavily tutored by his supervisor. He stopped short, but only just, of saying that the supervisor had written the thesis.

This is, I suppose, the sort of issue that a viva might explore: it is certainly the job of a viva to test the candidate's knowledge beyond the immediate confines of the thesis, and his/her capacity to interrogate the premises on which the thesis was written. So I had to rethink my original proposition that a second viva was not necessary. But, first, it seemed to me that a second viva with an internal examiner who felt this way was not only going to be difficult for all concerned but might well be positively counter-productive: how was it going to be possible to disentangle the issue of the candidate's degree of dependence on the supervisor from that of the internal examiner's patent resentment of that supervisor for other reasons? Second, if the internal examiner felt that the level of dependence on the supervisor really was such as to invalidate the degree, why was s/he not insisting (as s/he had the right to) on a second viva? Third, could I envisage any outcome in a viva that was going to change my original conviction that the thesis as presented warranted the award of a degree?

Some weeks later I received the 'joint report', which was in fact my own report with a brief final paragraph by the internal examiner endorsing my conclusions.

The whole business was both unsettling and unsatisfactory. I was reasonably happy in my own mind that the award of the PhD to the candidate, on the basis of what I had read, was the proper outcome. But everything else left a lot of questions hanging in the air. Because the head of department was also the candidate's supervisor, I could not turn to him/her for an impartial review of the internal examiner's views and action. For that I should have had to approach either the Dean of Graduate Studies (assuming they have such a person) or even the Vice-Chancellor. And I could not convince myself that such a drastic move was in the best interests of the candidate, which I took to be the primary consideration in the case.

We are grateful to Professor Wakeford for permission to use this extract from a case study. © John Wakeford

7.5 Summary

Every examination is different and therefore a decision whether to serve as an examiner needs to be considered carefully. In this chapter we have looked at the decision to examine from the perspectives of external and internal examiners. We have mapped out potential benefits of examining a PhD, as well as important considerations that should be thought through before an appointment is accepted. Issues that may confront replacement and additional examiners have also been addressed.

8

Examiners – Assessing a Doctoral Thesis

Chapter overview

Assessing the candidate's thesis is the first major task that confronts a PhD examiner, but most examiners receive no training or guidance on how to do this. In this chapter we do not attempt to provide a model of assessment. Instead we draw upon sources of available guidance to provide a toolkit that examiners can adapt to their individual needs. We begin by considering what examiners need to look for when assessing a thesis and then discuss strategies for reading and preparing a report on it.

Examiners ☺☺☺   Students ☺☺   Supervisors ☺☺

Chapter contents

8.1 How to assess a thesis

Currently, when examining, most academics rely on their own, usually limited, experiences and on the advice of colleagues; 92 per cent of the academics that we surveyed had received no formal training for examining a PhD. In this section we introduce some of the published formal guidelines on PhD assessment and then supplement these with the experiences of examiners. Following this, we look at issues specific to the assessment of practice-based PhD submissions, the key criteria of 'originality' and 'contribution to knowledge', and, finally, the range of standards in PhD theses.

Formal guidelines on assessment

Institutional guidelines
When you accept the job of examining a PhD thesis you agree to comply with the rules of the appointing institution. This means that the criteria you use to assess the thesis must be those set out in the institution's policy – it is important to read these carefully *before* reading the thesis and *before* agreeing to be an examiner (see Chapter 7). It is erroneous to assume that the regulations in place at your own institution, or those that were used to assess your own PhD, are standard. Institutions vary considerably in the ways that they define a PhD and in the criteria they present for assessing a doctoral thesis. Bear in mind, though, that although some policy guidelines are very specific, some (probably most) are extremely vague.

Discipline guidelines
Institutional criteria are ignored by some examiners who assess a thesis according to their own views of appropriate standards for their discipline. This practice is justified by these academics on the grounds that (1) a PhD provides access to a discipline and (2) institutional assessment criteria are scant. Examiners often rely on tacit knowledge about what a PhD in their discipline should be like, although there are a few discipline-based guides to doctoral assessment. At a general level, discipline-based guidelines identify similar points. We include examples from the sciences (see Boxes 8.1 and 8.2) and social sciences (see BPS/UCoSDA, discussed later). In the case of interdisciplinary and multidisciplinary PhDs there are, of course, no discipline-specific criteria.

Where they exist, discipline guidelines can provide a useful *supplement* to institutional policy, as the Royal Society of Chemists (1995: 9) states: 'Every institution will have its own formal regulations regarding the final examination for the PhD. It is not the intention of these guidelines to seek to supersede such regulations, though they may serve to inform their interpretation.'

Box 8.1   Case study

EXAMINING A CHEMISTRY THESIS

Examiners in the final examination for the PhD will be expected:

- to consider a candidate's thesis with care and to examine him or her in depth;
- to establish that the candidate is able to plan and execute a substantial piece of research in chemistry, and to interpret and report the results of such a study;
- to establish that the candidate has a deep understanding of the topic of the thesis and that the work is embedded in an appropriate general understanding of its wider chemical context;
- to assure themselves that the candidate has fully satisfied the requirements of the specified programme of study and has used the opportunities afforded to him or her by participation in research seminars and comparable activities;
- to assure themselves that the candidate possesses the necessary professional competencies, both those specific to a chemist (such as safety consciousness) and those of a more general professional kind (such as communication skills).

Source: Royal Society of Chemists 1995

Box 8.2   Case study

EXAMINING A PHD IN THE MOLECULAR BIOSCIENCES

Wood and Vella (2000: 772) report on the standards for a PhD in molecular biosciences as agreed by the Education Committee of the International Union of Biochemistry. Six points are identified, all of which are equally important.

- The candidate should demonstrate a general knowledge of physics, chemistry, biology and cell biology, biochemistry and molecular biology, the particular molecular bioscience in which s/he is being trained, and a detailed knowledge of her/his area of research.
- The candidate should be familiar with the research literature of the particular bioscience and should have the ability to keep abreast of major developments and to acquire a working background in any area.
- The candidate should demonstrate skill in the recognition of meaningful problems and questions for research in the particular bioscience.

- The candidate should possess technical skill in laboratory manipulation.
- The candidate should demonstrate that oral, written and visual communication skills have been acquired.
- The candidate should demonstrate skill in designing experimental protocols and in conducting productive self-directed research.

Guidelines from research funding bodies and the Quality Assurance Agency
In recent years the Research Councils and the Arts and Humanities Research Board (AHRB) have assumed a central role in shaping the content and delivery of education at doctoral level. A joint statement issued in 2001 identifies seven sets of skills that students are expected to develop during their research training. It also specifies that 'PhD students are expected to make a substantial, original contribution to knowledge in their areas, normally leading to published work'. The examination of the PhD has not, however, been the subject of guidance or regulation from these bodies and, at the time of writing, they are not intent on intervening in this area. Nevertheless, the joint statement contains a useful breakdown of skill areas, some of which apply, or can be applied, to assessing doctoral theses and viva performances (sections A, C and E of the joint statement are reproduced in Box 8.3). It makes sense that by the time a PhD student has completed research training modules and then proceeded to conduct and write up their own research, many of the skills identified by the Research Councils and the AHRB should be apparent in her/his thesis and viva performance.

Learning objectives for doctoral work have been suggested by the Quality Assurance Agency (QAA). Those relating to knowledge and research skills are of particular salience for the assessment of a thesis and are consistent with the statement of the research funding bodies.

Doctorates are awarded to students who have demonstrated:

i) the creation and interpretation of new knowledge, through original research or other advanced scholarship, of a quality to satisfy peer review, extend the forefront of the discipline, and merit publication;

ii) a systematic acquisition and understanding of a substantial body of knowledge which is at the forefront of an academic discipline or area of professional practice;

iii) the general ability to conceptualise, design and implement a project for the generation of new knowledge, applications or understanding at the forefront of the discipline, and to adjust the project design in the light of unforeseen problems;

iv) a detailed understanding of applicable techniques for research and advanced academic enquiry.

(QAA, 2001)

Doctoral students are also expected to be able 'to make informed judgements on complex issues in specialist fields, often in the absence of complete data' and 'to communicate their ideas and conclusions clearly and effectively to specialist and non-specialist audiences' (QAA 2001). These objectives articulate, at a general level, current good practice.

Box 8.3   Case study

EXTRACTS FROM *SKILLS TRAINING REQUIREMENTS FOR RESEARCH STUDENTS*, JOINT STATEMENT OF THE RESEARCH COUNCILS/AHRB (2001)

(A) Research skills and techniques – to be able to demonstrate:

1. The ability to recognise and validate problems.
2. Original, independent and critical thinking, and the ability to develop theoretical concepts.
3. A knowledge of recent advances within one's field and in related areas.
4. An understanding of relevant research methodologies and techniques and their appropriate application within one's research field.
5. The ability to critically analyse and evaluate one's findings and those of others.
6. An ability to summarise, document, report and reflect on progress.

(C) Research management – to be able to:

1. Apply effective project management through the setting of research goals, intermediate milestones and prioritisation of activities.
2. Design and execute systems for the acquisition and collation of information through the effective use of appropriate resources and equipment.
3. Identify and access appropriate bibliographical resources, archives, and other sources of relevant information.
4. Use information technology appropriately for database management, recording and presenting information.

(E) Communication skills – to be able to:

1. Write clearly and in a style appropriate to purpose, e.g. progress reports, published documents, thesis.
2. Construct coherent arguments and articulate ideas clearly to a range of audiences, formally and informally through a variety of techniques.
3. Constructively defend research outcomes at seminars and viva examination.

4. Contribute to promoting the public understanding of one's research field.
5. Effectively support the learning of others when involved in teaching, mentoring or demonstrating activities.

An examiner's guide to assessing a thesis
Although there are some formal guidelines on assessing a doctoral thesis these are not comprehensive or widely available. In this section we offer detailed guidance on working through a thesis by supplementing formal sources of guidance with the experiences of examiners.

The criteria outlined by the British Psychological Society (BPS/UCoSDA 1995: 11–12) for assessing written submissions within psychology and related disciplines, provides a particularly clear and comprehensive basic model and one which addresses the main points raised in other discipline-specific guidelines. These guidelines identify four 'overall attributes' of a PhD thesis:

1. presentation and clarity;
2. integration and coherence;
3. contribution to knowledge;
4. originality and creativity.

They also list five key types of work that should be presented in the thesis. These 'sectional attributes' include:

1. review of relevant literature;
2. statement of the research problem;
3. methods of enquiry adopted;
4. analysis of data;
5. discussion of outcomes.

Disciplines express 'sectional attributes' in different ways and include additional discipline-specific 'overall attributes' or refinements (see, for example, Boxes 8.1 and 8.2).

So far we have looked at the general attributes of a PhD thesis, but how can this general model translate into practice? In Box 8.4, Pam Denicolo, director of a social sciences graduate school, sets out a detailed and systematic breakdown of attributes that examiners in the social sciences usually look for in assessing a PhD thesis. This account of practice shows how basic assessment criteria (similar to those set out by the BPS/UCoSDA) are broken down into specific questions that examiners can ask themselves as they work through a thesis. This model must always be used within the specifications provided by the appointing institution. Although based on the collective experience of social science examiners, Denicolo's model of how to unpack each component of the thesis may provide examiners in other disciplines with a useful framework. A similar but less detailed breakdown of what to look for in a thesis is offered by Arthur Georges (1996) of the Applied Ecology Research Group.

Box 8.4   Case study

CRITERIA FOR ASSESSING THE WRITTEN THESIS IN THE SOCIAL
SCIENCES

by Dr Pam Denicolo, Director of the Social Sciences Graduate School, University of Reading

After many years of supervising and examining PhD theses using few, and rather generalized, guidelines, I responded to requests from students and colleagues training to be supervisors to put my implicit knowledge down on paper. The first draft was distributed to a range of experienced colleagues who added to and amended it, the results can be found below. They are summarized as attributes examiners look for in a thesis.

Overall

- Careful, clear presentation that has the reader's needs in mind.
- If necessary, or helpful, a glossary of terms and/or acronyms preceding the main text and succeeding the contents list.
- The contribution to knowledge expected and achieved should be made explicit.
- Each chapter should be coherent in itself and contribute to an integrated whole; all parts of the thesis should contribute explicitly to the 'story line'.

Sectional attributes

Introduction

- Rationale for study clearly explicated.
- The appropriateness of this researcher conducting this study made clear.
- Brief overview of thesis provided, clear outline of the 'story line'.

Review of relevant literature

- Succinct, penetrating, challenging, critical, analytical approach.
- Demonstrates thorough knowledge of field.
- Primary rather than secondary sources used.
- Quotations used to illustrate and exemplify rather than substitute for own words in argument (page numbers required).

Statement of research problems

- Clear and succinct hypotheses or questions derived from/revealed by the literature review.

- Should have a novel theoretical or methodological slant and/or bring together previously unrelated fields and/or a new area of application.
- Well articulated rationale for 'worthwhileness' of research.

Approach and methods of enquiry adopted (theoretical argument)

- Rationale of general approach closely argued giving reasoned case for rejecting other possible approaches.
- Justification of research design presented, taking account of potential advantages and limitations.
- Research techniques argued as theoretically and practically relevant to research problem; reasons given for rejection of possible alternatives; rationale provided for amendments to standard tests and procedures or for detailed design of innovative techniques.

Fieldwork/labwork (description of actual process)

- Clearly set out and easy to follow.
- Relevant details included (number of subjects/respondents, relevant profiles, timing of interventions, duration of interventions etc.).
- Information about the difficulties encountered and how they were dealt with so that the research was not compromised.

Analysis of data

- Mode of analysis theoretically justified.
- Any assumptions stated and justified.
- Congruent with research questions/hypotheses and approach adopted.
- Details of procedure clearly presented.

Presentation of data

- Clearly structured.
- Data 'trail' evident.
- Details of why, who, what, when and where provided.
- Tables, figures, diagrams to summarize all data clearly numbered and titled and referred to in the text.

Discussion of outcomes

- Main points summarized and evaluated, interpretations made of raw data;
- Links made to literature previously presented, e.g. what previous research/theory has been supported, substantiated, challenged, amended, rejected etc.

- Reflections on the research process – limitations addressed and consequent implications for results.
- Suggestions for repeat or further research based on this research.
- Implications of results for theory and practice.

Clear articulation of contribution to knowledge
Some examiners like to see a final section or postscript that discusses what the researcher has learnt from the process of the research.

Reference list or bibliography

- All references in text included with no additions.
- Any seminal or influential texts not referred to in text listed separately.

Appendices

- Referred to in text and clearly numbered in order of presentation in text.

Practice-based PhDs – the relationship between the written and practice components of a submission

> 'Practice' must represent an answer, or a contribution to the answer, of the research question(s).
>
> (Senior Lecturer, Drama)

In practice-based PhD examinations examiners usually assess a written thesis and some form of practice (for instance a performance or exhibition of work), they also viva the candidate. (Durling (2002) notes that at one art school there is no requirement for a written thesis.) The relative weighting of the practice and the thesis is not usually regulated by institutions and it is debatable whether this is necessary or even desirable. For example, as the head of one art school explained to us: 'each submission is assessed on an individual basis in terms of how much of the research question has to be dealt with in a particular way'. The thesis and the practice need to be approached as integral to one another; the relationship between these elements varies depending on the research question(s). A key question that examiners of practice-related PhDs need to address is: does the combination of submissions (thesis plus practice) answer the research question? The other main question is whether the thesis demonstrates adequately the processes of the research and critical reflection on the results.

The status of practice and its assessment are the subjects of much debate in the creative and performing arts and design. See Durling (2002) for an introduction.

'Originality' and 'a contribution to knowledge'

Two criteria are commonly employed to define a PhD submission, these are 'originality' and 'a contribution to knowledge'. Both criteria are vague and it is usually left to examiners to derive their own interpretations. To assist you in this task we now consider both of these concepts.

'Originality'

A spark of inspiration as well as perspiration.

(Winter *et al.* 2000: 35)

Originality is one of the most frequently stipulated criteria for the award of a PhD. But what constitutes originality and how much of a thesis should be 'original' to qualify for a PhD? 'Originality' is a slippery and potentially all-embracing term and one that academics interpret in diverse ways. For instance, as the UK Council for Graduate Education (2001: 17) note, there is 'broad debate' about 'how the originality in creative work might be tested, measured or demonstrated in the different artistic fields' and, in particular, the field of interpretative performance (see also Winter *et al.* 2000).

'Originality' is not routinely defined in institutional policy and this can pose problems for examiners. The guidelines at Leeds Metropolitan University are atypical as they list some of the ways in which a PhD thesis can be judged to be 'original', 'creative' or 'novel'. As this list, and recent published accounts suggest, 'originality' can take a multitude of forms in doctoral work (Cryer 2000; Delamont *et al.* 2000; Winter *et al.* 2000). Drawing on these sources we identify three main ways in which a PhD thesis can be original.

1. Research topics:

   - Research on new: areas of study, data sets, questions, hypotheses, problems, links between topics/data sets and so on. Research on significantly changed contexts as in the replication of a study.

2. Research processes:

   - New applications of established research tools – for instance, methods, instruments, conceptual tools, modes of analysis, procedures, theories, 'practice' – to different or new research topics.
   - Significant refinement of established research tools, or development of new research tools, applied to established or new research topics.
   - The application of new perspectives to research topics.

3. Research outcomes (intentional and unintentional):

- New or substantially revised solutions, products, theories, knowledge, interpretations, approaches, ways of doing research (methods, instruments, conceptual tools, modes of analysis, procedures, application of theory, 'practice').
- New syntheses of theory or knowledge or ways of doing research.
- The opening up of new and/or neglected areas for fundamental and significant further research.

This list provides a guide for identifying originality, one that embraces the diverse ways in which examiners interpret the term when assessing doctoral theses, including practice-based submissions (Winter *et al.* 2000). Unless the appointing institution identifies a particular interpretation of the word 'original', you can assume a submission qualifies as original if it meets one or more of the above criteria. However, as with most areas of academic life, there can be lively debate about whether aspects of a thesis/submission can be classified as original or new in any of the above senses. Cryer (2000: 197) argues that originality may be particularly contentious and/or contested by examiners if a thesis is potentially 'highly original': 'Really original research is all too often slow to be accepted.'

Originality is more important in some disciplines than in others. Expectations of originality may be quite modest in some branches of science; interestingly, the standards for a PhD in the molecular biosciences do not include reference to 'originality' (see Box 8.2). Although the focus on behavioural criteria may explain this omission, it seems more likely that originality is not an important and distinctive criterion in this discipline. Proof that a candidate is a 'self-directed scientist' seems to be of more import and relevance in this subject area (Wood and Vella 2000).

'A contribution to knowledge'

The requirement that a thesis should represent a contribution to knowledge is usually coupled with the criterion that it should be original/new. This coupling prevents ill-conceived or trivial projects – that might be new or original – from qualifying as worthy of a PhD. For example, the University of Cambridge (2003: 2) states that a thesis should make a 'significant contribution to knowledge' through, for example, 'new knowledge', 'new theory', new 'connections' and/or the 'revision' of older views. As with originality, a contribution to knowledge can be rather elusive for PhD students in some areas of science. A candidate who has worked on a large project may make a substantial contribution to the group's work, but their contribution to disciplinary knowledge may be limited. In some branches of science, projects are passed on from one doctoral student to another, and this compounds the difficulty of identifying a distinctive contribution to knowledge. This is conveyed clearly in the following example.

Tim ... was also funded to do his PhD on this enzyme. There was a person working on the enzyme before him. That was Connor. Connor started off by trying to purify the enzyme and he came quite close. Then a year later Tim started and actually purified the enzyme and started working on it. Now I shall be taking that work a little bit further. Maybe if they get another award there'll be someone carrying on my work in the same way.

(Delamont *et al.* 1997c: 326)

Publishability is a way of measuring contribution to knowledge. This measure is to the fore in the definition of a PhD espoused by the Research Councils/AHRB (2001): 'PhD students are expected to make a substantial, original contribution to knowledge in their areas, normally leading to published work.' This statement is rather vague about the quantity or quality of published work, presumably to embrace discipline differences. The BPS/UCoSDA (1995: 29) are more precise: a PhD submission should be 'equivalent in quantity and quality to at least two articles of a standard acceptable to a fully refereed journal', or 'substantial enough to be able to form the basis of a book or research monograph which could meet the standards of an established academic publisher operating a system of critical peer review for book proposals and drafts'.

Range of standards

It was clear that this was a weak thesis, the question was how weak can it be and still pass?

(Lecturer, Women's Studies)

What standard should a thesis meet in order to merit the award of a PhD? 'Excellence' may be the answer that rolls off the tongue, but in fact standards of British PhD theses are highly variable. In 1988 the Committee of Vice-Chancellors and Principals (CVCP) noted the 'diversity of quality' evident in doctoral theses. In order to distinguish between the different standards of PhD, the CVCP recommended the introduction of a 'PhD with distinction' for those theses with particular merit. It estimated that roughly 10 per cent of successful PhD candidates should receive this accolade (Committee of Vice-Chancellors and Principals 1988). This recommendation was not adopted, although BPS/UCoSDA have since reiterated the need for ways of commending outstanding candidates. This discussion does draw attention to a matter of importance for all PhD examiners, namely that there is a broad range of standards embraced by the award of PhD.

On the basis of interviews with external examiners, Phillips noted two ways in which academics judged the range of PhD standards. The first strategy involved 'mental yardsticks of undergraduate degrees'.

Using the idea of undergraduate degree grades (2/2, 2/1, etc.) as a guide that standards were not raised too high was a popular strategy to help decision making. By keeping these divisions as a yardstick in their mind, examiners were able to acknowledge that it was possible to gain a PhD for a piece of work that was less than 'excellent' although it was excellence that they were really looking for.

(Phillips 1994: 137)

The second strategy involved working with the 'analogy of peer reviewing of journal articles'. As we have seen, the potential publishability of all, or parts, of a thesis is sometimes stipulated as a measure of PhD standards. Whilst this criterion can help to establish a bottom line, it does not prevent divergent standards nor does it preclude diverse academic judgements of quality; books and articles in refereed journals vary considerably in their rigour, originality and accomplishment.

What, then, does the bottom line look like? Drawing upon interviews with examiners of Australian PhD theses, Mullins and Kiley (2002: 378–80) list the characteristics of a 'poor' (referred or failed) thesis, a 'standard' (pass) thesis and an 'outstanding one'. The characteristics of a 'poor' thesis include:

- lack of coherence;
- lack of understanding of the theory;
- lack of confidence;
- researching the wrong problem;
- mixed or confused theoretical and methodological perspectives;
- work that is not original;
- not being able to explain at the end of the thesis what had actually been argued in the thesis.

The characteristics of a 'standard' thesis are, as one would expect, positive and include:

- 'scholarship', defined in terms of originality, coherence, a 'sense of student autonomy or independence';
- the development of a well-structured argument;
- 'sufficient quantity as well as quality of work';
- publishability;
- evidence of critical reflection.

Interestingly, academics from across the disciplines used artistic metaphors to describe an 'outstanding' thesis – 'creativity', 'elegant', 'a well-sculpted piece of work', 'an artistic endeavour where the student is designing the work and there is elegance of design, of the synthesis, and executions' (this last quote was from a scientist). As these lists of characteristics indicate, academics are usually able to identify the technical skills that should be present in a thesis but, as Delamont *et al.* (2000: 35) point out, 'there are also indeterminate qualities which examiners can recognize but not itemize precisely because, by their very indeterminacy, they are resistant to precise explication.' Shaw and Green (2002) argue that the QAA framework (2001) provides a basis for benchmarking the standards of a PhD, and they offer suggestions about how to do this.

8.2 Strategies for reading the thesis

There is no standard method of reading a thesis; the time that it takes and the way it is done vary between examiners. They may also vary by discipline because of variations in the length and format of theses. For example, a thesis in mathematics or physics may be 80–100 pages in length and dominated by equations which need to be worked through, whereas in the arts, humanities and social sciences a thesis is likely to be a prose document of 80,000 words, or roughly 300 pages. The standard of the thesis is also significant. For example, a poorly presented thesis with many weak areas may require more time and attention than a strong and well-written one.

Mullins and Kiley (2002: 376–7) provide interesting examples of different 'reading styles' that PhD examiners employ. Although based on the examination of Australian PhDs, the range of practices they describe is not specific to Australian examiners and includes the following:

> . . . sets aside time to read the thesis. He checks who is in the references to see that the writers are there who should be there. Then he reads slowly, from the beginning like a book, but taking copious notes. (Humanities)

> . . . reads the thesis from cover to cover first without doing anything else. For the first read he is just trying to gain a general impression of what the thesis is about and whether it is a good thesis – that is, are the results worthwhile. He can also tell how much work has actually been done. After the first read he then 'sits on it' for a while. During the second reading he starts making notes and reading more critically. If it is an area with which he is not very familiar, he might read some of the references. He marks typographical errors, mistakes in calculations, etc., and makes a list of them. He also checks several of the references just to be sure they have been used appropriately. (Science)

> . . . reads the abstract first and then the introduction and the conclusion, as well as the table of contents to see how the thesis is structured; and she familiarises herself with the appendices so that she knows where everything is. Then she starts reading through; generally the literature review, and methodology, in the first weekend, and the findings, analysis and conclusions in the second weekend. The intervening week allows time for ideas to mull over in her mind. In the third weekend she writes the report. (Social Science)

In these examples, the examiner spends a couple of weeks reading and rereading the thesis. For some academics the thesis has to be read as close to the viva as possible, as in this example from our interview with a professor of government.

> I leave it very late to read a PhD. I'm quite obsessive when I examine them . . . It sounds obvious, but I do read it [the thesis] all the way

through, right to the very end, and make notes on it and everything. Which I know not everybody does . . . I'd be so embarrassed to be in an exam and say something, and the student say 'hang on a minute' . . . I've got a very good short-term memory, I haven't got a very good long-term one, but if I've read it [the thesis] over 36 hours before, or 24, which I often do, and they [the candidate] say 'blah di blah di blah', I can say 'hang on a minute on page 47 you say this', because it'll be in my notes and I'll remember it . . . A week later I've forgotten it.

If this is your first time examining a PhD, devise a strategy that is feasible for you and make sure you allow plenty of time to work through the thesis. In the next section we look at preparing a report on the thesis.

8.3 Pre-viva reports

Having read the thesis the next stage is to clarify your thoughts on it and prepare a report. Institutions vary as to whether an independent report must be submitted formally before the viva. Even where a formal report is not required it is useful to write an informal one that you are happy to pass to your co-examiner(s) prior to, or even during (subject to institutional guidelines), the pre-viva meeting (see Chapter 12). Often the report is a condensed version of a more detailed document that you have prepared to assist you in the viva. Being clear what you think about the thesis, and preparing a written account of your position, is *vital* to good preparation as a professor of history explains:

> I've learned over the years to be very clear about my judgement before the viva, even when this is necessarily provisional, depending in part on how the student responds to questions in the viva. Early experiences of being steam-rollered into agreeing to pass a thesis that I would have preferred to refer, by the combined mass of the other examiner and the supervisor, convinced me always to go prepared in this way, and to make clear where I stood from the start. The rule that many universities have, that examiners have to write their reports in advance of the viva, and even submit them a few days beforehand, in some ways makes this easier. By the same token, if a thesis needs some repair work before it is passed, I think it is only fair to have worked out just what this should be in advance, so that clear guidance can be given to the student (even if the requirements are modified by the viva performance and the views of the other examiner).

Purposes of the pre-viva report

Depending on institutional arrangements, the pre-viva report can serve several purposes for different audiences.

- For the examiners, it serves to present and justify their preliminary judgement of the thesis. It also identifies points for discussion in the viva – these form the basis of the agenda (see Chapter 12).
- For administrators, a formal pre-viva report can be part of quality procedures. In this case, the pre-viva reports can be used to check that the examiners' concerns have been addressed in the viva and taken into account in forming the recommendation of award.
- In at least one institution, the pre-viva report also serves an important purpose for the candidate in that s/he is informed in advance, via the supervisor, of the topics that will be discussed in the viva. See Box 2.3 for discussion of this practice.

What to include in the report

- You should provide a clear account of your evaluation of the thesis. This account should explicitly address institutional criteria and/or guidelines (see section 8.1) but, as previously mentioned, these may need to be interpreted through a discipline-specific lens and/or broken down to cover the different components of the thesis.
- A recommendation of the award, either definite or provisional (depending on the regulations at the appointing institution), needs to be recorded and justified by your evaluative comments.
- The report should also state clearly what purposes you think that the candidate's viva should serve (see Chapter 12).

8.4 Summary

In this chapter we have considered how to assess a PhD thesis and prepare a report on it. Strategies for reading the thesis have also been addressed. Although institutions usually provide little guidance on these matters, we have combined available guidelines and the experience of examiners to offer suggestions about how to approach this task. Preparing for, and conducting, the viva is discussed in Chapter 12.

9

Viva Preparation – Short Term

Chapter overview

The candidate's preparation for the viva is an ongoing process although it is useful to think in terms of three stages of preparation: long-term, short-term and final-stage. In Chapter 4 we examined the importance of long-term preparation and explored ways that students can develop skills that are essential for a good viva performance. In this chapter we focus on the second stage of student preparation that occurs around the time of thesis submission. We discuss different types of short-term preparation and ways in which sources of information and experience can be used constructively. The distinction we draw between short-term and final-stage preparations is necessarily arbitrary. In practice, some aspects of short-term preparation, in particular mock vivas, may take place in the weeks or even days before the viva. This chapter on short-term preparations is, therefore, useful to candidates on the verge of their viva.

Students ☺☺☺   Supervisors ☺☺☺

Chapter contents

9.1 Supervisors and peer support

The relationship between supervisor and student is of paramount importance throughout the course of doctoral study (see Delamont *et al.* 1997a). The relationship may change once the thesis has been submitted but it does not disappear. Our questionnaires to candidates revealed that most rely principally on their supervisor(s) for support and advice concerning viva preparation. Supervisors need to ensure that their students are engaged in constructive forms of short-term preparation for the oral examination and they should assist in providing these. One form of short-term preparation that some supervisors provide is a mock viva, which we discuss later in this chapter. Supervisors are also a major source of reassurance to students approaching the viva and they therefore need to be available in person or by email to address their students' anxieties. Myths and grapevine stories about the viva are often a source of concern for students and we discuss these in the next section. Although supervisors have an important role to play in preparing students for the viva, they can only do so much; students should be encouraged to also draw upon other sources of support.

Most students benefit from being encouraged early in their PhD studies to develop networks of support amongst fellow students within the institution and/or within the postgraduate forum of a professional organization (see Box 4.4 in Chapter 4 for an account of support provided by one professional organization). Later in the PhD process, an informal support group composed of students approaching their vivas within a particular department, school or faculty, can provide a useful forum in which students can discuss and manage concerns. Contact can be based on face-to-face meetings or email.

Box 9.1   Task for students

STUDENT SUPPORT GROUP

Find out whether there is a formal or informal student support group in your department, school or faculty. If there is not, and you think that you and others would benefit from one, set one up. Ask your postgraduate secretary to send out a mailing asking interested PhD students to get in touch. Then set up a meeting.

9.2 Viva stories and myths

Over half of the candidates we surveyed revealed that grapevine stories and fellow students' experiences were sources of information on vivas. But what are these viva stories and how should students and supervisors interpret them?

Peer and grapevine stories usually focus on the conduct of the examination and how the candidate was made to feel during their viva.

> I asked them [recently graduated PhD students] and I asked the junior lecturers – what was it like and do you have any advice kind of thing – it's really random. Like some people said, 'I walked in and they gave me a bottle of champagne and said, "relax you've passed" ', and other people said they left crying after four hours.
>
> (Carla, PhD student, Art History)

> Everyone's got a nightmare PhD story. One of my friends in History passed his about a month/two months ago and it was fine, basically they were lovely. Another friend of mine in Anthropology walked in and they said, 'Oh it's great, don't worry, let's talk about how to turn this into a book', and it was fine. And then another two friends of mine had horrendous, absolutely horrendous experiences where they've just been unable to speak properly for hours, and one of them for days, because they had such an upsetting time. [They had] aggressive, nasty, demoralising external examiners who just seemed to think their job was to make the person at the other side of the table feel like they'd done a shite piece of work.
>
> (Leila, PhD student, Sociology)

As these quotes illustrate, peer and grapevine stories often provide extreme examples. As Sorrel, a government studies candidate, put it: 'I've heard some very nice and some very awful stories . . . I've heard people who've failed with no good reasons, according to them, and I've heard people who are very happy.' This polarization is also evident in published accounts of PhD vivas. For example, Jeremy Quale (1999: 46) in his graphically entitled 'Return of the runny bottom: my PhD viva experience', refers to: 'Stories ranging from: "I walked in and they said 'congratulations, let's have an informal chat about your research', at one end of the continuum, to: 'They went through my thesis word by word, and I've been in counselling ever since' " at the other end.'

Implicit in many viva stories is the myth that the examination outcome is either a pass or fail, or, more accurately, that either the candidate passes and their thesis is described as 'fantastic' or the candidate fails – often a referral is interpreted as a major humiliation and disaster. In reality, the viva outcome is rarely either pass or fail (see Chapter 1):

- There is usually more than one pass category.
- It is common for successful PhD candidates to do corrections or more work on the thesis.
- A referral is not a fail but an opportunity to develop aspects of the thesis in ways that will, hopefully, raise it to the required standard.
- Few PhD examination candidates are not awarded a PhD in the end.

Grapevine stories also inflate the significance of the viva in the examination process and frequently suggest that everything hinges on the candidate's viva performance. In fact, as we saw in Chapter 3, the examiners' recommendation is shaped principally by their assessment of the thesis. However, although the viva is not of paramount importance in determining the examiners' recommendation it is usually important for how candidates feel about themselves, their research and their future prospects in academia (see Chapter 13).

Viva accounts, whilst often dramatic, do represent legitimate anxieties about having an unpleasant and/or unprofessional examiner. These concerns are fuelled by the mystery surrounding doctoral examinations and the scant regulation of oral examinations. These accounts also symbolize candidates' feelings of powerlessness as Carla, an art history student, explained: 'The thought of being examined on your own work, potentially by people who aren't necessarily fair, is very scary for most people I think, because it's really out of your hands at that point no matter how hard you've worked.'

Candidates' feelings of powerlessness are not surprising. Considerable time, money and effort is usually invested in doing a PhD. There are other costs too, particularly for ethnic minority students, working-class women and overseas students (Okorocha 1997; Leonard 2001). These costs include: the consequences of separation from family and friends and/or the tensions that can arise in attempting to juggle domestic and family responsibilities with the demands of academic life; the stress of managing the 'chilly climate' of sexism and racism in higher education institutions; the demands of coping in an alien culture. Despite the investment, the final stage of the doctorate threatens to be beyond the candidate's control.

Supervisors can help their supervisees put grapevine stories and the experiences of fellow students in perspective. Supervisors can also help students to unpack their reactions to these often unsettling accounts as Andrew, a physiotherapy candidate, revealed when we asked him how confident he was about the outcome of his viva:

It fluctuates. Some days you think, yes this will be OK, and then other days . . . Like after this chap had a disaster [in his viva] I sort of moped round for days thinking this is going to happen to me, I can see it now. And it was only later on, when we had a tutorial about what had happened to this guy, that I suddenly realized, well, actually, I could have answered all those questions really in a reasonable manner and it was the way in which he [the candidate] *didn't* answer them.

Box 9.2   Task for students

TALKING POINTS

Talk to your supervisor(s) about stories, or fellow students' experiences, that concern you.

Supervisors and candidates – six points to remember when thinking about viva stories

1. The majority of examiners are pleasant and fair in PhD vivas even if they are often rigorous and challenging in their questioning.
2. A candidate who is well prepared, and who has worked to develop their viva skills (see Chapter 4), is less likely to feel powerless in the viva than one who is poorly prepared.
3. Candidates never fail outright solely on viva performance unless the examiners are convinced that the thesis is not the candidate's own work. Usually, the viva is not the main site of decision making. As we saw in Chapter 2, the thesis is usually deemed to be of more weight than the candidate's performance in a decision to award or withhold a doctorate. In the case of a very poor viva performance and a good thesis, a candidate can be required to do a second viva (this is subject to institutional policy).
4. The outcome of a doctoral examination is rarely either pass or fail.
5. Many theses require further work and the extent of revision may depend on the candidate's performance in the viva. The viva provides an opportunity for the candidate to convey their understanding of the topic, convince the examiners of the value of their work and the approach they have taken even if, with hindsight, they may have done some things differently.
6. Although the viva is a formal examination it also serves other purposes (see Chapter 2). Importantly it provides an opportunity for the candidate to discuss their work with a 'captive audience' and to elicit information on future possibilities.

9.3 Mock vivas

Some academics favour mock vivas as a means of preparing students for their oral examination. But what is a mock viva? In the next section we map out briefly the main characteristics of mock vivas. Following this we consider ways in which mock vivas are valuable to students. We then outline the different purposes that mock vivas can serve and discuss the advantages and limitations in relation to questions that students and supervisors commonly ask. Actual examples of mock vivas currently in use in Britain are described in detail in three case studies, with comments on each. The use of oral examinations to decide whether a student can upgrade, or convert, from a master's degree to a doctorate are not included in this chapter. Although upgrading and conversion events can enable students to develop skills that are useful in the PhD viva (see Chapter 4), these events are important and real assessments in their own right – they are not *mock* examinations.

What are mock vivas? What forms can they take?

Mock vivas take a variety of forms depending on: who is being given the mock examination; what text is being examined; who the 'examiners' are; the audience; the timing of the mock relative to submission of the thesis and the actual viva. Mock vivas can also vary by length and setting. In their recent survey of 24 UK postgraduates from across institutions and disciplines, Hartley and Fox (2004) discovered that the time spent on mocks ranged from 25 minutes to four-and-a-half hours, with one hour as the average. Whilst the supervisor's office or a university seminar room seem obvious settings for mock vivas, they can also be conducted over the telephone: 'I did my mock viva over the telephone with one supervisor. She prompted me with questions and responded to my answers for about 50 minutes' (Hartley and Fox 2004). The principal differences between mock vivas are mapped out in Table 9.1; specific examples of the diversity of types of mock vivas are presented in the case studies (see Boxes 9.3–9.5 later in this chapter). As Table 9.1 shows, students can experience mock vivas in a range of forms. A principal variation is whether the candidate is (1) the 'candidate' in the mock viva, (2) the observer of another student's mock viva, (3) a member of an audience watching a performance of a mock viva, or (4) an 'examiner'. Students can also watch a video recording of a performance of a mock viva or of a student undertaking a mock viva.

Table 9.1   Variable features of mock vivas

Variables	*Possibilities*
Person being examined	Member of academic staff Candidate
Text being examined	Whole thesis Part of the thesis or thesis-related document Published piece
The 'mock' examiners	Supervisor(s) Supervisor and other academic staff Two academic staff (not supervisor) Academic staff and peer group
Audience (apart from 'examiners')	Supervisor(s)/supervisory team Students Other academics No one
Scheduling relative to submission of thesis and date of actual viva	Before submission of thesis After submission, at least a week before the actual viva After submission, only 1–2 days prior to the actual viva

Are mock vivas useful?

Views are divided on the value of mock vivas. On the one hand, mock vivas are promoted by some academics as a useful form of viva preparation. Roughly one-quarter of the psychology candidates surveyed by Hartley and Jory (2000) had experienced mock vivas, although practices seem to vary considerably between disciplines. On the other hand, some academics and students are unconvinced that mock vivas have much to offer and prefer not to hold them. As a theology candidate explained: 'Essentially, I was informed that formal guidance/training was not of much use because a viva could take any form.'

Important points are raised by those in favour of mock vivas, as well as by those who are sceptical of their value. For the sake of clarity we refer to these two groups as the pro-mock group and the sceptics. In our view, the sceptics are right to stress that a mock viva cannot be a trial run for an actual viva because vivas are highly variable in form and content. However, we also agree with the pro-mock group that mock vivas can be a useful form of viva preparation *as long as their limitations are recognized by all parties, especially the candidate.* As we explained in Chapter 3, there are six factors that shape the three components of an oral examination (the basic skills, content and conduct components). Once these factors are isolated and understood, it is possible for students and supervisors to (1) identify what components of the viva candidates can prepare for, and (2) work out how, if at all, different types of mock viva can contribute to this preparation.

What purposes can mock vivas serve?

The purposes served by a mock viva vary depending on the form it takes. Whether the student is the 'candidate' or an observer will shape what the student can gain from the experience. In cases where the student is the candidate, the value of the mock depends on three main factors:

- The scheduling of the mock viva relative to the submission of the thesis and the date of the actual viva is highly variable; a recent study reports a range from one day to approximately six months (Hartley and Fox 2004). Scheduling has important implications for other forms of examination preparation. When mock vivas are held prior to submission of the thesis they allow students to revise their work in light of the mock viva experience. After submission, however, a mock viva cannot lead to changes to the thesis although, if held a week or so in advance of the actual viva, there is still time for the candidate to work further on viva preparations. A mock viva held a day or two before the actual viva allows insufficient time for a candidate to address issues raised by the mock.
- Different benefits accrue to students from being 'examined' on the whole of their thesis, a part of it, or some other piece of writing.

- Students gain different insights into their work and how to 'defend' it depending on whether they are being 'examined' by their supervisor(s), whose approach(es) they are already familiar with, or by other people offering new, perhaps unexpected, perspectives and approaches.

Supervisors and students are advised to reflect on what they want to achieve from a mock viva and to tailor the format of it to meet these specific ends. Table 9.2 suggests ways in which the different characteristics of mock vivas meet different objectives. The first objective is specific to the thesis, the remaining three objectives relate directly to the components of the viva discussed in Chapter 3.

Advantages and limitations

As the case studies later in this chapter demonstrate, the advantages and limitations of mock vivas vary according to the form that they take. In the following we consider in detail the advantages and limitations of mock vivas by reflecting on some of the main questions that students and supervisors ask about them. Answers to these questions are not straightforward. In the following we adopt a question-and-answer format. The answers highlight the positive features – the 'Yes' features – as well as the important 'But' features. Students and supervisors are encouraged to heed both sets of responses.

- *Does participation in, or observation of, a mock viva help to demystify the oral examination?*

Yes – candidates usually approach their viva with a certain amount of trepidation; supervisors are often anxious on behalf of their students. Mock vivas can be an important way for candidates to see, and sometimes experience, what is regarded as usual and/or professional examining practice in their department. A mock viva modelled on the format of an actual viva also provides candidates with information about the usual procedures and roles of participants.

    But – in order for a mock viva to fulfil these purposes it must be organized in accordance with the policy on PhD examining in place at the institution where the viva will take place. Further, unless there is someone in the actual viva to monitor it, perhaps an independent chair, it cannot be assumed that the conduct of the actual viva will conform to institutional guidelines.

- *When candidates receive a mock viva that addresses their thesis (whole or part), does this prepare them to answer questions about their work in the actual oral examination?*

Yes – opportunities to talk about one's thesis and to explain and justify the approach taken are valuable preparation for the viva. A mock viva can also alert a candidate to different, and unexpected, perspectives on their work, particularly if the mock examiners are not the candidate's supervisors. 'The

Table 9.2   The relationship between specific objectives and the organization of a mock viva

Objectives of a mock viva with student as 'candidate'	Organization of mock viva
Refine aspects of the thesis	• Schedule – before submission • Text – whole, or key parts of, thesis • 'Examiners' – academic staff other than supervisor(s); peer group
Foster skills useful in the viva – *viva basic skills*	• Schedule – before or after submission • Text – whole, or part of, thesis; published piece not written by 'candidate' • 'Examiners' – ideally other academic staff, although members of the peer group can also be very effective. Supervisor(s) can be very helpful but they may be too familiar and/or 'safe' so that the 'candidate' does not gain experience of working under stress
Provide experience of thinking deeply about, focusing upon and answering different types of questions about the thesis – *viva content*	• Schedule – before or after submission • Text – ideally whole of thesis, although using part(s) of the thesis is still useful • 'Examiners' – ideally academic staff other than supervisor(s); members of peer group can also be effective; supervisor(s) may be too predictable, and/or reinforce a particular approach to the candidate's work
Provide experience of managing different types of behaviour – *viva conduct*	• Schedule – before or after submission • Text – thesis or other published piece. However, this objective is most likely to be achieved if the 'candidate' is examined on their thesis, or aspects of it, because the exam is experienced as far more personal (this is, of course, an important feature of the actual viva which encourages some candidates to be defensive – see Chapter 11) • 'Examiners' – some supervisors can be very adept at playing a different character in a mock viva, but not all supervisors are born thespians. To foster a student's skills at managing viva conduct it is best to expose them to the different styles of questioning and behaviour of other academic staff and peer group members

mock viva was certainly a useful experience as it was the first time that my thesis had been organized into a "whole beast" rather than discrete chapters . . . It was also a good experience to discuss the work in detail with an "outsider", i.e. not my supervisor, who had a different take on the issues raised'

(Hartley and Fox 2003: 10). If the supervisor acts the part of examiner, s/he may be able, if s/he is familiar with the approaches of the actual examiners, to ask questions that are similar to those that may be asked in the actual viva, *but this cannot be taken for granted.*

But – mock vivas are not a good substitute for long-term preparation as described in Chapter 4. Further, and most importantly, students should not regard a mock viva that examines the whole, or part, of the thesis as a trial run for the content of the actual oral examination. The specific questions asked in mock vivas and actual vivas are frequently very different (see also Wallace and Marsh 2001; Hartley and Fox 2004). As we saw in Chapter 3, vivas can have diverse content depending on the examiners' views of the standard of the thesis being examined and about what types of knowledge a PhD candidate should possess. So, for example, a candidate whose thesis is judged to be borderline may receive a very different type of viva in terms of content from a candidate whose thesis is judged as strong. Further, a candidate who has submitted an excellent thesis may be examined very differently by two examiners depending on the ideas that they each have about what contextual knowledge the candidate should possess – this is, of course, linked to the examiners' different approaches and interests. If these points are not familiar to you, return to Chapter 3 for a full account.

The following quote from a successful social science PhD candidate hints at some of the limitations of the mock viva as a preparation for the content of the actual viva. Asked after the viva how she could have been prepared better, Leila replied:

> I don't know really. I suppose a better mock viva might have helped. Like a really sort of full on, proper, you know let's read this as if we're not your supervisor and we don't like what you've done sort of thing. That maybe would have given me a bit more of a sense of where the kinds of questions might come from, or where the difficulties might lie. So I don't know, it's difficult. It's not something that you can necessarily prepare for because you're talking about two individual people with particular perspectives on their own work and that's what they are going to bring in. So I'm not sure you ever can [prepare]. A viva that you had with two other people would have been completely and utterly different. So I'm not sure it is possible to prepare because it's down to whoever you are fortunate or unfortunate enough to have as your internal or external examiners. Two other people would have given me a significantly easier time, two other people might have given me a significantly harder time, but I'm not sure.

Retrospectively, Leila thought that a more challenging mock viva may have prepared her better for the oral examination. However, she also recognized that the content of the viva was subject to the interests and approaches of the examiners, and this could not be predicted accurately and replicated in a mock viva. Samantha, a psychology candidate, requested a mock viva, 'but', she reported to us, 'the real thing was nothing like the mock!' In retrospect she specified that 'a more detailed, thorough, accurate-likeness mock' should be provided 'i.e. specific questions rather than the general "tell us about your PhD" mock viva question'.

Samantha's request for preparation that included specific and challenging questions is a fair one. Doctoral students should have a range of experiences, including a mock viva, in which they can practise addressing questions about their thesis and related topics; this is best achieved through a long-term strategy of preparation (see Chapter 4). However, Samantha's assumption that more specific questions in her mock would have prepared her better for the viva ignores the fact that it is only in retrospect that she can identify what her examiners expected of her. To reiterate the point made by Leila: 'Two other people would have given me a significantly easier time, two other people might have given me a significantly harder time.'

- *When candidates are given, or observe, a mock viva apparently modelled on the structure of the actual examination, does this provide them with insight into the way that examiners behave and give them practice at managing conduct?*

Yes – when the student is the 'candidate' a mock viva can contribute to her/his experience of managing different kinds of academic exchange. This type of experience is always valuable in preparing for the viva. Similarly, observing a public performance of a mock does contribute to the candidate's knowledge of how academics engage in intellectual exchange. Also, where supervisors are familiar with the examining styles of the actual examiners, they may be able to conduct a mock viva that is similar in conduct to the 'real thing', *but this cannot be taken for granted.*

But – this aspect of mock vivas is valuable only if it is seen as *an example* of an academic exchange; it does not provide illustration of the way that the actual examiners will behave. A history student recalled how 'my supervisor's mock viva was rather intense and made me unnecessarily defensive'. Whereas he expected his actual viva to be 'a grilling', 'formal', 'exhaustive' and preoccupied with 'specifics', it was actually 'relaxed', and focused on themes. As we have already seen, viva conduct varies according to examiners' personal/political agendas and interpersonal dynamics. It also varies depending on the examiners' views about what PhD candidates should be able to cope with (their examining style).

- *Does a mock viva, in which the candidate is examined, offer an opportunity to rehearse skills that are key to the viva performance?*

Yes – irrespective of the content and conduct of a mock viva, candidate's experiences of undergoing a mock viva can provide an important contribution to the development of skills required in the actual viva: being able to think under pressure, managing demanding questions, debating a point, communicating clearly, asking for clarification and so on. As one respondent in Hartley and Fox's (2004) study commented: 'It was a good preparation as this was the first time that I had "spoken" the answers. This allowed me to listen to myself and to see the effect of my answer on someone else.' This type of mock viva is most useful when the student receives feedback on their performance. Feedback can help candidates to see ways of communicating their ideas more clearly, think of ways of handling difficult questions or situations, and confront aspects of preparation that they have previously avoided (see also Chapter 4).

But – one viva is no substitute for longer-term preparation. As we saw in Chapter 4, students are best equipped for the skills demands of the viva by regular practice of talking about, and debating aspects of, their work. Conference and seminar presentations, upgrading and conversion panels, as well as mock-viva-style exchanges, are all ways in which students develop crucial skills and confidence. Mock vivas are the cherry on the icing on the cake.

Case studies: examples of different types of mock viva

So far we have considered the advantages and disadvantages of mock vivas in general. In this section we introduce three case studies of different types of mock viva in use in the UK and identify their specific strengths and limitations – see Boxes 9.3–9.5. To avoid repetition we focus only on strengths and limitations that are specific to each type of mock and advise you to read these in conjunction with the earlier discussion of mock vivas. Supervisors may find that these examples provide ideas for developing, or refining, their own repertoire of support for doctoral students.

Box 9.3   Case study 1

VIDEOTAPED 'REALISTIC' MOCK VIVA WITH STUDENT AUDIENCE

by Professor Liz Stanley, University of Newcastle (formerly of the University of Manchester)

At a previous point in its existence, the Women's Studies Centre at the University of Manchester made a 'Mock Viva Kit' of a 'mock but realistic' viva that PhD students could borrow and watch either individually or in groups with a member of staff present to discuss points that arose.

The initial 'viva' involved a doctoral student volunteering to have parts of their draft thesis examined, with another member of the Centre videotaping proceedings (there were in fact quite a number of volunteers, the person closest to completion was chosen). Some draft chapters together with an introduction and conclusion were made available to two members of staff who acted as an external and an internal examiner. A date was arranged for the 'viva', to which all graduate student members of the Centre were invited. The conduct of the viva was as realistic as possible under the circumstances, and all the formal requirements of the University of Manchester were fulfilled.

The 'examiners' held a 'preliminary meeting' to discuss the thesis and how to organize the viva in the 'examination room' with the student audience present (but not the 'candidate'). The 'examiners' brought with them their written initial responses to the 'thesis', which they swapped and read before conducting their preliminary discussions. Then at the appointed time the candidate arrived with the 'supervisor' (present in a non-speaking role to take notes of the proceedings for the candidate). At the end of the viva, the candidate and the supervisor were asked to leave, whilst the examiners discussed the candidate's performance during the viva in relation to their initial responses to the thesis. The candidate was then invited back into the room and the result given; this was a pass subject to some additions to the introduction and a new and more substantial conclusion. There was then a discussion of the entire proceedings, involving the candidate and the student audience as well as the examiners, and this too was videotaped. Following the videoed viva, the two people who acted as the examiners wrote formal reports, just as for a real viva, again in the form required by University of Manchester regulations.

The examiners' preliminary and final reports, the work that formed the thesis, and the video of the mock viva and the discussions around it, were all part of the Mock Viva Kit.

Advantages

- The students involved in producing the Mock Viva Kit, and also those who used it subsequently, were able to observe the entire oral examination process.
- It showed how the thesis and the viva are used together to inform the results that examiners reach.
- It gave students ideas about appropriate behaviour in a viva.
- It showed clearly what a viva under University of Manchester regulations entailed.
- Student participants were able to reflect on different kinds of questions and to discuss the different approaches of the internal examiner and the external examiner with the people concerned.
- The mock viva exercise was accessible, via the video, to students who were unable to attend the event (in particular part-time students) and to future cohorts of doctoral students.

Limitations

- The format was not able to convey how variable vivas and examiners can be.

- The experience of being the candidate was very different from being an observer.
- Using the Mock Viva Kit was less realistic/helpful than participating in the mock viva proceedings.

Box 9.4   Case study 2

MOCK VIVA OF STUDENT WITH PEER AUDIENCE

Peer observed mock vivas are a feature of short-term viva preparation for students on the doctoral programme in the Department of Educational Research at Lancaster University. Once a year the department arranges mock vivas for all doctoral programme students in their final stage of study – usually about 15 students. Each student is allocated two examiners, one academic staff member (not a supervisor) and one member of their peer group. The 'examiners' are presented with university guidelines. The 'candidate' has to submit, in advance of their mock viva, two copies of a piece of writing relating to their research – this is then examined in the mock viva. The mock, which takes roughly 30 minutes, is observed by an audience of doctoral students. It focuses solely on examining the 'candidate' and their work and does not include procedures prior to examining the candidate or the examiners' deliberation and feedback after the candidate has been examined. Following the mock viva there is usually 15 minutes of general discussion involving the candidate, examiners and the audience. Candidates are given the option of speaking to the examiners in private about their performance.

Advantages

- Students can observe different styles of examining. This diversity is always a source of surprise to students, even though they are told that vivas and mock vivas are highly variable.
- Observing, and then discussing, other people's mock vivas provides an opportunity for students to reflect on how they might handle different types of questions and styles of conduct in their actual viva.
- Candidates have the opportunity to refine their skill, address questions about their work and gain further experience of academic exchanges.
- This model gives the student examiner the opportunity to develop their questioning skills and to reflect on what it is like to be on the 'other side of the fence'.
- Academics, perhaps those with little or no experience of PhD examining, can gain ideas to inform their own practice.

Limitations

- It does not cover the whole oral examination procedure, although this can be discussed before or after the mock viva takes place.
- This type of mock viva is necessarily rather short in order to allow all students to experience being the candidate.
- The mock does not address all the thesis or, because of time constraints, contextual matters.

Box 9.5   Case study 3

PUBLIC PERFORMANCE OF A MOCK VIVA

Some departments provide public performances of mock vivas in which academic staff act the parts of the various participants in a PhD oral examination. These are regular events in the Sociology Department at Cardiff, University of Wales, and are described by Delamont *et al.* in *Supervising the PhD: A Guide to Success* (1997a: 151–3):

> First a staff member who has a PhD 'volunteers' to be a candidate. She chooses a published article, held in the university library, and it is designated 'the thesis'. Other staff are chosen to act as external examiner, internal examiner, supervisor and chair. A date is set, invitations are issued to postgraduates and posters are put up . . .
>
> On the appointed day, the cast assembles in the lecture room, and the chairperson explains what is going to happen. The 'candidate' waits outside the room, while the chair introduces the panel to the audience explaining their roles. Then the viva begins. The chair reminds the panel of their duties – quoting the university's rules – and then asks to have the candidate brought in. We then have a viva, lasting forty minutes or so, with the candidate trying to answer the panel's questions as well as possible, and the panel asking supportive questions. That is, the first performance is a successful viva: the thesis is a pass and the candidate is trying hard to be a 'good' student.
>
> After the first enactment of a viva, we stop and send the candidate out. The lecturer alters his or her appearance – swapping the smart suit for a t-shirt and jeans – and is again brought in. This time the 'candidate' acts bad student, and the panel are forced to fail the thesis. Different staff play 'bad' student in different styles – weeping, monosyllabic, depressed, aggressive, drunk, elaborately flippant . . .
>
> A few people find the mock viva frightening, but most respond that it is both entertaining and informative. It takes a good deal of organizing, but the benefits are worth it. The event is demystified.

Advantages

- It allows students to observe the examining styles of two 'examiners'.
- It provides knowledge about usual PhD examination procedures and practices at the institution.
- It provides students with an opportunity to reflect on how they might handle different types of questions and styles of examining in their actual viva.
- It provides students with ideas about how to behave in a viva.
- Academics, perhaps those with little or no experience of PhD examining, can gain ideas to inform their own practice.
- The text that is 'examined' is available for all the audience to read in advance. This facilitates audience engagement and it helps illuminate the different ways in which examiners may approach the same text.

Limitations

- It suggests that the difference between a successful and unsuccessful viva depends largely on the conduct and dress of the candidate.
- It suggests that a candidate can be failed on the basis of their viva – candidates could not be failed outright on the basis of viva performance alone unless the examiners were convinced that the thesis was not the candidate's own work.
- Students do not gain experience of being examined.

Making the most of mock vivas – tips for supervisors

Mock vivas can make an important contribution to the short-term viva preparation of students, although their limitations must be kept in mind and discussed by the supervisor and student. The following points are suggestions about ways that supervisors can maximize the benefits of mock vivas for their students:

- Consider and identify the objectives of a mock viva for each student and choose a style of mock viva that meets these objectives.
- Encourage your students to prepare thoroughly for their mock viva(s); the process of preparation can be as illuminating as the mock viva itself (Hartley and Fox 2004).
- Ensure that the mock viva 'examiners' are well prepared and that the event is taken seriously.
- Caution students not to think of their mock viva as a trial run for the real thing. Emphasize that a mock viva will not, indeed cannot, be the same as the actual viva in terms of content or conduct. Vivas are

like interviews and driving tests – you can have a pretty good idea of what is likely to happen, but neither the content nor conduct of the examination can be guaranteed in advance (see Chapter 11). The experience of Carlos (see Chapter 3), who was shocked by his oral examination because it did not correspond with his expectations, is an important reminder of this.

- Give students specific feedback on their mock viva performance. If the student has undergone a mock viva in front of an audience, give them the option of audience and/or private feedback. This also emerged as important for the respondents in Hartley and Fox's (2004) study.
- Discuss *ways* of answering questions, as well as actual answers. Delamont *et al.* (1997a) suggest that supervisors make a tape-recording or video of the mock viva, especially in cases where the student's first language is not English.
- Check your institution's viva regulations and ensure that students are familiar with these and with guidance given to examiners. Point out that examiners do sometimes stray from official procedures and recommendations.
- Consider using different types of mock viva as short-term preparation. For example, Delamont *et al.* (1997a) advocate a combination of individual vivas (where the supervisor 'examines' their student) and the public performance mock viva (see Box 9.5).
- Watching other students undergo a mock can be as instructive as doing one, particularly if students are given the opportunity to discuss it (see Boxes 9.3 and 9.4). A video of a student undergoing a mock viva can also serve this purpose if there is an opportunity for the student to discuss the proceedings with their supervisor.
- Commercial videos of mock vivas should always be used with caution as they may not depict viva procedures and practices at your institution.
- View mock vivas as one part of a package of preparations.

Making the most of mock vivas – tips for candidates

Most of the tips for supervisors apply also to candidates. However, there are five points that are of particular salience.

- Think about what you want to get out of the mock viva. What are your strengths and weaknesses? What do you need to practise? It may help to revisit the self-assessment chart in Box 4.2, Chapter 4.
- Prepare thoroughly for the mock viva; the process of preparation can be as illuminating as the mock viva itself. You may identify weak areas that need more attention or parts of your thesis that you are unclear about. This is best discovered before the viva.
- Do not think of the mock viva as a trial run for the real thing. A mock viva will not, indeed cannot, be the same as the actual viva in terms of content or conduct.

- If you are not given feedback on your mock viva performance, ask for it. How did you fare in handling the skills demands, the content of the questions, the conduct of the exchange? (See Chapter 4.)
- View mock vivas as one part of a package of preparations.

9.4 Summary

In this chapter we have looked at three aspects of short-term preparation:

- the relationship between the student and their supervisor;
- ways of dealing constructively with viva stories and myths;
- the uses of mock vivas.

In the next chapter we consider final-stage preparations, that is those that occur during the fortnight prior to the viva.

10

Viva Preparation – Final Stage

Chapter overview

Student preparation for the viva shifts into a third and final phase in the weeks before the viva. In Chapter 4 we looked at ways of preparing for the viva throughout the course of PhD registration, and in Chapter 9 we focused on short-term preparations that take place around the time that the thesis is submitted. This chapter concentrates on practical and academic preparations in the fortnight before the viva. The guidance we offer on final-stage preparations, especially on 'knowing the thesis' may, however, be useful to students preparing for a mock viva several months before the 'real thing'.

Students ☺☺☺   Supervisors ☺☺☺

Chapter contents

10.1 Countdown to the viva

Due to various admin. problems there was a considerable delay between submitting my PhD thesis and my viva voce exam – several months in fact! During those months I had been doing many different things, including teaching, teaching and more teaching. Unfortunately, one of the things I hadn't been doing was thinking about my PhD research. Although I had spent a number of years reading, writing, experimenting and dreaming about my research, I realised a couple of weeks before my exam that I could remember very little about what I had done! . . .

I've heard various academics say that for at least the brief period of time leading up to and during your viva you'll be the world's leading expert in your field of research. The task before me, therefore, was somewhat daunting. I sprang into immediate action and began to procrastinate like mad. One week later I'd finished my revision timetable and was ready to put it into action. I began to reread all those journal articles I'd been citing all the way through my thesis – hoping that they still said what I thought they said. I took my thesis down from the top shelf, blew the dust off, and opened it. Then I decided to treat myself and have two cups of tea and nine digestive biscuits.

(Quale 1999: 45)

Jeremy Quale's account sums up neatly the experiences and feelings that many candidates have as the viva approaches. Although the final stage of viva preparation is very important, candidates are often unsure about what to do and where to start. The challenge of final-stage preparation is often exacerbated by the time between submission and the viva: 50 per cent of respondents in Hartley and Jory's (2000) survey experienced a waiting time that exceeded three months.

The final stage of viva preparation involves academic and practical matters:

- practical arrangements;
- supervisor/student meeting;
- academic preparations.

Each of these requires advance planning.

Practical arrangements

As soon as a date for the viva has been announced, candidates are advised to draw up a list of practical arrangements that need attending to and to identify appropriate dates for completing each of these arrangements – see Box 10.1. Final checks on all arrangements should be made a few days before the viva.

Box 10.1   Task for candidates

PRACTICAL ARRANGEMENTS

Check through the following list of practical arrangements. What arrangements will you need to make and by when?

- *Travel.* If you need to travel to the place of your viva, you may need to organize this in advance (train and plane tickets, check car is in working order, car parking, a lift). Always leave yourself plenty of time for travel and parking. For long journeys, plan to arrive at least a day in advance, especially if jet lag is likely to be a problem.
- *Paid work commitments.* If you require time off work, organize this well in advance. It is best to have a whole day off even if the viva is in the afternoon.
- *Domestic responsibilities.* If you have responsibility for children or adults ensure that alternative care and/or supervision arrangements are in place well in advance. If possible, have a back-up plan. Do a final check on domestic arrangements the day before the viva.
- *Viva arrangements.* Check the time and venue of your viva. If you have not visited the room before, ensure that you know how to find it and, if possible, visit the room in advance to check its location and layout.
- *Stress.* What are your 'stress busters'? If you are likely to get stressed by the prospect of your viva, think in advance of how you can manage this. Some universities offer workshops on managing stress. Hopefully, your experience of facing stressful academic situations (conference presentations, upgradings, mock vivas, teaching) during the course of your PhD will have led you to work out successful coping strategies.

People have different 'stress busters' – what works for one person does not necessarily work for another. However, there are general stress busters that you can incorporate into daily life the week before the viva. Cottrell's (1999) advice to undergraduate students on managing stress before an exam is also applicable to PhD candidates:

- Drink plenty of fresh water.
- Undertake some form of exercise – walking, playing Frisbee, swimming, working out at a gym.
- Make time, even a small pocket each day, to relax.
- Eat healthily.

Some candidates may find that herbal remedies work well as a means of coping with stress but it is advisable not to experiment with these on the day of your viva. Try these remedies at an earlier stage to discover what works best for you.

- *Clothes.* Ensure that you have organized what you will wear to your viva. A few institutions provide strict guidelines on the dress of candidates and examiners; meeting these requires forward planning. At the University of Oxford, for example, the formality of the occasion is underscored by a strict academic dress code.

'For the *viva* itself, which is a formal examination of the University, you will be expected to wear *subfusc* [formal academic dress at Oxford University]. This is defined as follows: for men dark suit, dark socks, black shoes, plain white shirt and collar, and white bow tie: for women dark skirt or trousers, dark coat (if desired), black stockings and shoes, white blouse and black tie. In addition, you should wear the Oxford gown of your present status (i.e. Student for the Degree of Doctor of Philosophy), or the gown and hood of the degree held from your own university, or, if an Oxford graduate, the gown and hood of your Oxford degree.'

(University of Oxford 1997: 4)

Most institutions leave dress to the discretion of the participants. Although some books advise candidates to dress smartly, it is best for you to wear what you find comfortable, bearing in mind that the viva is a formal occasion. In other words, do not dress casually if you are likely to feel underdressed and uncomfortable.

Supervisor–candidate meeting

A meeting between the candidate and supervisor is essential during the final stage to ensure that the candidate is clear about oral examination procedures at their institution. It is useful if the candidate knows in advance who will attend the viva and who, if anyone, will take notes in it. At this meeting the supervisor can also advise the candidate on final-stage academic preparations. If these preparations include a mock viva, read Chapter 9. Last-minute concerns that the candidate has about their thesis and/or about the demands of doing an oral examination can be discussed. The supervisor can also help boost their student's confidence by reminding them of the strengths of their thesis.

Academic preparations

Many types of academic preparation will have been completed prior to the final stage (see Chapters 4 and 9). The scheduling of final-stage academic preparations will depend on personal preference, needs and available time.

The final stage of preparation usually involves rereading the thesis. Students that we interviewed and surveyed, from across the disciplines, mentioned this as their primary form of final preparation; 85 per cent of the psychologists in Hartley and Jory's (2000) study also reread their theses. We advise candidates to start rereading their theses roughly two weeks prior to the viva and to make a list of corrections and typographical errors as they do this. Two weeks should provide enough time to complete final-stage academic preparations for the viva (we discuss these further below), although it is still close enough to the viva that the thesis will be fresh in the candidate's mind on the day.

10.2 Rereading the thesis

The main purpose of this exercise is to ensure that you are familiar with what you have written, that you 'know your thesis'. At the point of submission a candidate is, usually, extremely well informed about their work. However, as in Quale's case (see above), there can be a sizeable gap between submission and the oral examination during which your attentions may be directed away from the thesis. In these cases, it is likely that you will forget aspects of the thesis. Whatever the gap between submission and the oral examination it is sensible to reread the thesis. Examiners expect you to know your thesis in detail and to be able to respond to very specific, as well as general, questions. Further, in order to address some of the examiner's points you may need to refer to a specific sentence or equation and to reconstruct the process leading up to its inclusion. Examining practices vary considerably, but some examiners, particularly in certain branches of the sciences, approach the task by requiring the candidate to talk through their thesis, or parts of it, line by line.

There is a range of ways in which candidates approach the task of getting to 'know their thesis'. At one end of the spectrum a candidate can reread merely to refresh their memory. More usually candidates use rereading as an opportunity to identify mistakes, weaknesses, contentious points, key stages in their argument and to think about how to manage questions. Being clear about the purposes of rereading can help to focus the exercise.

'Know your thesis'

In Chapter 2 we looked in detail at what academics see as the purposes of the PhD viva. Most of these purposes require that the student should 'know their thesis' well. For example, authentication of the thesis, which is a key purpose of the viva even when the thesis is deemed strong, depends on the candidate showing that they 'know their thesis'. But what does this mean? What should you be able to do at the end of the final stage of academic preparation? We have identified seven objectives that you should work towards when rereading your thesis:

1. Know what is written in the thesis.
2. Know the layout of the thesis.
3. Understand what is presented in the thesis.
4. Justify and defend the thesis.
5. Identify, and be prepared to discuss, weak areas, gaps and mistakes.
6. Identify the originality, contribution to knowledge and implications of the thesis.
7. Reflect on what could be done differently if starting again.

Each of these objectives is now addressed in turn.

Know what is written in the thesis
At the most basic, examiners expect candidates to know what they have written. What arguments are presented in the thesis? What literatures and debates are referred to? What approaches have been used and discussed (theories, concepts, methodology)? What findings and conclusions are presented? Some of the strategies discussed in the following section on knowing your way around the thesis can help you revise what is, quite literally, presented in the thesis.

Know the layout of the thesis
You may need to locate specific sections in the thesis quickly during the viva. This is primarily a practical matter as it can reduce delays. More importantly, knowing the layout of your thesis can help you to feel in control in the viva and to focus your energies on the examiners' questions rather than on how to locate particular sections of the thesis. As one chair noted of a successful PhD candidate: 'The candidate had a very clear view of what was where in the bound document so that flow was never interrupted by any pauses' (Trafford and Leshem 2002: 34).

You can use several strategies to ensure that you know your way around the thesis, but whatever you do will be easier if your thesis is clearly structured with detailed section summaries and a comprehensive table of contents. A careful reread can reacquaint you with the layout of the thesis; some candidates may prefer various memory aids. Cryer (2000) suggests attaching Post-it-style stickers to a copy of the thesis. Another suggestion for quickly producing a guide to the thesis and an aid to revision is to cut and paste the introduction and conclusion to each chapter, plus chapter sub-headings, into a single computer file. Rereading can also be used to generate a detailed summary of the content of the thesis.

> A couple of people said to me, 'What you need to do is you need to read each page and you pick out three key words', it's in a textbook this. You pick three key words on each page and you write those down and then you do sheets of paper with these words on. And then, if you get a question, you ask them what page it is and then you can tell them what the page is about.
>
> (Douglas, PhD student, Sociology)

The method described by Douglas is a variant of the system advocated by Phillips and Pugh (2000: 153–5). Their system of viva preparation involves two or three sheets of lined paper, each divided into two columns. Each half line is numbered and each number corresponds to a page of the thesis. Over a period of roughly two weeks the candidate writes a summary of each page of the thesis on the appropriate half line. Phillips and Pugh claim three advantages for their system: (1) the candidate will have revised the thesis 'in the most detailed way possible'; (2) s/he will be 'in a position to pinpoint – at a glance – the precise location of any argument, reference or explanation'; (3) they will have prepared a handy aid to revision, one that does not require revisiting the whole of the thesis.

Phillips and Pugh's system helps you become familiar with what you have written, it also generates a useful list of thesis contents. For some students this exercise can be very reassuring. However, *there are two main limitations* to this approach. First, the system does not prioritize understanding. There is a danger that you may become overly concerned with knowing your way around the thesis at the expense of understanding what you have written and why. Second, used in isolation this system encourages a myopic view of the thesis; it fails to bring into focus the thesis as a whole and its place in the broader intellectual context.

Understand what is presented in the thesis

Thirty-six per cent of examiners in our survey described the viva as an opportunity to check the candidate's understanding of different aspects of their thesis. You therefore need to ensure that you *understand* (1) the theories, concepts and methods used, (2) your own arguments and conclusions, and (3) the arguments of key scholars in your field (particularly if you make extensive use of this literature in the thesis). If the thesis involves the presentation of tables, graphs, statistics or equations then you must be able to explain their construction and meaning. Our successful interviewees frequently used rereading as an opportunity to check their understanding of what they had written in the thesis. 'I'll write some sort of summary of my PhD. Basically there are three sorts of core chapters in it, and I'll summarize those research chapters on to a couple of pages and make sure I understand it all' (Bob, PhD student, Chemistry).

Checking understanding was also a key task that Andrew, a physiotherapy candidate, set himself when he reread his thesis. Importantly Andrew did not neglect to work through what he described as his weakest area – statistics:

> I think reading through the thesis isn't enough. I think self-inquisition and self-testing are probably the way I've often done things. I'd had a bit of a funny experience about three years ago when somebody asked me a question and I didn't know the answer to it and I looked like an idiot. Since then I've gone into everything, even the lines of the bar chart. You go back and check the data, so if someone asks you what it is you can explain it.

Rereading to check understanding is a useful strategy. For example, when Gary, a pharmacy student, reflected on his viva, he described how 'I'd put quite a lot of work in just looking back or expanding on things I'd written about that I didn't understand in quite as much depth as I thought I should. And two of those things came up.'

Box 10.2   Task for candidates

CHECK THAT YOU UNDERSTAND, AND CAN EXPLAIN, THE DIFFERENT ASPECTS OF YOUR WORK

Understanding is conveyed primarily through your explanations so it is useful to check that you can provide clear and full verbal explanations of your approach, findings and conclusions. If you have experienced a mock viva this may have highlighted sections of the thesis that you are less clear about (see Chapter 9).

Ways of checking that you understand, and can explain, different aspects of your PhD research are:

- explain aspects of your work to fellow students or your supervisor;
- write down brief explanations and reread them the next day;
- tape record your explanations and then play them back to yourself a few days later.

You may find it convenient to work through the thesis one chapter at a time, or you may prefer to tackle the thesis as a whole. Whichever method you adopt, you need to consider carefully and critically whether your explanations are full and make sense.

Justify and defend the thesis

You need to know, and also show, why you have adopted a particular approach (perspective, methods, theories), made certain claims and arrived at specific conclusions. In other words, you need to ensure you can address the 'why' questions (see Box 10.3). In practice-related PhDs, candidates also need to demonstrate that they know why they have presented various submissions aside from the written thesis. A 'why' question that is frequently used by examiners as a way of starting a viva is, 'why did you choose this topic for doctoral research?' (Trafford 2002: 5). Whilst this is usually regarded as a 'gentle' question (subject, of course, to the examiner's style of questioning), most other 'why' questions are designed to be more probing. Being able to provide reasonable and clear answers to the 'why' questions is an essential component of an informed and convincing defence of the thesis. As we saw in Chapter 2, roughly one-quarter of the examiners in our survey identified defence of the thesis as a purpose of the viva.

Box 10.3   Task for candidates

JUSTIFY AND DEFEND YOUR THESIS: THE 'WHY' QUESTIONS

Identify key 'why' questions relating to your thesis. Then write down brief answers to these questions (these are probably addressed in more detail in your thesis). Likely 'why' questions are:

- Why this topic?
- Why this angle on the topic, rather than some other?
- Why the use of certain literatures and theories and not others?
- Why these methods, sources and techniques, as opposed to others?
- Why these modes of analyses?
- Why these conclusions?

Remember that the most convincing answers to 'why' questions are those that engage with alternative approaches and, following from this, identify the merits of the particular choices that you made in producing the thesis.

When tackling this task pay special attention to rehearsing your rationale for sections of the thesis that you are least confident about.

Preparing to defend the thesis is not just a matter of rehearsing arguments, it also requires tackling questions relating to the weaker parts of your work: 'I know where I think the argument's a bit weak in the thesis, or where I'm least comfortable, and I need to have a look at that again, see how I arrived at that kind of conclusion' (Douglas, PhD student, Sociology). Sometimes, when candidates return to their work they realize that their thinking has shifted on certain aspects of it. This is not a cause for panic or alarm. The important point is that you can: (1) justify the thesis within the context that it was produced, i.e. defend the decisions that were made at the time of doing, and writing up, the research; and (2) explain why you now have different views about this aspect of your work. Critical reflection on, and evaluation of, your research is an important skill. Another aspect of preparing a defence is deciding how far to go in defending different aspects of the thesis. As we discuss in Chapter 11, it may be appropriate to defend some aspects of the thesis with more vigour than others (see also Box 10.4). Grix (2001) suggests that candidates should not concede too much concerning the originality of the thesis and its contribution to knowledge because they are crucial to the award of PhD.

Box 10.4   Task for candidates

HOW FAR SHOULD YOU GO?

Think about what aspects of your work you would be prepared to defend to the hilt and what aspects you would defend less strongly if pressed by the examiners.

Identify, and be prepared to discuss, weak areas, gaps and mistakes
In some cases, usually owing to time constraints, a candidate will feel that they have submitted a thesis with a gap or weakness. Following submission, candidates are advised to attend to such gaps or weaknesses and to ensure, if possible, that they have a good idea of how these shortfalls in the thesis can be addressed.

> . . . reread the PhD and collect information about those parts where I think there are gaping holes, things that ought to have been in there but are not in there, things that I think will probably be asked.
> (Kali, PhD student, English)

> I had prepared quite well. I had anticipated largely what they would ask me and, to some extent, I mean I knew she'd say I had to write the conclusion again because it was three sides long and I hadn't really concluded it properly because I ran out of time. So I knew, and to some extent I'd anticipated that, and I'd already done more reading.
> (Angela, PhD student, Women's Studies)

This type of preparation is very useful because examiners often ask candidates to talk about weak or missing areas. Indeed, roughly one-third of the examiners in our survey mentioned that the viva provided an opportunity for the candidate to clarify areas of weakness in their thesis. Cryer (2000: 242) provides useful advice to candidates on this matter: 'If criticisms seems valid, prepare responses to show that you recognise this by saying, for example, what you would have liked to be able to do about them if there were more resources or if you had thought about them at the right time, or what you hope that other workers may still do about them.'

Identify the originality, contribution to knowledge and implications of the thesis
What is original about your thesis? How does it contribute to knowledge?
What implications does the thesis have for future work in the area? These
three questions should all be addressed in a PhD thesis but, in the time
between submission and the oral examination, you may discover new or
fresh perspectives. You are therefore advised to revisit these three questions
in the weeks preceding your viva. Although these questions are often
explored with rigour, they can also serve as a warm-up at the beginning of the
viva. Wolfe (2003) suggests that it is worth being prepared for this type of
question:

> Be ready for a 'free kick'. It is relatively common that a panel will ask
> one (or more) questions that, whatever the actual wording may be, are
> essentially an invitation to you to tell them (briefly) what is important,
> new and good in the thesis. You ought not to stumble at this stage, so
> you should rehearse this. You should be able to produce on demand
> (say) a one minute speech and a five minute speech, and be prepared to
> extend them if invited by further questions. Do not try to recite your
> abstract: written and spoken styles should be rather different. Rather,
> rehearse the answers to the questions: 'What is your thesis about, and
> what have you done that merits a PhD?'

Although most institutions do not define 'originality', some do. If your
institution provides a definition, check that you can articulate the originality
of your thesis within this framework. If you are uncertain about how your
thesis is original, take a look at Cryer's (2000) analogy of an explorer on an
expedition; see also Chapter 8 of this book.

Being able to identify what is original about a thesis requires being
informed about the broader discipline – topics, approaches, theories,
methods, debates and so on. This awareness is also fundamental to assessing
how the thesis contributes to knowledge; many institutions require examiners to test the candidate's knowledge of the broader context during the viva.
If you have kept abreast of key journals and attended the main conferences
in your field you will probably have a reasonably good overview of your
discipline and the place of the thesis within it.

Following on from the identification of the ways in which the thesis contributes to knowledge, it is also useful to reflect on the implications of your
work. Typically, you need to consider the implications of your work for knowledge and/or research practice in your field. Burnham's (1994: 32) advice is
that 'it is not necessary to rush out and digest the latest textbook offering an
overview of your discipline. Examiners simply wish to see that candidates are
able to discuss what implications the thesis in question may have for their
broader discipline.' Depending on the topic, it may also be appropriate for
you to consider the implications of your research findings for policy and
practice outside the academy.

If, after submitting the thesis, you feel unsure of your answers to questions about the originality, contribution and implications of your thesis

you should arrange to discuss this with your supervisor. The two tasks in Boxes 10.5 and 10.6 may help to generate reflection on these three questions.

Box 10.5 Task for candidates

DRAFT A BOOK PROPOSAL

An interesting way of revisiting the three questions of originality, contribution and implications prior to the viva, and of rehearsing the main concerns and findings presented in the thesis, is to write a book proposal based on the thesis. Book proposals usually have two parts: a rationale for the book and an outline of contents. For the purposes of viva preparation, you need only write the book rationale. This exercise entails reflection on what is original about your work, how your 'book' contributes to the discipline and compares with competitors. Publishers' guidelines for prospective authors can be downloaded from the web and used to structure this exercise and make it more realistic. This task is based on a suggestion contained in the Institute of Education's (2003) guidelines for their PhD students.

Box 10.6 Task for candidates

MAKING HEADLINES

Write a 500 word newspaper article in which you outline your key research findings. What would the headline be? Why is your research important and to whom? If you want to take a particularly light approach to this task, you could try penning a piece for a tabloid as well as a broadsheet.

A variant of this task is to imagine being interviewed about your research on Radio 4 – you never know, this may actually happen.

Reflect on what could be done differently if starting again

Examiners frequently ask candidates to reflect on how they would tackle their PhD research if they were to start again. It is therefore sensible to think about this question in advance. It can be very difficult, after investing so much time and energy in a thesis, to imagine it done differently. Considering this question should not lead you to lose faith in your thesis but rather to stand back from your accomplishment and to critically evaluate it. What have you learned from this experience and how would these lessons help you to design another project in the area? See Box 10.7.

Box 10.7 Task for candidates

TIME TRAVEL: STARTING AGAIN WITH THE BENEFIT OF HINDSIGHT

How would you tackle your PhD research if you were to start again?
   To think through a response to this question you first need to unpack
it. Reflect on each of the following:

- Did you encounter particular difficulties in the process of doing
  your research that an alternative approach (methods, sources,
  instruments, use of concepts etc.) would avoid?
- Have your findings addressed your research question(s) as fully as
  you would like? What might you have done differently to shed more
  light on your topic?
- Do recent developments in your field have implications for your
  research question(s)? Do these new developments suggest fruitful
  new directions for research?

The limits of 'knowing your thesis'

'Knowing your thesis' is not the same as knowing what the examiners will
make of it, because people read in different ways and for different purposes.
Moreover, as we stress throughout this book, the content of the viva can vary
considerably (see especially Chapters 2 and 3). Nevertheless, it is sensible to
consider how your work relates to your examiners' interests and relevant
literature written by them. Ideally this literature should be cited in the thesis
because, as Delamont *et al.* (1997a: 145) point out, 'if the external is relevant
enough to the thesis to examine it, then his or her work should probably be
cited'.

Likely questions

Rereading strategies often involve predicting the questions that the examiners will ask and preparing responses to them. Broad (2003) suggests compil-
ing a file of anticipated questions that you can add to in the lead up to the
viva; his PhD file consisted of questions from his supervisor as well as those
he had been asked at the end of presentations. The students we interviewed
generally adopted a shorter-term approach:

   I'm going to go and read it [the thesis] in the library a couple of times
   and just kind of mark anything that I think is problematic or where I
   think I might be picked up.

   (Leila, PhD Student, Sociology)

... try and foresee the questions they are going to ask me and know the weaknesses in what I've done.

(Bob, PhD student, Chemistry)

I mean, if I was looking at this thesis, what would I want to pick out and ask about?

(Kali, PhD student, English)

The approach adopted by Kali reveals one important limitation of this exercise, your reading of the thesis will not necessarily be the same as those of your examiners. Even in cases where you try to anticipate the examiners' perspectives this is inevitably a prediction. It is therefore advisable *not* to allow your rereading of the thesis to be constrained by predictions about the examiners' questions. As Gary, a pharmacy candidate, recognized: 'I went through my thesis and tried to look at it as if I was an external examiner and what would I ask ... I'm going through the list of that, and reading up on things. But they [the examiners] might ask something different.'

Asking friends or colleagues to pose questions is another common strategy. Jan (Religious Studies) drew upon several sources of help to develop competence and confidence in addressing questions about her work. 'My husband has set me a few questions. It's about Plato my thesis, so he's asked me questions about translation, things that I wouldn't dream of in a million years ... A friend of mine has sent me some questions that she thought would help me because she's just recently gone through her viva.'

Reflecting on the thesis from different perspectives, gaining practice at answering questions, rehearsing ways of answering demanding and/or unexpected questions are all excellent forms of viva preparation (see Chapters 8 and 12 on how examiners approach their job). It is also a good idea to ask yourself the questions you most fear an examiner asking and to work through responses to these. Second guessing the specific interests of your examiners provides good practice at answering questions but this strategy is not a reliable guide to the questions you will be asked in the viva. Further, as Kate, a psychiatry candidate, explained, 'there's only so many questions you can sit and guess before you go in there'.

Although you may have prepared carefully, you must not assume that you have anticipated all the important questions. The experience of Carlos (described in Chapter 4) is a salutary reminder of the vulnerability that can follow from assuming that viva preparation equips you to tackle all questions. Carlos, an education candidate, relied heavily on a strategy of predicting questions to prepare for the viva. He asked his supervisor and another lecturer to list possible questions which he then revised. The examiners asked Carlos only a few of the questions that he had anticipated and prepared for; all their other questions were unpredicted because Carlos was unaware, prior to the viva, of the weaknesses that the examiners found in the thesis. As we saw in Chapter 3, vivas are highly variable and unpredictable. Candidates who have fixed expectations are likely to be surprised and possibly disadvantaged by their viva experience. *You need to keep a flexible approach to the viva. You need not only to prepare well throughout the course of your PhD – as suggested in this chapter and in Chapters 4 and 9 – but also to keep an open mind about the questions that will be asked in the viva.*

Bored with the thesis

> You know when you've finished writing it you get fed up looking at it . . . It was all I could do to pick it up again and read it. There were bits I was quite proud of, where I'd drawn in a bit of literature and I would reread those because it was a nice warm thing, but other stuff was a bit tortuous.
>
> (Douglas, PhD student, Sociology)

Rereading the thesis is a widely recommended form of preparation, although some candidates tremble at the prospect of reading their thesis 'yet again'. Rereading after submission is, however, different from reading the thesis prior to submission; students that Phillips (1994: 133) interviewed described the former as 'illuminating' and 'quite different'.

Although you need to know your thesis very well, it is difficult to concentrate fully when you are bored with your work. One candidate used the analogy of 'eating cold porridge' to describe her experience of returning to an old project. If the prospect of rereading your thesis is as unattractive as eating cold porridge you may find that the tasks in this chapter provide ideas to get you started.

The limits of rereading

Rereading is valuable, but it is *not* advisable to keep rereading your thesis – once, possibly twice, should be sufficient. It is also *not* usually advisable to reread the thesis a day or two before the viva. Rereading should not be a last-minute activity because

- it can lead to overload;
- it does not allow you time to reflect on how to manage questions;
- it can lead to panic.

10.3 Literature update

Keeping abreast of relevant literature is an important aspect of viva preparation. Examiners may ask you directly about new literature or developments in key debates, particularly if these pose a challenge to your work. Although it may be tempting to hide your head in the sand, it is best to be aware of these developments, and to think through a response before the viva. This response may take several forms:

- a critique;
- an acknowledgement of the merits of the work;
- reflection on how new developments might influence how you would approach your thesis if starting again.

If the developments are very recent, examiners will not usually expect you to have a sophisticated response. Informed comment, and some preliminary reflections on the implications for the thesis will be sufficient to indicate to the examiners that you are able to actively engage with developments.

Keeping up to date with relevant literature should be an ongoing form of preparation, but for candidates who have other demands on their time following the submission of the thesis, it is a job for the final stage:

Figure 10.1 Don't bury your head in the sand – keep abreast of relevant literature between submission and viva. © Andrew Jackson

I'll probably have a scan of the relevant journals in the field, the current issues, just to make sure that I'm on top of current knowledge, especially of any developments that have happened since the thesis was submitted. Just to show that I have an understanding of the direction in which scholarship has been going since I submitted . . . just making sure that I know what other people were doing in the field at the time of the viva just in case I was asked about that.

(Tony, PhD student, History)

Tony's strategy is a sensible one – scanning relevant journals is an excellent and relatively quick form of preparation. Reviews and abstracts are also useful sources of concise information on recent developments. If, in the weeks before the viva, you discover a book that you feel you must read, it may be appropriate to use a quick reading strategy. Blaxter *et al.* (1996) offer useful tips on reading a book in five minutes.

10.4 Questions to ask examiners

Think about what *you* want to get out of the viva.

Examiners often invite the candidate to ask them questions at some point in the viva, usually towards the end of the proceedings. Burnham (1994: 33) advises that 'supine candidates never impress, so prepare a series of searching questions for the examiners'. Although it is not necessary for you to worry about finding 'searching' questions to 'impress', the viva can provide a valuable opportunity to get advice on several matters (this is obviously dependent on how the viva proceeds):

- the development of ideas relating to aspects of your research;
- future research directions;
- career development;
- publishing and other forms of dissemination.

Aside from advice you may also want to talk about an aspect, or implication, of your work that is particularly important to you. This may be addressed by the examiners' questions and/or the examiners may invite you to suggest topics for discussion (see Chapter 12). If you are not given an opportunity to talk about this matter it can still be appropriate to indicate that you want to do so.

10.5 Less than 24 hours to go

The night before

Ideally, you should *not* read the thesis the night before the viva; this should have been done already. Candidates can sometimes feel tempted to revisit their work because they fear that they do not remember it. This is usually an effect of anxiety. Carla's supervisor advised her to 'go to a movie the night before, . . . just relax the night before and have a good night's sleep'. This is sound advice.

The morning before

At this stage in the countdown check that you have everything that you need to take into the viva. Here is a checklist:

- The thesis – with identical pagination to the examiners' copies. Just imagine the confusion, delay and stress that can arise in the viva if the examiners work with pages that are numbered differently from yours.
- Paper.
- Pens or pencils.
- List of typographical errors and corrections.
- Notes, perhaps your revision aid.
- Tissues.
- Water.
- Any medication that you require.

Five minutes before

Turn off your mobile phone when you arrive outside the examination room.

10.6 Summary

Candidates – summary of final-stage preparation

Practical matters
- *As soon as the thesis is submitted* draw up a list of practical matters and work out a timescale for attending to these – travel, paid work commitments, domestic responsibilities, viva arrangements, stress, clothes.

Academic matters
- Read your thesis carefully roughly two weeks prior to the viva – check that you *know* what you have presented.
- Check that you know the *layout* of your thesis – possibly, prepare an overview of the contents of your thesis.
- Check that you *understand* the theories, concepts and methods used, your arguments and conclusions and the arguments of key writers in your field. If your thesis involves the presentation of tables, graphs, statistics or equations then check that you can explain their construction and that you understand what they are saying.

- Get to grips with weak areas, or gaps, in your thesis.
- Check that you can justify, that is *defend,* your approach, claims and conclusions (see Chapter 11 on the *process* of defending the thesis in the viva).
- Revisit the ways in which your thesis is *original* and *contributes to knowledge* and be clear about the *implications* of your work for future research.
- Be prepared to comment on how you would tackle your research if starting again.
- Keep a note of the mistakes and typographical errors in your thesis.
- *Scan* the latest journals, books and book reviews to keep informed of developments in your field.
- Practise answering questions about your thesis and the broader context. Ask yourself the questions you most fear an examiner asking and work through responses.
- *Do not* assume that, after final-stage preparation, you have all questions covered. Adopt a flexible approach.

Supervisors – summary of final-stage preparation

- As soon as the thesis is submitted remind your student to draw up a list of practical matters and decide on a timescale for attending to these – travel, paid work commitments, domestic responsibilities, viva arrangements, stress, clothes.
- Advise your student about organizing final-stage academic preparations. If this includes a mock viva, see Chapter 9.
- Meet, or communicate via email, with your student a few days prior to the viva to check that they:

  - 'know their thesis', the broader context of literature, and the limitations of their preparations;
  - are familiar with the usual procedures for PhD vivas at your institution.

11

In the Viva – Candidates' Perspectives

Mostly the viva is a journey into the unknown.

(Phillips 1994: 133)

Chapter overview

This chapter addresses the questions that candidates frequently ask about the viva. It outlines examination procedures and offers guidance to candidates about how to handle the demands made of them and how to 'squeeze' maximum value out of the experience. This chapter will not, however, tell you all that you need to know about the viva; you should read this chapter in conjunction with Chapters 2, 3, 4, 9 and 10. The chapter is illustrated liberally with the experiences of a diversity of candidates, including mature students, women and men, home and overseas students, and students from different disciplines and institutions.

Students	☺☺☺	Supervisors	☺☺
Examiners	☺☺	Chairs	☺☺

Chapter contents

Most vivas are awkward affairs. The candidate is ushered into the internal's office to shake hands with the external he/she may have cited (even revered) but in all probability never met.

This is followed by approximately two/three hours of fitful conversation in which the candidate makes numerous nervous gaffes and the examiners mechanically take turns probing areas that are often peripheral to the thesis but reflect their specialisms.

(Burnham 1994: 31)

Peter Burnham's portrayal of vivas will be little comfort to candidates approaching a viva. In this chapter we explore in detail candidates' experiences of the viva, which set in context Burnham's caricature. We start at the beginning of the viva.

11.1 First few minutes

The viva typically starts with the chair (an independent chairperson or, more usually, an examiner) introducing the viva participants to one another and then outlining how the viva will proceed. The examiners may or may not offer comments on the thesis at this stage and candidates should *not* interpret a lack of comments at this point as a negative sign. It is good practice for the chair to outline how the viva will be conducted, and most of our interviewees reported that the viva started in this way.

They started off by just sort of general comments about my thesis and they said they'd read through it and enjoyed it. They were just trying to put me at ease and then Sarah, my internal, said 'The external's going to run the examination and I'll chip in with bits'.

(Matt, PhD student, Chemistry)

They laid out the procedure; they said my dissertation was divided into three main sections and they said they wanted to talk about each section individually although there were certain overarching questions that they wanted to address as well. And they said that they were going to address sections one and three first and then come back to section two, maybe having a break in between if it went on too long.

(Kali, PhD student, English)

In some cases the chair may explain what the main purposes of the viva will be; Gary, a pharmacy candidate, recounts below what his examiners told him about the purposes. However, most examiners are not this explicit.

They said the first purpose is to make sure that the person sitting in front of them was the person who both wrote the thesis and did the experimental work. They said secondly it was to determine if I had an appropriate level of background knowledge. And the last one was about the thought processes that had gone on behind the work, if the hypothesis had been developed in a manner appropriate to the degree.

Will the provisional decision be released at the outset?

This is a key question for many candidates, so we explore possible answers and the implications of them.

Our questionnaires to candidates revealed that 32 per cent were informed of their examiners' decision at the start of the viva. Hartley and Jory's (2000) survey of 100 psychology doctoral graduates revealed a similar finding; one-third of their respondents were told the examiners' recommendation at the start.

Our research also revealed notable discipline differences: 47 per cent of candidates in the arts, humanities or social sciences were informed of the examiners' decision at the start of the viva compared with only 15 per cent in the natural sciences.

If the provisional decision was indicated at the outset, what would this mean?
Some examiners argue that telling successful candidates their decision at the start of the viva puts the candidate at ease, reduces the pressure in the viva and hence enables a more relaxed and productive discussion. This can work

in some cases; however, some candidates have built themselves up to such a degree to defend their thesis that even being told at the start of the viva that they have passed does not relax them.

> [At the start] they said, 'We want you to know before your viva that we're satisfied with your thesis.'
> *Interviewer: That's brilliant and how did you feel when that happened?*
> I didn't read the signals and I wasn't sure what it meant.
> *Interviewer: So you didn't know whether you'd passed or not?*
> No, and then Pam said to Andrew, 'I don't think Jan has fully understood what you've said', because it was obvious, and I must have looked a bit dense. And then he said ... 'You do realize we're saying that you've got your doctorate so what happens now is with regard to publication?'
> *Interviewer: That must have been a relief.*
> You're not kidding!
> *Interviewer: How did you feel?*
> Well, because I was so geared up for the viva, it was like trying to stop the Titanic. I couldn't reconfigure my head to think about anything other than defending my thesis. So every time they spoke to me I was defending my thesis even though I didn't have to.
>
> (Jan, PhD student, Religious Studies)

Some candidates are so intent on defending their thesis even after being told that they have passed, that they miss out on opportunities for developmental discussion: 'I treated each question or observation as potentially hostile, playing very safe and proper and consequently missed the opportunity to discuss my research with willing and interested experts in my field' (Denicolo *et al.* 2000: 13).

For some successful candidates, however, hearing a positive (provisional) decision at the outset does mean that the viva process is more relaxed and the discussion geared more towards development than examination. Advanced developmental discussion can be very rewarding for successful candidates and so they should be ready to make the most of it, thus maximizing the benefits of the viva for themselves. Remember though, that the viva should always serve to authenticate the thesis, so any provisional decision released at the outset is contingent upon this role being fulfilled.

If the provisional decision was not indicated at the outset, what would this mean?
Many examiners will not release a provisional decision to the candidate at the start of a viva, even if they judge the thesis to be excellent. This may be because the viva should always act as a site for authenticating the thesis and/ or institutional policy prohibits it. Variations in practice within and between institutions mean that candidates do not know how to interpret the 'silence'

when examiners make no comment about their decision at the start of a viva; candidates should *not* interpret this silence as bad news (see Chapter 12 on considerations for examiners).

Questions – easy openers?

Many candidates that we interviewed had been told by their supervisors to expect one or two 'easy' opening questions that would put them at their ease. Whilst many of our respondents said that they were asked 'easy openers', others, who had been led to believe that they would have a gentle introduction to the viva were shocked when their opening questions were anything but gentle.

> First I went in and I was introduced to them both and it was fairly formal and straight into sort of specific questions, not the questions I thought they were going to be asking it has to be said, they were very specific . . . I thought their first question might be 'What are the applications of your research?', just to sort of give a broad outline about what it was all about, but they didn't, they just went straight for some maths and papers and stuff that I cited.
>
> (Bob, PhD student, Chemistry)

> They just made me comfortable and they asked me questions, actually not very general questions, quite specific. I was expecting more general questions instead but almost immediately they went straight into the details.
>
> (Silvo, PhD student, Economics)

Gary, a pharmacy candidate, was asked a general question at the start of his viva, but it was certainly not the sort of question he was expecting, and he found it rather disorienting: '[The examiners] asked me to come in the room and explained who they were, explained what the purpose of the viva was and then started with some general questions like – "What's the difference between a PhD and a master's?", which kind of threw me.'

Andrew (Physiotherapy) was asked a general, introductory question, but he suggested that it did not really work to put him at ease, as he knew that it would be followed by many, more difficult questions:

> They offered a gentle question to start with but that didn't put you at your ease because you knew that was the gentle question to start with. You thought that's the rubbish out of the way, what are they really going to be asking because you know the first question they ask is always 'How would you summarize this work in general?' And it doesn't fool you into thinking 'Oh, this is a nice question' because you know this is just a gentle wind-up.

Summary – what types of questions should candidates expect in the first few minutes?

- Most examiners ask a general introductory question in an attempt to put candidates at ease. Trafford's (2002: 5) exploration of 25 vivas in a number of disciplines revealed that after the start-of-viva introductions, 84 per cent of candidates (21 out of 25) were asked a question along the lines of 'Why did you choose this topic for your doctoral research?' As we said in Chapter 10, it is worth being prepared for this type of question.
- But, not all vivas start with 'gentle', general opening questions.

  - Some candidates report general questions that are not gentle and are very unexpected, for example, Gary, quoted earlier.
  - Some examiners go straight into very specific and detailed questions.
  - What questions are perceived as 'easy' is always relative and context dependent; what is easy to one person may not be to another.

- In other words, to some degree you must expect the unexpected.

11.2 Factors shaping the viva – reminder

In Chapter 2 we outlined and discussed the ways in which the purposes of the viva (examination, development, ritual) vary depending upon institutional policy, and more importantly, the views of the examiners about what a viva is for. Building upon this discussion, in Chapter 3 we explored in detail the ways in which the components of the viva (skills, content, conduct) are shaped by: (1) the structure of the viva; (2) examiners' assessments of the thesis; (3) examiners' knowledge expectations; (4) examining styles; (5) personal/political agendas, (6) interpersonal dynamics. If these ideas are unfamiliar to you we recommend that you revisit Chapters 2 and 3.

In the next section on viva interactions we address candidates directly.

11.3 Interactions in the viva

The viva as an 'academic interview'

University College London (2002) describes the viva as an academic interview: 'A viva is an academic interview at which the examiners will be looking for an understanding of the subject matter of your thesis, an appreciation [of] its significance to established knowledge in the field, and an awareness of the breadth of the subject area.'

This description of the viva as an academic interview is useful, as there are many parallels between a PhD viva and a selection interview. As such, whilst you may have no personal experiences of vivas to draw upon when thinking about and approaching the viva, you are likely to have some interview experiences that you can reflect upon. It is useful then, for you to consider the parallels, to think about your experiences of interviews and to reflect upon your strengths and weaknesses in interview situations. Some of these parallels are delineated below.

- Both sets of parties are trying to impress each other. In a job or selection interview, the interviewee is trying to impress the interviewer in order to get the job; the interviewer is trying to impress the interviewee so that the interviewee will want to work for her/him. In a PhD viva the candidate is trying to impress the examiners so that they will be awarded a PhD; the examiners are trying to impress the candidate (and each other) in order to maintain their standing as 'experts'.
- There are complex power relations at play. In a job or selection interview, the interviewer is seen to have more power than the interviewee. However, this power relation can shift once an interviewee is offered the job and is 'in demand', it is the interviewee who then can accept or refuse the offer and can sometimes negotiate pay and conditions of service. In a PhD viva the examiners have considerable amounts of power – the power to pass or fail the candidate. But whilst candidates may be relatively powerless in one sense, they are still likely to be the most knowledgeable person in the room about their specific research topic, and it is important not to forget this.
- In job or selection interviews the interviewers may use different 'tactics' and ask different types of questions depending on what they are trying to find out about the interviewee and what 'skills' they are attempting to assess. For example, Higham (1983) discusses the use of 'stress interviewing' where interviewees are 'tested' to see how they respond to strains and tensions. Stress interview methods might involve: asking very blunt questions that verge on the offensive; focusing on weaknesses in the application and almost badgering the interviewee about them; the interviewer being silent for long periods of time to see how the interviewee responds, and so on. In the viva the examiners' questions and questioning style will also be shaped by what they are trying to find out and what types of 'skill' they are attempting to assess. For example, an examiner who regards the viva as an appropriate place to test whether the candidate can withstand the rigours of academic debate and argument may ask more 'challenging' and confrontational questions than an examiner who is concerned to hold a relaxed discussion. See Chapter 2 for a discussion of examiners' views about the purposes of the viva and Chapter 3 for discussion of viva examination styles.
- In job or selection interviews there are certain types of question that are likely to be asked. For example, why do you think that you are well suited to this particular post? Why would you like this job? However, there is no guarantee that these questions will be asked, and a host of unpredictable questions may be included. The case is similar for the viva. There are

certain types of question that are likely to arise (see Trafford and Leshem 2002). For example, 'What shaped your choice of topic for doctoral study?' However, predicting questions is difficult and there is no guarantee that any of them will arise in the viva. Furthermore, in both selection interviews and the viva one might predict that most of the questions would relate to the job or the thesis, respectively. However, this cannot be guaranteed and interviewers and examiners may ask questions outside of these domains and expect interviewees and candidates to respond knowledgeably.

- Some of the skills tested in a job interview are the same as those tested in a viva. For example, in both cases the interviewee's/candidate's verbal skills are explicitly or implicitly crucial to the assessment (see Chapter 3). In both cases interviewees/candidates are required to 'think on their feet', perform/communicate clearly whilst under pressure, and to explain and justify their work and ideas.
- Selection interviews and vivas are not one-way processes where interviewees or candidates simply respond to questions. In both situations the interviewee or candidate can act to shape the proceedings. The extent to which this is possible will be influenced, in part, by the interviewers or examiners, but interviewees and candidates should not be afraid to work towards meeting their own agendas.

Box 11.1   Task for candidates

FLASHBACK TO PAST INTERVIEW EXPERIENCES

Think about how you have performed in selection interviews. What are you particularly good at? What do you need to improve? Think about how you might work to improve aspects that are weak.

Whilst there are important similarities between selection interviews and PhD vivas, there are also a number of differences. For example, the viva might be regarded as more stressful than a job interview as the viva examines three or more years' work, and so a great deal is invested in it. However, there are parallels, and by reflecting upon your experiences of selection interviews, you may be able to think about, and relate to, key aspects of the viva in advance of it.

Posture

Social psychologists suggest that posture is an important aspect of non-verbal communication. Argyle (1992: 11), for instance, argues that posture 'indicates degree of alertness or sleepiness, and some more specific reactions as well. If listeners are bored they prop their heads up, if interested they lean forwards, if they disagree they tend to fold their arms.' It seems unlikely that candidates would display signs of sleepiness in the viva. However, an upright position slightly leaning forwards should convince the examiners that you are alert and interested: 'Those who have to appear on television are told to lean slightly forward and assume an air of relaxed alertness. This is probably the ideal pose for being interviewed too!' (Higham 1983: 62–3).

The body language of the candidate in an account by Trafford and Lesham (2002: 34) seemed to impress the viva chair who, after the viva, provided the following comment: 'I could see confidence in the candidate's body language – leaning forward to emphasise best points and make clear eye contact with the examiners, literally straight between the eyes!'

Listen

> Listen – to the questions – don't answer the question that you want to hear.
>
> (University College London 2002)

A lot of candidates that we interviewed suggested that their head was in a whirl at the start of the viva, and that it was difficult to 'take in' the questions being asked. Usually, nerves settle down as the viva progresses. It is important that you listen carefully to examiners' questions, and address the question posed rather than one you would like to answer (rather like politicians do). Ideally, examiners should avoid asking multi-part questions, but if they do ask more than one question at once it can be useful to write down the questions (or an abbreviated version of them) as the examiner is speaking. If you miss the point of a question or get lost in a long question, ask for clarification – this is much better than starting to answer a question that you are not sure about and getting lost along the way. As Grix (2001: 109) says: 'at all costs avoid going off into a long soliloquy which has little or nothing to do with the original question asked'.

Take time to think

> In a curious relativistic effect, time expands in the mind of the student. A few seconds pause to reflect before answering seems eminently reasonable to the panel, but to the defender it seems like minutes of mute failure. Take your time.
>
> (Wolfe 2003)

Wolfe's advice is good advice – it is legitimate to take time to think about a question before responding to it. It is also legitimate to pause for a short time during your response whilst you work out what to say next.

Working through the thesis

> Some examiners prefer to work through the thesis in the order in which it is written. Other examiners prefer to discuss topics. Very few examiners will perform a page by page criticism.
>
> (University College London 2002)

Examiners discuss the thesis in different ways. However, University College London's statement that 'very few examiners will perform a page by page criticism' is too general and fails to acknowledge discipline differences in the ways that examiners work. Whilst few of our candidates experienced a 'page by page' approach, academics in the area of pure maths have told us that a 'page by page' or even 'line by line' approach would not be unusual within their discipline. So it is worth talking to your supervisor about whether one particular approach is common in your discipline area. Bear in mind, though, that you cannot be sure what approach your examiners will adopt.

Answering questions

'What if I can't answer a question?' 'Should I defend my work to the hilt?' These are the types of question that PhD candidates frequently ask in relation to the viva, and so they are amongst the questions that we will address in this section. How, then, should you converse and answer questions in the viva?

Writing about conversations, Grice put forward a set of conversational rules which Argyle (1992: 12) summarizes as follows:

- provide no more and no less information than is needed.
- Be relevant.
- Tell the truth.
- Be clear.

Whilst these 'rules', as they relate to everyday conversation, have been challenged by some psychologists, they are useful guidelines for answering questions in a viva. They are, however, rather general, so we now consider more specific issues and questions.

Broad questions

Remember that some examiners may not be particularly good at asking questions. In some cases, the questions asked may be broad. Higham (1983) points out that the difficulty with some broad questions can be knowing where to begin, and so he suggests that if candidates are faced with very broad questions they should throw them back to get them more narrowly defined.

Questions the candidate cannot answer

In some cases, there may be questions that you cannot answer. If this happens you need to work out *why* you cannot answer and respond accordingly.

- *You don't understand the question.* Ask for the question to be repeated and clarified. Douglas, a sociology candidate, told us that he wished that he had asked for clarification of some points: 'There were some questions that I simply couldn't answer, and with hindsight now I wish I'd said, "Can you rephrase that because I simply don't understand the question?".'
- *The question is outside your area of expertise.* It is legitimate to suggest that the question is outside the remit of your work. However, don't use this response too often and bear in mind that you need to display knowledge of the 'broader context' (which is ill defined).
- *The answer is not straightforward.* Here you may need a little extra time to think, so take it. Wolfe (2003) also suggests that:

> The phrase 'That's a good question' is exceedingly useful. It flatters the asker and may get him/her onside, or less offside; it gives you time to think; it implies that you have understood the question and assessed it already and that you have probably thought about it before. If necessary, it can be followed by a bit more stalling 'Now the answer to that is not obvious/straightforward . . .' which has the same advantages.

How to 'defend'

> I suppose I truly believed that a defence of one's thesis was exactly that – a confrontation in which the biggest bully won.
>
> (Denicolo *et al.* 2000:13)

In Chapter 2 we reported that approximately one-quarter of our academic respondents thought that a purpose of the viva was to allow the candidate to defend her/his thesis. It can be difficult to gauge what 'defend' means – should candidates stick to what they have written in the thesis in a terrier-like fashion even if the examiners put forward convincing opposition to it? Continuing the battle metaphor, to what extent should candidates 'stand and fight' and to what extent should they 'give ground'? The advice provided by University College London (2002) is helpful in answering these questions:

> Be prepared to justify your ideas and conclusions. If the examiners challenge your interpretation but you feel that your case is a good one, muster your arguments and be willing to present your case firmly but courteously. However, if the examiners have identified a genuine weakness, concede the point gracefully. Even if you feel the examiners are unreasonably critical do not become argumentative or allow the discussion to become heated. You can agree to differ and to reconsider the point.

Kali, an English candidate, told us in his post-viva interview that he had adopted this approach, which he felt was successful:

> A tip that my brother gave me – because his supervisor had told him this – was not to be too defensive. So where there was an obvious problem, and when they pointed it out, to go with it and to admit it, and say 'Well, yes, I realize this is a problem and I had thought about it and I couldn't see any way around it and that's why it's there the way it is.' And there were a couple of points where they did that and I said that. So they said, 'So you admit it?', and I said, 'Yes, I do', and they were really pleased about that and they would just go on.

In Box 12.3 we provide a case study of a candidate who was *very* defensive in the viva and this caused considerable problems for the examiners and the candidate. One of the examiners told us:

> The candidate's reaction to critical points wasn't good. I thought on a number of occasions that she simply needed to acknowledge the weaknesses and say more about how she had coped with these, how she would improve things given a second chance. But she didn't do this, and so it was very difficult to have a *conversation* about the thesis which showed her as someone who had academic insight, which would have made us decide that some of the flaws mattered less. After all, nothing's perfect and the main thing is to show that you can see that and deal with it . . . Advice for the candidate – admit that there are flaws in your thesis, and also have an answer as to why they are there, why they are flaws, and what you would do about it given a second chance. Don't think you have to die in a ditch defending it.

Grix (2001: 109) offers good advice about defending the thesis in the viva that reinforces our earlier points, but he also offers guidance about areas where candidates should not concede too much.

> Do not become defensive, but try to reflect on the questions that are put to you, regardless of the manner in which they are expressed. The examiners will be more impressed with someone who can take on board criticism or suggestions than with someone who is adamant that his or her approach is unimpeachable. You need to get the balance right on what you can and cannot afford to concede in the viva. Obviously, with questions concerning the originality of the thesis and its contribution to knowledge you ought not to concede too much, given that these are crucial to actually gaining a PhD. Conceding on areas where you might have done something differently and *even better* than you actually did is probably safe, provided that you are confident that your thesis, as it stands, is good enough to pass.

See also Chapter 10 on preparing to justify and defend the thesis, particularly Box 10.4.

11.4 How long will the viva last?

Often candidates are provided with guidance about how long the viva is likely to last that ignores discipline differences. Such 'discipline-blind' guidance is misleading because, as our questionnaires to candidates revealed, there are substantial differences in the average length of vivas in the natural and applied sciences compared with those in the arts, humanities and social sciences (see Table 11.1). As Table 11.1 shows, most natural and applied sciences vivas were completed in one to three hours, whereas arts, humanities and social science vivas were typically less than two hours long. In the natural and applied sciences, 43 per cent of vivas lasted two hours or less, compared with 83 per cent in arts, humanities and social sciences.

Table 11.1 Proportion of candidates in natural and applied sciences, and arts, humanities and social sciences having vivas of up to one hour, one to two hours, two to three hours and three+ hours

Length of viva	Natural and applied sciences (%)	Arts, humanities and social sciences (%)
Up to 1 hour	3	27
1–2 hours	40	56
2–3 hours	43	15
3+ hours	15	2

Breaks

If the viva is going to extend beyond two hours, it is good practice for examiners to offer the candidate a rest pause after two hours; BPS/UCoSDA, amongst others, specify this. It is legitimate for candidates to request a short break during the viva, particularly if it has been in progress for two hours or more. Obviously, the timetable of the examiners needs to be borne in mind (some have trains to catch), but candidates who feel in need of a break should ask the person who is chairing the viva.

11.5 What does it feel like to have a viva?

How candidates feel in the viva varies tremendously, and is shaped by a range of factors. In this section we provide examples of descriptions offered by candidates (mainly, although not exclusively, our interviewees) when they were asked how they felt during the viva. Although we have attempted to categorize these responses, a number of them fit into more than one of the categories. We include these descriptions so that candidates, supervisors, examiners and independent chairs can gain insights into the range of different emotions experienced during the viva; clearly, there is no common 'viva feeling'.

Tough and frazzling

. . . it was a really tough viva, it was really hard . . . it was, you know, BOMB, BOMB, difficult question BOMB, another difficult question. So lots of people had said, 'Oh, after ten minutes, fifteen minutes you'll calm down and it'll just be really nice and you'll get on with it'. It was sort of palpitating, dry mouth, drinking lots of water from start to finish. It was really tough. The questions were very difficult but they didn't ask them in a kind of dismissive or nasty or confrontational tone. It was a bit of wolf-in-sheep's-clothing-style questions. They were asked very kind of positively and constructively as opposed to aggressively . . . It was tough. It was really tough. I was quite surprised at how hard it was because it was stuff you thought you'd thought of, and then they were kind of digging and digging and digging. So I was quite surprised that it was that hard.

(Leila, PhD student, Sociology)

I did find it quite frazzling . . . I think I imagined it wouldn't be so frazzling. I really did think 'Oh, my god, not another question'. Yes, I did actually find it quite hard going. Not answering the questions. I can't explain it. It's just they keep coming and coming and it's endless . . . It's very intense. I could answer the questions, I had prepared quite well, I had anticipated largely what they would ask . . . so it's not that I wasn't prepared. I don't think I could have prepared myself better. It was just the intensity of the experience I did find quite frazzling . . . When I came out I felt like I'd been dragged through a hedge backwards.

(Angela, PhD student, Women's Studies)

Nerve-wracking

Well, I was nervous, even though I knew it wasn't going to be too bad [it had been made clear at the start that the examiners felt there were no major problems]. So I was very nervous and my heart was absolutely pounding. I had to sit on my hands to stop them trembling and all that, but it was OK. I suppose it was a bit mixed. I was kind of excited thinking 'Crikey, I've done it, I've done it', and I suppose you have a whole mix of emotions going on.

(Alice, PhD student, Geography)

Mixed emotions

Different sorts of emotions really . . . Sometimes you'd think, 'OK, things are going OK', and then they'd ask something and you'd think,

'Boy, I'm struggling with this'. So it was mixed emotions throughout. But I found myself taking big breaths and having to drink the water because my mouth did get dry – two-and-a-half hours [in an] oral is a long flipping time.

(Andrew, PhD student, Physiotherapy)

Surprisingly all right

I went in with no nerves at all and was completely surprised. I must be a cold person or something, but it just didn't get me at all. I think because I'd spent the three weeks kind of building up, revising, that I went in quite confident knowing a lot ... [The tone of the exam was] very informal and very pleasant, very supportive. It didn't really deserve to be called an examination really.

(Dan, PhD student, Chemistry)

[In the viva I felt] surprisingly all right. I was really, really nervous before I went in. But once I actually sat down and had a few questions thrown at me I just got into it. You have to talk about your PhD so many times, you kind of just get into that kind of mode and just click into it. I had a glass of water, which was a good job because I was getting a very dry throat.

(Kate, PhD student, Psychology)

I felt very comfortable, extremely comfortable in fact. I was nervous beforehand because I thought they were going to ask me things and I wasn't going to remember them, and I wasn't going to know the answers. But once we got talking about it I just realized that I had been living with this material for four years and anything they could throw at me I could answer, and once we got on that it was fine.

(Kali, PhD student, English)

Painful

The external examiner came with a list of hundreds of comments, some minor typos, others deeply-profound criticisms, and proceeded to fire them at me in the order in which they arose in the text. He gave no indication by his tone of voice, by his manner or by his response to my replies, as to whether he was making a profound or a superficial criticism. He made not one single comment of praise, not even a 'This part was alright, but . . .' Clearly, the entire viva was some sort of power game, in which the external used his power to show me who was in charge . . . For the next three months, I did no research work of consequence, so deeply affected was I by this experience. As I told my supervisor afterwards, if the external had treated a dog in this fashion, he would have been hauled before the RSPCA for cruelty.

(quoted by Wakeford 2002)

When I try to tell the story of what happened to me, so many colleagues don't hear it. They think that what I'm complaining about is that the questioning was difficult. That's not what I'm saying. What I'm saying is that it was aggressive and it was rude. If it had been difficult I would have been delighted because I would have been able to defend the stuff I'd been working on for four years. But it wasn't. It was barked at me aggressively and it was about piffling, minor things.

(Barbara, candidate who passed her PhD with minor corrections, quoted in Wallace and Marsh 2001: 49)

11.6 What happens at the end of the viva?

Confidential exchange between examiners and candidate

If the supervisor has been present for the viva, *sometimes* s/he will be asked to leave the room so that the candidate can speak to the examiners in private about supervision issues. This is good practice as it allows candidates to raise any issues about supervision that they would like to draw to the attention of the examiners.

Examiners' deliberations

At the end of the examination the candidate (and the supervisor if s/he is there at this point, and any other observers) is usually asked to leave the room whist the examiners confer. Candidates should not be alarmed by this practice, as it is very common. Unfortunately, Leila, a sociology candidate, was not made aware of this practice and as a result interpreted the procedure in a rather negative way: 'Why had they made me leave the room? Had I done something wrong? Why didn't they just tell me at the end? Making you leave makes you think, 'Oh God, they're reassessing their assessment'. Leila's concerns were unnecessary – this is very common practice. During the time conferring after the viva the examiners are likely to discuss what decision they will recommend to the university, whether any corrections are required, and if they are, the nature of, and timescale for, them.

The examiners' recommendation

Usually, after the necessary discussion by examiners, the candidate (and supervisor if involved) is invited back into the room and told what the examiners will recommend to the university. If further work is required from the candidate the examiners should map out: (1) the nature of this further work, (2) a deadline for it and (3) the way(s) in which it will be re-examined (for example, whether another viva will be required). See Chapter 1 for a discussion of possible outcomes/recommendations.

When examiners do inform candidates of their recommendation at the end of the viva, it is important the candidates realize that it is a *recommendation*. As the BPS/UCoSDA (1995: 15) guidelines point out: 'Such recommendations can be, and on rare occasions have been, rejected by the relevant University Committee. The candidate should be advised to await formal written communication from the University before taking any major steps.'

In some institutions, examiners are not obliged to inform the candidate of their recommendation even after the viva. If they wish, they can let the university inform the candidate in due course. For example, at the University of Cambridge (2003: 6), examiners are provided with the following guidelines.

> The board recognises that the oral is a useful forum for giving positive feedback as well as for discussing corrections and more serious shortcomings such that it is impossible to avoid giving the candidate at least some indication of the likely outcome. **However, you are asked to exercise great discretion in deciding whether to indicate what your joint recommendation is likely to be. If you decide to do so, please make it clear that it is a *recommendation only* as the *official outcome will not be certain* until after the Degree Committee and Board of Graduate Studies have considered your Reports.**

However, it is common practice in universities for examiners to inform candidates of their recommendation after the viva (even where examiners are not obliged to).

11.7 Summary

In this chapter we have addressed questions commonly asked by candidates about what happens in the viva, how to handle the demands of it, and how to make the most of the opportunities offered. Events in the period immediately after the viva, including the post-viva debriefing and the work and responsibilities of candidates and supervisors, are discussed later, in Chapter 13. How candidates feel after the viva, and what they can do if they are unhappy about (aspects of) the examination process, is also addressed in Chapter 13.

12

The Viva – Tips and Issues for Examiners

PhD examining . . . it's the same principle as your First Aid Certificate.
We've all done them, but if I broke my arm now you couldn't do me a
three-part sling, could you?

(Professor, Management)

Chapter overview

This chapter explores examiners' perspectives on the viva and
provides guidance for novice examiners as well as tips and suggestions for experienced ones. Building upon the discussion in
Chapter 8 about assessing the thesis, we consider how examiners
prepare for the viva, conduct the oral examination and make a
recommendation of award. Most academics are, quite rightly,
wary of attempts to standardize vivas. However, whilst we are not
proposing a model of uniformity, there is a surprising degree
of consensus amongst experienced examiners about what, in
general, constitutes good practice. This chapter therefore offers
guidance and 'tips' on vivas drawn from the diverse experiences of
academics from across the disciplines.

Examiners ☺☺☺   Chairs   ☺☺
Students ☺   Supervisors   ☺

Chapter contents

12.1 Before the day of the viva

Forward planning is key to making the viva as stress-free as possible for you and your co-examiner. It is important to be clear about (1) what you need to *do* before the day of the viva and (2) what you need to *think about* prior to the day of the viva. Clearly, reading and assessing the thesis is the main pre-viva job, but there may be others. For example, internal examiners are sometimes responsible for scheduling the viva and finding a venue for it. Frequently, both examiners are required to submit a pre-viva report (see Chapter 8); this depends on the institution, but in some universities the viva cannot go ahead until this is received. As such, it is important to be clear about what you need to do and when you need to do it.

The things that you need to *think* about before the day of the viva are as important as the things that you need to *do*. We suggest that there are two key matters for most examiners to consider, and an additional one if you are examining a practice-related doctorate. These are: (1) the purposes of the particular viva; (2) working with your co-examiner; and (3) for practice-related PhDs the examiners must decide procedures for the assessment of the full submission (thesis plus practice).

All these matters are important, but probably the most important is thinking about, and being clear about, the purposes of the viva. Clarity about purpose is particularly important in cases where co-examiners and supervisors try to railroad you into passing a thesis that you are not entirely happy with (see Box 12.1).

What are the purposes of this particular viva?

The examiners' judgement about the standard of the thesis will necessarily shape the purposes of the viva and its content.

Prior to meeting with your co-examiner it is imperative that you reflect upon the purposes of the viva as these have important implications for the organization of the oral examination and what each of you do in it. As we saw in Chapter 2, the viva can serve a number of different purposes. If you have not already done so, you are strongly advised to read Chapter 2, although a summary of the key purposes is provided below.

Reminder – key purposes of the viva

Examination purposes
- Authentication of the thesis. This may be particularly important where the candidate works as part of a team.
- Assess ability of candidate to locate research in broader context.
- Check candidate's understanding.
- Clarification of obscurities and/or areas of weakness in the thesis.
- Defence of the approach, methodology and conclusions presented in the thesis.
- Decision making in borderline cases.
- Gatekeeping – check on supervision and on PhD standards across institutions.
- Test candidate's oral skills.

Developmental purposes
- Basic development – explore ways that a thesis may be raised to doctoral standard.
- Advanced development – explore ideas and discuss the development of the candidate's research beyond the requirements of a doctoral thesis; discuss future work and publishing opportunities.

Ritual purposes
- Rite of passage.
- Reward.

In thinking about purposes you need to consider two agendas (see Box 12.1). First, you must attend to the agenda of the appointing institution as it may identify purposes for the viva. Second, there is your own agenda. Your agenda is likely to depend primarily on your assessment of the thesis. For instance, you are unlikely to discuss publication plans with a candidate whose thesis you judge to be a fail. As we saw in Chapter 3, examiners' assessments of the thesis fall into one of three main categories; as a reminder, we have reproduced Table 3.2 as Table 12.1.

Table 12.1   Model of the key purposes of vivas depending upon the examiners' assessments of the thesis

Examiners' assessments of the thesis	Key purposes of the viva
Good thesis	The viva is used to authenticate the thesis, explore the broader context, clarify points, develop ideas and offer advice on publication
Borderline/referred thesis	The viva is used to authenticate the thesis and to: 1. decide whether the candidate has done sufficient research of an appropriate standard to produce a thesis for the award of PhD 2. decide whether the candidate understands and can reflect critically on their research, and the broader context, in ways that are appropriate at PhD level 3. explore ways in which the thesis can be raised to PhD standard
Failed thesis/award of lower degree	The viva is used to confirm the fail and explore why the candidate has failed. The examiners will also determine whether a lower award is appropriate, for example, an MPhil

---

Box 12.1   Task for examiners

WHAT ARE THE PURPOSES OF THIS PARTICULAR VIVA?

Being clear about what you want to do in a particular viva, and why, is essential preparation for both the pre-viva discussion and the actual viva.

Take ten minutes to reflect on what you want to achieve in this particular viva.

- Identify the different tasks that you want, or have, to fulfil in the viva (for example, various examination, developmental and/or ritual purposes). Ensure that you attend to both your own agenda and that of the institution that has appointed you.
- Once this is done, you can then map out the specific points you want to raise with the candidate about their work and broader knowledge.

Thinking about your relationship with the co-examiner(s)

The viva can be especially stressful when there are differences in hierarchy and gender that are acting contrary to convention. For example, a candidate older than the examiner, the external examiner less senior than the internal examiner. It is important to be clear about the seniority of roles within the viva.

(Senior Lecturer, Education)

It helps if you are clear about your status as an examiner in advance of the pre-viva meeting, and have time to think through the implications of this for how you will work with your co-examiner(s). This may be particularly important if your relative status as examiners is inconsistent with your relative status as academics. For example, the appointing institution may expect you, a senior lecturer, to act as the 'senior' examiner and yet your co-examiner – perhaps a professor – is actually the senior academic. Careful advance preparation and, in particular, being clear about your assessment of the thesis, are ways of boosting your confidence and your ability to negotiate with your co-examiner(s). The importance of this preparation is conveyed clearly in the case study reported in Box 12.2 later in the chapter.

Should the supervisor be allowed to attend?

This question is appropriate only if examining at an institution that permits the supervisor to attend subject to the wishes of the examiners and/or the candidate. The pros and cons of the supervisor attending the viva, from the perspectives of examiners, are discussed in Chapter 6.

Practice-based PhDs – arranging to examine the full submission

In practice-based PhD examinations, examiners almost always assess a written thesis and some form of practice (for instance a performance or exhibition of work) as well as viva the candidate. The viva includes discussion of the thesis and the practice, and the candidate should have an opportunity in the viva to answer questions about their practice and to explore the practice–theory interface. A key question that candidates doing practice-related doctorates need to be able to answer is 'why have I approached my research question(s) in this particular (range of) way(s)?' Some vivas are in two parts to accommodate discussion of the thesis and practice; part one may be concerned with the thesis and in part two the candidate is 'with' the practice so that they can discuss it with their examiners. Alternatively, a candidate's practice, perhaps a performance, is viewed in an evening, and then discussed in the viva on the following day.

It is important to consider how to organize the examination so that you can experience the practice and assess it in relation to the thesis and the candidate's oral performance. As the following example illustrates, this decision is not always straightforward.

I was an internal examiner for a PhD about a year or two ago where there was actually a thesis written in relation to an exhibition. We did actually manage to arrange the exhibition to be going on at the same time as the oral examination. So the examination included walking round the exhibition at the installation, looking at that, talking to the candidate about that and then looking at the written work . . . We did wonder later whether it might have been better to have looked at the exhibition on one day and come back to the written work on another day. Then the written work could have been reread in the light of looking at the exhibition.

(Professor, Cultural Studies)

A two-day process, with a review of the practice on one day and the viva on the next, is preferred by some examiners of practice-related PhDs because it allows time for the examiners to 'absorb' the candidate's work. It does, however, make the examination process more protracted and time consuming.

12.2 Pre-viva meeting

At this meeting the examiners should address four main matters: the content of the viva, the conduct of the viva, the investigation of extenuating circumstances and the management of post-viva business. It is usual for this meeting to take place in private, although we are aware of one university where an administrator minutes the discussion.

Content of the viva – producing an agenda

Agree an order of questions with all examiners and try to stick to these unless the candidate brings up a new issue.

(Professor, Education)

[The agenda] needs careful negotiation before the viva to ensure how the process of the conversation will take place. List the question that you'll each ask and probes or sub-questions.

(Professor, Policy Studies)

Ensure that the procedures for conducting the viva are agreed in advance, i.e. who deals with what, when, to ensure that the viva flows smoothly.

(Reader, Psychology)

Constructing a clear, well-ordered agenda for the viva is the primary task in the pre-viva meeting. The agenda is structured by the different purposes that the viva has to serve. Within this framework, decide how to address specific points about the candidate's work and decide who will broach which main questions and in which order. At this stage it is useful to reflect on whether there are any questions that are pivotal to your final decision. If there are, it is best to raise them relatively early in the viva.

Academics adopt different strategies for asking the candidate questions about the thesis. Some prefer to tackle the big themes of a thesis, others feel more comfortable working through the specifics of the thesis.

> Not a page-by-page criticism. I prefer to develop themes from the text – and follow them up, or take a particular line of reasoning and follow it throughout the thesis. *Don't* comment on every typo or reference error – but at some point, make general comments about either the excellent presentation, or the need to stick to a common citation system.
>
> (Professor, Urban Planning)

Differences in approach can be a matter of personal preference, although there are discipline differences. Three common approaches to asking questions about the thesis are the thematic approach, the process approach and the page-by-page approach.

- *Thematic approach.* The examiner focuses on the broad themes of the thesis; this can be supplemented with detailed discussion about specific sections of the thesis.
- *Process approach.* 'They sort of worked their way through my thesis by going through the literature review and then asking about the methodology' (Kate, PhD student, Psychiatry). The examiner focuses on the research process – formulation of research problem, theory/approaches, methods, data analysis, conclusions. This process often mirrors the organization of the thesis. This approach can be supplemented with discussion of specific sections of the thesis and/or the broader themes.
- *Page-by-page approach.* The examiner works systematically through the thesis, page by page, or line by line. In some subjects, such as mathematics, this approach can enable the examiner to follow in detail the research process, perhaps the explication of a solution to a problem. However, in the arts, humanities and social sciences this approach is often equated with 'nit picking' and is associated with a preoccupation with spelling and punctuation. Candidates in the latter disciplines often report being unhappy with this approach to their work: 'The external examiner came with a list of hundreds of comments, some minor typos, others deeply profound criticisms, and proceeded to fire them at me in the order [in] which they arose in the text' (Wakeford 2002).

It is important to consider whether your approach gives priority to your main concerns and questions. For example, if you use a page-by-page approach and your most important questions relate to the conclusions, the candidate may be tired by the time they address them and so perform less well than if they had answered these questions earlier. It is also useful to think about whether your approach will encourage the candidate to respond well to your questions. For example, candidates in the arts, humanities and social sciences may experience a page-by-page approach as inhibiting and undermining and, therefore, it may prompt stilted answers.

Below is a checklist of questions about content that you should address in the pre-viva meeting:

1. What is the (agreed?) provisional decision – good thesis, borderline thesis, failed thesis?
2. What are the agreed purposes? Be very clear about these and ready to communicate them to the candidate. Check that these purposes are consistent with your provisional decision about the thesis.
3. What specific questions do you want to ask? Highlight any pivotal questions and ensure that these are raised relatively early in the viva. Check that your list of questions is consistent with your agreed purposes for the viva.
4. What question(s) will be used to begin the viva discussion?

Conduct of the viva – the behaviour, roles and responsibilities of viva participants

The roles of each examiner need to be clarified in the pre-viva meeting. As we saw in Chapter 6, there is considerable variation between institutions regarding examiners' responsibilities during the viva. You need to be aware of the institution's regulations and the implications of these for how you conduct the oral examination.

Below is a checklist of questions about conduct that you should address in the pre-viva meeting:

1. Is there a lead, or 'senior', examiner?
2. Will one of you serve as chair and what will this entail?
3. Who will introduce the participants, and the structure of the viva to the candidate?
4. Who will introduce the purposes of the viva to the candidate and what will they say?
5. Is it appropriate to release the examiners' provisional decision at the start of the viva? Who will do this? What will they say? (See later.)
6. In the case of practice-based PhDs, will you need to conduct all, or part of, the oral examination in the presence of the practice? How will this be achieved?
7. Is one of you responsible for student support and, if so, what will this entail?
8. What positive feedback will you provide at the beginning?
9. If there is going to be advanced developmental discussion, will the shift from examination purposes be signalled clearly to the candidate so that they know they are not being assessed on this aspect of the viva discussion?

10. Who can attend the viva and in what capacities? You need to be clear about the institution's rules concerning viva attendance (see Chapter 6) so that you know what to expect from other attendees and what you are entitled to request of them. For example, if supervisors can participate in viva discussions it is helpful to know this before the viva begins.

11. How long should this viva last? If the viva is likely to exceed two hours, you may want to include a break in the proceedings.

12. How will you behave towards the candidate in the viva and what type of examining style will you employ? The answer to this question may be linked to the purposes that you think are important, such as ritual purposes (celebratory or challenging), the assessment of the candidate's oral skills, and/or a test of the candidate's ability to manage certain types of academic exchange. Not all types of academic conduct and examining style are appropriate in a viva (see Chapter 3) and some institutions prohibit certain behaviour, for instance, 'aggressive' questioning styles.

Investigating extenuating circumstances

When examining a PhD thesis that is borderline or very weak it may be appropriate to investigate why the thesis is of a low standard. Extenuating circumstances are not, in themselves, justification for awarding a PhD. However, you can take account of some extenuating circumstances when you make recommendations for further work. BPS/UCoSDA (1995: 17) identify four factors that examiners may need to consider before preparing their final report and recommendation: (1) the personal circumstances of the candidate; (2) the candidate's access to research facilities; (3) supervision; (4) factors related to research procedures. In order to address these factors you may need to talk to the candidate in private during the viva; some institutions expect examiners to do this as a matter of course. A number of institutions require the supervisor to notify the examiners before the viva of any extenuating circumstances, and/or they expect the supervisor to be available on the day of the viva to answer examiners' questions. If you are concerned about a candidate's work you should check on investigation procedures at the appointing institution and, if necessary, ensure that you speak to appropriate people (for example, the supervisor) before preparing your post-viva report.

Post-viva business to consider in the pre-viva meeting

Two main post-viva matters must be addressed at the pre-viva meeting. First, you need to agree how you will tackle the post-viva paperwork, usually a joint report and recommendation of award. Second, consider whether you will attend, or initiate, a post-viva celebration.

Box 12.2   Case study

UNDER PRESSURE FROM THE START

I was approached by the main supervisor to be an examiner on the basis of one of my long-standing research specialisms. I was also, I believe, recommended by a more senior member of staff with some responsibility for postgraduate students. Because the PhD candidate was a member of staff at the institution in question, I was one of two externals, the second being someone I knew slightly. Before the viva took place there were several phone calls and emails from the main supervisor about arrangements for the examination. All these communications stressed how excellent the candidate was and how good the thesis was – in retrospect, this was perhaps a warning sign. The supervisor also suggested that s/he might attend the pre-viva discussion, but both the other external and I pointed out that this was problematical, although we had no objection to the individual concerned eating lunch with us after the pre-viva discussion (this invitation was declined).

Whilst reading the thesis prior to the viva, it quickly became clear to me that the thesis was far from excellent. The research itself was quite weak and the methods chapter omitted key details about the methodology. The theoretical framework was very thin and tended to mention key writers without adequate elaboration. The tone of the thesis implied that the writer had alighted on a topic and an academic area that were 'soft'; thus, by implication, no high standards were involved and anything would do.

On the day, the pre-viva discussion revealed that whilst I and the other external thought the thesis was poor (not even worthy of an MPhil as it stood) the internal thought it a brilliant pass. The internal was at pains to let me know at this preliminary pre-viva discussion how well connected he was in the academic world. In the viva itself (at which the supervisor was not present) the candidate proved unable to mount a spirited defence of the thesis and indeed stumbled over some very basic methodological and theoretical issues. Questioning about why particular things had been done revealed that the candidate appeared to have been poorly and badly advised by the supervisors, although with no supervisor present this was difficult to establish fully and is one reason why in my view supervisors should always be present at vivas.

The internal examiner, who was supposed to be chairing the viva, consistently went out of his way to stress to the candidate how good the thesis was and frequently departed from the list of possible questions that we had agreed for each examiner during the pre-viva discussion. The other external examiner and I tried to ignore this, but it was potentially very embarrassing given the internal's chairing role. At the end of the viva when we asked the candidate to withdraw, the internal engaged in a long wrangle about how us two externals were prejudiced against the candidate and the topic, and lacked the necessary academic expertise to judge it. However, we both persisted in outlining the reasons for a decision requiring major revisions to the thesis. The candidate then returned for the verdict and was visibly shaken by the outcome, and kept saying 'but X [supervisor] said I'd be sure to pass'. Horror was expressed at the extensive list of required changes we read out. The candidate and the internal examiner both fled the room at the same time, leaving me and the co-external to sort out the examination paperwork and take it to an administrator.

In retrospect, we should have insisted on the supervisor being present at the viva (since the regulations did permit this), and perhaps should have found some tactful way of keeping the discussion to the agreed topics and issues – a neutral chair would have helped us to do this. We should perhaps also have advised the institution that the internal examiner did not behave appropriately. The candidate, after a year of extensive revisions under a new supervisor (an approach suggested by the externals to the institutional administration), did get a PhD.

12.3 In the viva – first impressions

Room and layout

Ideally, the viva venue should be an office or small meeting or teaching room. A science professor that we interviewed recalled an unusual, and very uncomfortable, experience as external examiner. When she arrived to conduct the viva she was taken to the private quarters of the internal examiner. Perched on the internal examiner's bed, amidst various cuddly toys, she then had to examine the candidate. This viva, she recalled, seemed to last for ever.

Ensure that the seating is arranged to promote communication. There should also be enough table space for at least three copies of the thesis, notes, water and so on. In cases where the supervisor can attend, even other observers, it is important to ensure that they will not distract the candidate or examiners. Although supervisors are often present to provide silent support for their student, their views can be proclaimed loudly through body language: 'If the supervisor is present it can be difficult to cope with their body language even if they are not permitted to speak. Position the seating so that neither the examiners nor the candidate are facing the supervisor' (Senior Lecturer, Education).

Below is a checklist of preparations for the viva venue:

1. Sufficient seating and table space.
2. Clock/watch.
3. Fresh water and glasses.
4. Adequate ventilation/heating.
5. Minimize outside noise.
6. Tissues.
7. Your notes and other examination paperwork.
8. Paper and pen/pencil.
9. 'Do Not Disturb' sign on the door.
10. Telephone unplugged.
11. Mobile phones switched off.

Introductions

His opening gambit was, 'It's OK. We need to ask you a few questions. Oh, and by the way, I find your writing style really irritating.'
(Douglas, PhD student, Sociology)

The first stage of the viva involves introducing the candidate and yourselves. Often, the candidate will already know the internal examiner. Whilst this can be reassuring, the candidate is not used to meeting this person in the role of examiner: 'Make sure that the candidate knows how you will expect them to address the examiners, including yourself, in the viva. If you are the internal examiner they may be used to using your first name to address you but be unsure in this special context' (Reader, Psychology). If you do not already know the candidate it is also good practice to check how they want to be addressed.

The second stage of introductions involves explaining the format and purposes of the viva to the candidate. It is of utmost importance that the purposes of the viva are made clear to the candidate. For example, if you think that the thesis is a pass but that there are some confused sections that need rewriting, you might tell the candidate that principally you want to establish that the thesis is their own work, but that there are a few sections of the thesis that need clarification and you would like to discuss these in detail. You might then say that once you have discussed these aspects of the thesis you will move on to consider the thesis in its broader context and discuss future possibilities.

A checklist of points to cover in the introduction is provided below:

1. Introduce the candidate, examiners and anyone else involved in the examination.
2. Purposes of the viva – introduce and explain.
3. Format and organization – clarify who will chair the viva, how you will approach the examination, the organization of the questions.
4. Duration of the viva (approximate).
5. Notify candidate that they can request a break if appropriate.

Should you release a provisional decision?

Some institutions discourage examiners from releasing a provisional decision until after the viva. However, many academics believe that this practice is unfair to the candidate as it does not allow her/him to make the most of the viva.

> If both examiners are agreed before the viva that the thesis should pass, it seems absolutely right to tell the candidate at the start of the viva, in the hope that they will then be able to enjoy and benefit from the occasion more than they otherwise would. If a thesis is almost certainly going to be referred but the candidate could redeem the situation in the viva, it seems fair to indicate this too, but it needs to be done in a sensitive way.
>
> (Professor, History)

One problem with informing the candidate about your provisional decision at the outset is that, whatever the standard of the thesis, the viva should serve as a site for checking that the candidate is the author of the work. If you commence by telling the candidate that s/he has passed, but then become doubtful as the viva progresses that the work for the thesis was actually conducted by the candidate, you would be placed in a difficult position. For this reason, it is risky for an examiner to declare unreservedly at the start of a viva that a candidate has passed.

Examiners have devised ways round this problem, particularly for strong candidates.

> An examiner of one of my own recent candidates said at the beginning of the viva: 'Unless you give me reason to believe that you did not write this thesis or conduct this research on your own, there is *nothing* you can say in this viva that will cause you to fail your PhD.' My student relaxed immediately and I thought it was a great way to start.
>
> (Reader, Psychology)

Another example is provided by a professor of earth sciences, who recalls how an external examiner began the viva by saying to the candidate, 'I think this is a wonderful piece of work. All I want to establish is, did you write it?' This examiner then proceeded to give the candidate 'a real grilling' for three hours but at least the candidate knew his thesis was judged worthy of a PhD before this began. Where the appointing institution allows you to inform the candidate of your provisional decision at the beginning of the viva it is still best to be cautious. As Loughborough University (2003: 20) advises: 'Examiners should be cautious about their comments on the potential outcome of the examination at the outset of the viva, given that the viva is an integral part of the examination process.'

If you do not release your provisional decision at the start of the viva, remember that candidates are often uncertain about how to interpret this and may read it as a bad sign. As one candidate explained to us: 'I was unaware that the examiners, if they wanted to follow strict procedure, could defer announcing the result until after the viva' (PhD student, English and American Studies). To avoid unnecessary anxiety, the BPS/UCoSDA (1995: 13) advise that 'at the outset of the examination the candidate should be explicitly told by the chair that no information about outcomes will be provided until the end of the examination, and that no conclusions should be drawn from this'.

12.4 In the viva – a productive exchange

We ask too many questions, often meaningless ones. We ask questions that confuse the interviewee, that interrupt him [sic]. We ask questions the interviewee cannot possibly answer. We even ask questions we don't want the answers to, and, consequently, we do not hear the answers when forthcoming.

(Benjamin 1981, cited in Millar *et al.* 1992: 128)

Opening questions

Making the candidate feel at ease is one of the first challenges for examiners in the viva. Some institutions specify that examiners should do this, although there is usually no guidance as to how. Examiners usually approach this task in a manner similar to interviewers, they try to find a gentle question.

[It is] very important to get the candidate to relax; some questions only loosely related to the thesis are helpful and then some questions about the reasons for the choice of topic. If appropriate, stress that the thesis was interesting or enjoyable to read.

(Professor, Education)

Let someone who knows the student kick off with general material – why the subject, what interested the candidate, what do they feel were the main conclusions etc.? Also make comment, if possible, about some strengths to reduce apprehension. If it is a good piece of work, say so; if not so good, say so but carefully.

(Professor, Urban Planning)

The opening question is very important although some candidates are, with hindsight, dismissive of these – see Chapter 11. Whilst there are some fairly standard opening lines, a few academics approach this part of the viva with a bit more creativity than is reassuring for the candidate. For example, Gary, a pharmacy candidate, was rather alarmed when his external examiner asked him, 'What's the difference between a PhD and a master's?'

Content questions – examination and developmental purposes

The main point of asking questions in a viva is to elicit information from the candidate. The type of question you use will depend on:

- your purpose or objective – clarification, to check understanding, to prompt a justification or defence, to explore capacity for making links, to elicit evaluation;
- how tightly you want to control what is talked about – this can range from the very specific to the very broad;
- how much information you want or how deeply you want to pursue a point.

The purposes you have identified for the viva should determine the viva content. For instance, if the thesis is fairly good but has some areas of weakness, likely purposes would be to authenticate, to check understanding, clarify obscurities/areas of weakness, assess ability to locate research in broader context and allow the candidate to defend the thesis. Aside from these examination purposes you will probably want to pursue at least one developmental purpose: in this case, ways in which the thesis can be raised to PhD standard.

Different types of question are suitable for these various purposes – an inappropriate type of question will close down, rather than open up, the scope for the candidate to respond in relevant and constructive ways. Therefore, it is useful in advance of the viva to think about the purposes of your particular questions and ensure that the questions you have in mind are fit for these purposes. In Table 12.2 we provide an overview of the types of question that most readily link to the different viva purposes. Clearly, these are not exhaustive, but provide a flavour of the possibilities.

Table 12.2   Questions fit for a purpose

Examination and developmental purposes	Types of questions
Clarification	'How many . . .?', 'How did . . .?', 'When . . .?', 'What . . .?', 'What do you mean by . . .?'
Check understanding	'Explain how . . .', 'Explain the meaning of . . .'
Prompt justification/ defence	'Why' types of question – 'Why did you . . .?', 'Can you explain why . . .?', 'Can you account for . . .?'
Link to broader context	Questions about application, relevance, contribution to field, originality. Also comparative questions – 'How does your approach compare with . . .?'
Prompt evaluation (judge in relation to own objectives); particularly valuable in pursuing developmental purposes	Questions that encourage reflection on the candidate's work and self-assessment: 'Can you reflect on . . .?', 'How would you assess . . .?', 'How might you . . .?', 'To what extent . . .?' Also hypothetical questions – 'What if you . . .?'

You will probably need, or want, to ask some searching, 'deep' questions in the viva. Our research suggests that most candidates (even those who are subsequently referred) want to discuss their work in detail with the examiners and to learn from the exchange. They often relish probing, challenging questions and, if successful, they want to feel that they have proved themselves in the viva. Searching questions, used in the right way, are perceived as: (1) an indication of the examiners' interest in, and engagement with, the candidate's work; (2) an opportunity for the candidate to demonstrate intellectual competences; (3) a test befitting the award of a PhD; and (4) a means to develop and/or expand thinking and knowledge. Vivas that lack opportunities to explore the thesis in depth are frequently viewed by candidates as 'superficial' and 'disappointing'. Having said this, unrelenting probing can be stressful for the candidate and interpreted as an indication of serious problems unless the conduct of the exchange is managed in ways that are affirming and which allow a shift in intensity.

Conduct – promoting a productive exchange

Examiners are often preoccupied with asking questions about the thesis and exploring the candidate's knowledge, this can be at the expense of attending to the conduct of the viva. Viva conduct is, however, of considerable importance for how candidates feel during the viva and has implications for how well they respond to your questions. The conduct of the viva exchange also shapes the candidate's post-viva perceptions of their viva performance, their PhD and themselves (see Chapter 13). It is good practice to promote a productive exchange in the viva, one that encourages the candidate to perform at their best and to get the most out of the viva, irrespective of the standard of the thesis.

There are five main ways in which you can promote a productive exchange:

1. Provide positive feedback on the thesis and the candidate's comments.
2. Show interest in, and engagement with, the candidate's thesis.
3. Actively listen to what the candidate has to say in the viva.
4. Ask questions that can be answered.
5. Avoid an aggressive or hostile tone when asking questions.

Positive feedback

We didn't spend enough time telling her what was good about her work. The external and I had agreed on what issues we wanted to raise, and although I had mentioned that we should say some positive things about the work, we did not start off with this. In the future, I would be more careful to be sure that this was done and to draw out what was good about the project and what we had enjoyed reading. The problem, I think, was that there was so much that we needed to cover that we slightly rushed over these points.

(Lecturer, Women's Studies)

It is important to provide positive feedback whatever the outcome. Affirming statements can take a range of forms – 'That's a very interesting comment', 'You seem to have coped well with that problem in data collection', 'I like your use of this analogy' – and can refer to specific or general aspects of the thesis. Comments about the strengths of the work are particularly important at the beginning of the viva exchange, even if followed by an indication that further work is required. Positive comments are also a useful way of signalling that a series of demanding and probing questions are not a sign of a fail, or an attempt by the examiners to demolish the thesis. One examiner told us how, in the viva, she keeps to hand a list of 'enthusiastic' questions that relate to parts of the thesis that she found 'interesting, challenging, enjoyable' (Professor, Sociology). She then draws on this list throughout the viva, particularly when candidates become tense, uncooperative or defensive (see also Box 12.3). Affirming feedback is particularly important in cases where you expect to ask for revisions – the candidate needs to feel that it is worthwhile investing more time in their thesis.

Interest and engagement

You can promote a productive exchange by showing interest in, and engagement with, the different aspects of the candidate's thesis. This can be achieved by asking different types of questions – explanation, justification, link and evaluative questions, as well as clarification ones. Some examiners prefer a question-and-answer approach in which the candidate is expected to speak only in response to the examiners' questions and prompts; the examiner does not enter into discussion. With this approach the agenda is firmly in the hands of the examiners, and candidates often perceive it as rigid, hierarchical, disempowering and belittling. Although the viva is a formal occasion which has important examination purposes, the style of exchange between the examiners and candidate can be relatively open. Many examiners like to generate discussion and encourage the candidate to raise questions for consideration: 'My approach to the oral is a bit like carrying out a qualitative interview . . . I often begin with some very general question asking the candidate to revisit the significant features of the thesis and take off from there. "A conversation with a purpose" sort of thing' (Professor, Sociology). Candidates regard this type of exchange as recognizing their achievements and facilitating communication and exchange of ideas – 'an interesting conversation between intelligent people' (Kali, PhD student, English), 'a discussion rather than a quiz' (Nigel, PhD student, Nursing).

Active listening

Examiners promote a productive exchange by showing that they are actively listening to the candidate. One way to demonstrate this is through your body language. Typically, an attentive posture involves: maintaining comfortable eye contact with the candidate; leaning forward slightly; an attentive facial expression; encouraging gestures, including head nods; the avoidance of fiddling and arm crossing. These affirmative cues are immensely reassuring. It is worth remembering, however, that the meanings of body language are culturally variable:

> Across cultures, gestures can easily communicate the opposite of what is intended . . . For example, in the West, the use of eye contact is a sign of attentive behaviour, whereas Africans 'listen' just with their ears and may or may not look at the speaker. For them the avoidance of eye contact is a culturally essential indication of politeness and respect for older or professionally superior person.
>
> (Okorocha 1997: 8)

Verbal prompts – 'yes', 'I see' – are other techniques of active listening. Reflective questions, ones that paraphrase what the candidate has just said, also show that you have listened. They also provide an opportunity for the candidate to check that you have understood them correctly and, if necessary, for them to clarify or expand points.

Questions that can be answered

It is vital that questions make sense and are answerable. The use of multiple-part questions, or a series of questions strung together as one, is not good practice. These questions are confusing and difficult to answer. Leading questions can also close down communication because it is unclear to the candidate how they should respond. Candidates who are not being examined in their first language may also find it difficult to understand complex expressions of English when coping with the stress of the viva. 'In each circumstance, the candidate's first language was not English. Under the pressure and stress of the viva, the facility with English seemed to evaporate. The candidate seemed not to understand the questions put forward, especially those questions asked by the external' (Reader, Gender Studies). In the case cited above, the examiner attempted to support the candidate and facilitate communication by rephrasing each question and by asking questions in several different ways. Slowing the pace of the dialogue is another helpful strategy.

Tone

Achieving the right tone is important because candidates use it as an indicator of your assessment of them and their thesis. Although some academics subscribe to the view that the viva should test the candidate's ability to survive an onslaught of aggressive questions and put-downs, this is not good practice. Although candidates in our research were often in favour of probing and demanding questions and discussion, no one wanted the 'tone' of the viva to be aggressive and hostile. Successful candidates who had been exposed to this type of exchange reported negative feelings about themselves, their work and academia as a result of this experience (see Chapter 13).

Troubleshooting

There are occasions when, in spite of all your attempts to provide a supportive environment, the candidate does not respond productively and is, for example, unresponsive or defensive (see Box 12.3). These candidates pose a particular challenge for examiners. There are no simple solutions. Being clear to the candidate about the purposes of the viva at the beginning, and explaining how the viva will need to proceed in order to fulfil these purposes, can reduce the chances of unhelpful behaviour. However, examiners also need to be supportive, as described earlier in this section.

> I have found that positive questions are very helpful when a student is defensive and uncooperative. While it is imperative that examiners push candidates on a point, no purpose is served listening to a student struggle or dig themselves into a hole. It is in these circumstances that I have found that moving on to one of my 'enthusiastic' questions eases the situation and allows me to return later to a more awkward issue from a different angle.
>
> (Professor, Sociology)

If the candidate is persistently unhelpful it may be appropriate to remind them directly of the purposes of the viva and to point out how their behaviour is not conducive to fulfilling these. You may find it useful to take a short break to discuss with your co-examiner(s) how to manage this situation and/or you may want to gently broach this matter with the candidate and then propose a short break to allow the candidate to adjust their approach.

Box 12.3 Case Study

WHATEVER IT TAKES, I'LL FIGHT TO THE END

It is not unusual for candidates to be defensive in the viva. In some cases this is because the candidate approaches the viva as an exercise in survival, one where they must 'defend' their work at all costs. Although Jan (Religious Studies) was told at the beginning of her viva that she had passed, she was so geared up to defend her thesis that she was unable to shift her approach: 'I couldn't reconfigure my head to think about anything other than defending my thesis. So every time they spoke to me I was defending my thesis even though I didn't have to'.

Defensiveness can also arise because the candidate has invested so much in their thesis that they cannot yet stand back and critically review their own work: 'Be prepared for strong reactions from the candidate to any comments made about their thesis. Sometimes "the baby" must be seen to be perfect and any comment or query is taken as criticism'

(Senior Lecturer, Education). Whilst some defensiveness is quite usual and should be expected, some candidates are persistently defensive. Extreme defensiveness can be highly unproductive, particularly when the examiners want to discuss ways of getting a thesis up to standard or they want to make a decision about a borderline case. Unhelpful interpersonal relations can also result when candidates constantly block the examiners' attempts to discuss the thesis, as in the following case.

The candidate was defensive in a mildly aggressive sort of way, which caused her to be somewhat dismissive of points raised by the examiners. She didn't enter into a dialogue, which I guess is what every candidate should attempt to do, because then they can shine as fellow academics engaged in the same enterprise and you can get somewhere. Before the viva we had agreed that . . . we would use the viva to make a decision about whether to recommend resubmission for an MPhil or PhD. We wanted the candidate to have the opportunity to show herself in the best light given the circumstances, and we thought that this would happen if she could choose the topic for discussion – then she could pick the one that she was strongest on, most inspired about, etc. So the idea was to let the candidate choose the topic by asking what she thought was most interesting/central, the main reason she had chosen to study and then pursue that topic. That's what we did, but it didn't go well. Her reaction to critical points wasn't good . . . In the end, one of the examiners became extremely persistent, largely out of frustration I think, and I would say s/he made matters worse – it got slightly adversarial. I tried to wade in when I could and ask an answerable question, but it was difficult to do this. I wanted to take the heat off. What I didn't have time to really think through as I tried to find ways to intervene, was how to get the candidate working better.

In this case the candidate did herself a great disservice because she needed to 'enter into a dialogue about the thesis and work with the examiners in identifying where it needed patching up. I guess if she had done this, she *might* have ended up in the position of rewriting chapters as opposed to total resubmission.'

With hindsight, this examiner would have tackled the situation slightly differently. 'I think if this happened again, I might be more direct in trying to get the candidate to see that problems in the thesis aren't necessarily fatal . . . Advice to the examiner: be patient and keep to good initial intentions even if it's difficult!' We would add that it could also be useful to remind the candidate of the purposes of the viva, and to make it clear (gently) what are helpful and unhelpful types of response.

12.5 At the end of the viva

Once the viva is over, you and your co-examiner(s) should be left in private to discuss your recommendation. However, before asking the candidate, and any other observers, to leave the room it is advisable to explain what you are doing. Candidates can, if uninformed, be very worried by a request to leave the room (see Chapter 11).

Difficult decisions

There are always going to be marginal cases, and in these circumstances a decision about an award can easily go either way.

> I think there is a need to accept that there is an enormous spectrum of quality in PhD theses. The difficulty that can arise is that you can have a relatively marginal student who is on the pass/fail border. What do you do if the supervisor says s/he has run out of money, s/he has a job in a poor country in Africa and s/he is under pressure to return etc. Alternatively, what if the student says s/he is leaving science and going into the City. Should these factors be allowed to colour decisions? In principle no, in reality possibly.
>
> (Professor, Neurochemistry)

> There's always these marginal calls . . . Sometimes you think, well it's a fairly slender research base and ideally they could have done a lot more, but you can see why they didn't and you can't really say 'well, go and do another year's work'. So you make a kind of judgement call. Those things in my experience get discussed very . . . seriously, and they [the examiners] reach credible judgements and outcomes, but the decision could often go the other way.
>
> (Professor, Government)

Pressure to make a particular recommendation is not usually brought to bear by the candidate but by their supervisor and/or other advocate, sometimes the internal examiner. As described in Box 12.2, these pressures can precede the viva and make the task of examining uncomfortable for all concerned. Whilst acknowledging that there is a 'spectrum of quality' in PhDs, and that candidates' circumstances vary, examiners need to feel that their final decision has been fair. This is a point that was repeatedly referred to by experienced examiners from across the disciplines. As one examiner told us: 'Don't allow pressure from the internal institution to force you to pass an inadequate thesis – it will stay on the shelves to haunt you.' Two case studies – Boxes 12.4 and 12.5 – provide illustration of examiners resisting pressures to pass weak theses and, subsequently, feeling vindicated in their actions.

If you feel that the candidate has extenuating circumstances, for example they have been poorly supervised, this should not influence your recommendation of award. You can, however, investigate these circumstances and suggest in your report that they be taken into account if further work on the thesis is required.

Box 12.4   Case study

FIRM BUT FLEXIBLE

Prelude
After agreeing to examine a PhD I was contacted to arrange a date for the viva. During the discussion I was urged to make an early date as 'the candidate's visa was running out and she needed to return home to Asia within a week of the viva'. The earliest date (heavily suggested) was the day after the internal examiner returned from an overseas visit, having taken the thesis along on the trip. I agreed, received the tome and began to examine it. Rapidly, it became clear that there were numerous typographical, punctuation and grammatical errors. In the absence of the internal I contacted the Registry with a list of these mistakes so that the candidate could begin to amend them before the viva. I made it clear that this was an exceptional gesture and it certainly did not preclude any further amendments, nor should any presumption be made about the outcome of the examining process.

The viva day
The internal examiner had arranged to contact me the evening before the viva, but failed to do this. So I arrived on the day with a list of questions and a list of possible further amendments. In the preliminary discussion the internal was shocked by my 'stringent requirements' though I felt them eminently reasonable if not a little generous. S/he was not familiar with the university regulations about time allowed for major or minor amendments, nor what criteria were used to differentiate them. We sought the advice of the Registrar who clarified the time allowance but again emphasized the need for the student to complete before returning home.

The viva process
The candidate responded reasonably well to the questions, though it was clear that some of the issues raised had not been considered previously nor apparently raised in supervision. This surprised me, as some seemed essential, for example the need to justify the choice of the methods used and the rejection of others that might have been suitable. There seemed to be an implicit assumption that if the supervisor had recommended or agreed particular methods then that was justification enough.

The post-viva discussion and decision
This was difficult to begin with as the internal had expected that, as the typos had been addressed, the student could be awarded a straight pass. However, even taking a benevolent stance, the best I could contemplate would be minor corrections, although I have seen many students do less work under the rubric of major corrections. The supervisor was called in to discuss practicalities. It emerged that though s/he was an expert in the field his/her supervision experience was very limited and there was no mentor system in place. However, it was also revealed that the candidate could extend her visa to stay in the country for the three months required for minor corrections and that the supervisor would be able to help with the task. I conceded to minor corrections and the next day I provided a detailed list of amendments.

The aftermath
I worried for several weeks that I had allowed myself to be pressurized into a less-than-just decision by sympathy for the candidate's plight of less-than-adequate supervision and her need to return home 'successful'. Also, I felt slightly pressured by the covert but obvious assumption of the internal and supervisor that any doctorate studied in their institution (which is prestigious) would automatically be deemed to meet standards. I was reassured after three months to receive a copy of the corrections (which was not a formal requirement) and also a letter of thanks from the supervisor which said that it had been a wonderful learning experience for him/her that would guide supervision in the future. I have since heard from the candidate on several occasions, to convey thanks but also to send copies of journal articles written from the thesis. I now feel that a blend of firmness and flexibility to circumstance is central to good examining.

Box 12.5   Case study

ASKING FOR REVISIONS IS NOT ALWAYS EASY

The candidate was a relatively young woman. Her male supervisor was very nice, very experienced and 'mature', but it seemed to me that he had not kept up with changes in quality assurance around PhDs and vivas. He tried to brief me, along with the internal examiner, who was a very able man but not well versed in the particular area.

I found negotiating with them and being fair to the student very difficult, and a complex political process. The student had not conducted a particularly feminist study but had ended up finding gender issues salient to her conclusions. I wanted, and insisted on, some revisions and rewriting of the thesis, but that was a very difficult process, as the internal and supervisor disagreed strongly with me. I was also told that the candidate would not do the amendments, but just leave as she was married and had other commitments. The situation was made worse as the internal examiner, whose responsibility it was to liaise with the candidate about corrections, lost my subsequent email correspondence for about a month.

However, in the event the candidate did revise and resubmit the thesis and it turned into a very creditable and good piece of work. So, having stuck to my guns, so to speak, I felt validated, *but* I had felt bad and guilty about it given how strongly the two men disagreed with my views.

Feedback to candidate

If you and your co-examiner are able to agree on a recommendation it is then necessary to decide what you will say to the candidate; note that at some institutions examiners are not required to release their recommendation to the candidate, this can be handled solely through formal channels. If you tell the candidate your decision, remember to point out to them that technically it is only a *recommendation* until formally ratified by an appropriate university committee. We are aware of one instance where a university committee did not accept the examiners' recommendation of 'pass subject to minor corrections', because the examiners' pre- and post-viva reports listed corrections that were deemed to constitute 'major' corrections.

In cases where further work of any kind is required it is usual to outline this to the candidate; specific details can be provided later in a written report. It is essential that you agree with your co-examiner the corrections that are required to raise the thesis to the appropriate standard and to detail these in the post-viva report. It is important to be clear about the corrections you require because the candidate's revised or resubmitted thesis will be judged against these. 'The examiners specify what the deficiencies of the thesis are and how they are to be tackled . . . What then happens is that the candidate addresses the deficiencies in a very narrow way. The result is a revised thesis that has attended to the letter of the required corrections but not their spirit' (Professor, Sociology). It is useful to be clear about the objectives of the corrections as well as the specifics.

Ideally you should finalize post-viva paperwork before you depart, although if you are in a rush this will have to be done later. If the candidate needs to do further work to the thesis it is usually left to the internal examiner or an administrator to liaise with the candidate, often via the candidate's supervisor. External examiners should not usually engage in dialogue or correspondence directly with the candidate or offer this. In cases where the internal examiner takes responsibility for liaising with the candidate over corrections, it is vital that this remains relatively formal.

12.6 Summary

In this chapter we have considered the viva from the perspectives of examiners; to do this we have drawn upon the experiences of examiners from across the disciplines. We have looked at how examiners can prepare for the viva: the decisions that need to be made before the day of the viva and the pre-viva meeting. We have also discussed how to conduct a viva, from managing first impressions to generating a productive exchange. Post-viva business has also been addressed, including the recommendation of award.

13

Post-viva

Chapter overview

This chapter focuses on the period immediately after the viva has finished (after the decision has been released) and the days following it. We examine how candidates feel after the viva, and outline and discuss the importance of post-viva debriefing. The work and responsibilities of candidates and supervisors in various post-viva stages are outlined. Finally, this chapter examines what candidates can do if they are unhappy about (aspects of) the examination process.

Students	☺☺☺	Examiners	☺☺
Supervisors	☺☺☺	Chairs	☺

Chapter contents

13.1 Candidates' post-viva feelings

> Perhaps one of the biggest surprises about doing a PhD is that many
> people feel anything but straightforwardly elated afterwards.
>
> (Leonard 2001: 258)

Leonard suggests that finishing a PhD can provoke complex sets of feelings and emotions for candidates. In one sense, this is unsurprising given that the completion of a PhD frequently leads to significant life changes, particularly for full-time students. On the other hand, it can come as quite a surprise for candidates who have invested a considerable amount of time, effort and often money to reach the point of finishing their PhD, and who may expect to feel elated if and when they are awarded their doctorate. In this section we explore the types of emotion encountered post-viva by the candidates that we interviewed. It is important to note that none of our interviewees failed their doctorate; most had corrections to do – these varied from a few typographical corrections to more substantial rewrites. Below, we map out some of the most common responses. Whilst we have attempted to categorize these, a number of candidates' comments fit into more than one category. However, these comments provide an indication of the range of responses that candidates described, and reinforce our point that there is no one type of response to a successful result.

Relief

An overwhelming sense of relief was a common post-viva feeling amongst our candidates:

> It's a strange feeling because you can't believe it and so you do not realize until a bit later on, but the most, how could I say, the prevailing feeling is the relief that you have finished.
>
> (Silvo, PhD student, Economics)

> [I felt] just really relieved. I just wanted to contact my family and friends and tell them I'd passed and I couldn't because I was still there [with the examiners and supervisor] and you can't, you're bursting inside but you feel like you need to keep that straight face. So yes, I felt absolutely on top of the world afterwards.
>
> (Alice, PhD student, Geography)

> *Interviewer: So what happened immediately after your viva finished?*
> I think I screamed! We had something to eat in actual fact; it was really nice because the department had organized . . . a small buffet there so we just had a bite to eat . . .

Interviewer: How did you feel at this point?
Relieved, I suppose. In truth it [the buffet] went on too long because I just wanted to get out of there and run about really.

(Nigel, PhD student, Nursing)

Delayed reactions . . . but then relieved and happy

A number of candidates said that they did not fully comprehend the outcome until some time after the viva, that it did not 'sink in' straight away:

It didn't sink in until Sunday [the viva was Friday] when I came back up and saw my family. The overwhelming emotion immediately after the viva was just relief that it was all over and I'd passed.

(Gary, PhD student, Pharmacy)

Interviewer: So what happened immediately after the viva finished?
A huge sense of relief. It was very strange, it took a while to sink in, to be honest.
Interviewer: So how did you feel at this point?
Great, really relieved, it was a huge weight off my mind. My friend said, 'Is it a bit of an anti-climax?', and it wasn't at all . . . I just felt good.

(Kate, PhD student, Psychology)

Excited and good

Carla and Kali both felt very pleased:

When they told me I'd passed I was excited, I couldn't believe it and I thought they were going to tell me, 'OK you passed, but you have to go and do this, this and this.' So I was just kind of waiting for them to say something else and then I realized they weren't. It was only afterwards when I was on the bus on the way home – I was like 'OK, this is done.'

(Carla, PhD student, Art History)

Interviewer: How did you feel once you heard you'd passed?
Oh God, this is it, it was all good.

(Kali, PhD student, English)

Delighted but . . . sick, weepy and tired

Jan was awarded her doctorate with no corrections, which is very unusual. She was very nervous before her viva partly because, like most candidates, she did not really know what to expect. After her viva Jan was clearly delighted, but overwrought:

I went over with my supervisor to see my husband in the restaurant where he was waiting, reading his books, or pretending to . . . We arrived and I looked at him and I immediately burst into tears and he thought I had failed and he cried and I cried and Gladys [her supervisor] cried. And then we got a cup of tea and some cake and then I felt sick. And then we went across the road to a funny little place . . . where you have wine and coffee and things, and we went there and we had champagne and I drank two glasses and wanted to be sick . . . I felt very drained, very as if it hadn't happened, very odd actually, and then we came home on the train and I felt bleary eyed on the train and then I wanted to sleep for a week.

(Jan, PhD student, Religious Studies)

Anticlimax

The build-up to the viva, and the expectations surrounding it, can leave candidates with a sense of anticlimax after the event. Shaun described this feeling,

I was certainly pleased that I'd got it, but not quite sure how I felt, a bit of an anticlimax because it's not like a pauper-against-the-odds win-through with some brilliant presentation that I'd come through, it was kind of 'great, yes I've got it'.

(Shaun, PhD student, Engineering)

Do I really deserve this? Am I an academic fraud?

In *A Woman's Guide to Doctoral Studies*, Leonard (2001: 230) notes that:

A theme throughout this book has been many women's chronic low self-esteem and lack of confidence. Many of us go on questioning whether we can manage a doctorate and whether it is worth its personal and professional costs throughout the time we are working on it (and beyond) – despite the good academic results we have achieved and/or professional expertise we displayed in our jobs before undertaking doctoral studies.

The lack of confidence that Leonard identifies as common amongst many women during doctoral study was also apparent post-viva in our research. Some of our successful candidates, all women, suggested in their post-viva interviews that they had questioned whether they really deserved a PhD, despite being awarded one. For example, Carla was awarded her doctorate subject to completing minor corrections, and she was given very positive feedback on her viva performance from her supervisor. Despite these affirmations of her academic competence, she was unsure about whether she deserved her PhD and whether she was a 'proper' academic:

That's funny, it was like, in a sense you have this pridal mound, but in another sense I was really numb after. I was really, really happy but then I was thinking, it was kind of like I can't believe it. And in a sense the problem was almost like, OK, yes, you have a PhD now but then . . . do I deserve it? The whole time you are studying to be this thing and then you get it, but then you're like, but do I really belong with these other people?

(Carla, PhD student, Art History)

Leila passed with no corrections, but she too doubted herself afterwards:

It [the viva] compounded a few things I felt, which was that you worry you've kind of got this fraud complex, that you're constantly winging it, you're constantly flying by the seat of your pants.

Interviewer: Even though you passed?
Yes, I know, I'm really crap like that. I do think I had to fight for it and I do think I deserved it and I'm really pleased I've got it, I really am. And I was really relieved when I came out and just wanted to kind of weep with relief, not because I was upset or anything but just because it was over and I'd passed and it was all right now and everything else. But it compounded, I think, a few of my doubts. That this kind of environment, I don't know, maybe it's the same with any environment you just seem to be constantly up against a series of pressures to prove your worthiness, to prove your worth and sometimes you think 'Oh God, I'd quite like to work in a shop'.

(Leila, PhD student, Sociology)

Leila doubted herself despite very positive feedback from her internal examiner about her viva performance:

Interviewer: Did you get much feedback on the viva and your performance?
Yes, I did actually. My internal told me that she thought she'd never seen anyone defend their thesis so well, which was really nice.

We return to Leila and the ways in which the viva can affect candidates' perceptions of their competence later in this chapter.

I'll be happier once the corrections are done . . .

A few of our candidates who had corrections to do either expressed displeasure at having to do the corrections and/or suggested that they would feel like they had really got the award only once the corrections were completed and approved. Angela, a women's studies candidate, falls into the first of these two camps:

After the viva my supervisor and I went for coffee and cake . . .
Interviewer: And how did you feel at this point?
Pissed off [at having to do the corrections].

Douglas, a sociology candidate, seemed on the other hand less unhappy about having to do the corrections (although he described them as 'petty') and more concerned about closure:

I didn't feel elated because I was conscious that there was still stuff to do and it's just the bitty, silly things. If it had been 'pass no corrections' I would have been a lot happier but it was the uncertainty over the corrections. I flicked through this thing full of Post-it notes seeing apostrophes marked and commas . . . I had this niggling kind of concern, doubt in my mind that the process was going to become a bit convoluted. I still do, as I sit here now. I mean people congratulate you, 'Oh, well done mate', but I won't be happy, I won't believe that the thing's out of the way until I hand in the hardbound copy to the exams office with the bit of paper from the internal.

13.2 Effects of the viva upon candidates

My viva was a real high – the pinnacle of the PhD process.
                    (PhD student, Nursing and Women's Studies)

The experiences of candidates in the viva often have significant implications for how they regard their intellectual competence and future academic prospects. Our questionnaires to candidates explored the effects of the viva upon their perceptions of academic competence; desire to continue work in the sphere of their PhD; desire to work within academia; and perceptions of the publishability of their PhD. Key results from these questions are presented in Table 13.1.

Table 13.1   The effect of the PhD viva upon candidates' self-perceptions and feelings in terms of: academic competence; desire to continue work in the sphere of their PhD; desire to work within academia; and publishability of the PhD

Candidates' self-perceptions	Increased (%)	Decreased (%)	No effect (%)
Perceptions of academic competence	53	17	30
Desire to continue work in sphere of PhD	39	9	52
Desire to work within academia	19	16	65
Perceptions of publishability of PhD	57	13	31

Source: Reproduced from Jackson and Tinkler 2001: 363

A notable feature of this table is that 17 per cent of candidates reported decreases in their perceptions of academic competence as a result of the viva and 16 per cent expressed a decreased desire to work within academia. These figures suggest that for one in six students the viva serves a negative function. A look at candidates' responses in relation to outcome reveals that a greater proportion of candidates who were referred reported a decline in perceptions of academic competence (47 per cent) and in their desire to work within academia (47 per cent) than those who passed (11 per cent and 10 per cent, respectively). Although it is not especially surprising that approximately half of the candidates who were referred reported the viva as having negative effects, it is more surprising that one-tenth of those candidates who passed also attributed a negative effect to it. In an attempt to shed light on this finding, we return to Leila, who earlier in this chapter reported feeling like an academic fraud. Leila was one of our interviewees who suggested that the viva impacted negatively upon her feelings of academic competence despite passing her PhD without the need for corrections. Her narrative below is a response to our question 'did the viva have any effect on your feelings of academic competence?'

> Yes. I find the academic environment one that doesn't necessarily foster a great deal of confidence. I've talked to a lot of people about this and you do most of the time feel like a total fraud who at any moment is going to be unmasked as a complete thickster, which you kind of logically know isn't the case but you kind of live with that. And so the viva, I suppose, does sort of loom as this moment at which the cape or the mask will finally be lifted . . . I mean, the kinds of questions that they were asking [in the viva] did make me at times feel quite stupid, but partly because every time they asked me a question I just assumed I'd got it wrong. So instead of just going 'Oh no, but', I'd think I did it wrong, I did it wrong and now I have to demonstrate that I do know what it means or that I do know how that works. So I just took every question as a criticism. So I think that's one of the things that the viva does, unless you're very supremely confident about your capabilities and supremely confident about what you've done, I think you just assume that they are pointing out all the mistakes and flaws in your thesis as opposed to actually wanting to engage with how you've used it.

Leila's description of the academic environment as 'one that doesn't necessarily foster a great deal of confidence' may have resonance for many people working within academia, but particularly for women. Whilst our questionnaire data suggested that women and men reported decreased self-perceptions following the viva (as outlined earlier), it was women who reported and talked about such decreases in our interviews. The lack of confidence reported by Leila here and by Carla earlier in this chapter may be attributed, in part, to 'the chilly climate for women' in universities. Leonard (2001: 202) discusses the ways in which women routinely encounter academic sexism, racism and homophobia in their interactions within institutions. She argues that 'we should not underestimate how much it drags us down; and how particularly disheartening (and hypocritical) it seems when it occurs in universities with their ideals of merit and intellectualism and Equal Opportunities policies'. Levels of confidence are important in shaping how candidates approach, perform in, and respond to the PhD viva. Our data, and the work of others (see, for example, Deem and Brehony 2000; Anderson and Williams 2001), suggest that levels of confidence are related in complex ways to gender. Thomas (1990: 181), in her book on gender and higher education, wrote: 'the one lasting impression I carry from this research is how much more self-confident the men were than the women [in higher education]'. Gender does not work in isolation though, and we have explored elsewhere the ways in which gender, social class, 'race' and fluency in English interrelate to influence the ways in which candidates approach and experience the viva in Britain (see Jackson and Tinkler 2001).

Issues of confidence are complex and we cannot offer straightforward advice about how to deal with post-viva uncertainties. We do not advocate approaches whereby individuals are targeted for 'confidence-boosting' training. Such approaches are problematical as they 'blame the individual' and ignore and deflect attention away from structural problems and inequalities. There is a tension for many within academia between fighting against and challenging systemic inequalities and yet surviving within the systems that exist at any given time. Peelo (2000: 126), a study counsellor argues that:

> There is something important for students to learn about entitlement, confidence to be and to act within a system which values the assertion of personal knowledge and viewpoint above all else. Learning, too, not to pin one's identity or sense of intellectual esteem on the marks and comments one receives. In coming to understand the reality of the academic environment one hopes that students learn that they have choices about how to negotiate a manageable path through their degrees, rather than feel helpless or, even, driven into inappropriate or unhelpful behaviours.

The question has not been answered in full as to why the viva serves to discourage one in ten successful candidates from remaining within academia. Some possibilities are outlined below, but we must stress that they are merely *possible* explanations.

- In some cases, there may be a mismatch between intention and practice on the part of examiners. Some examiners may appear to the candidate to be far more harsh or critical than they actually intend to be. In such cases, poor communication on the part of examiners and/or misunderstandings on the part of the candidate may deter candidates with excellent academic potential from staying in academia.
- Sometimes, examiners may be operating with an unspoken agenda to 'weed out' candidates that are unwilling, or unable, to tolerate the confrontational style that frequently characterizes academic engagement (see Chapter 3).
- Certain candidates may appear calm and robust in the viva, thus prompting the examiners to think that they are 'enjoying a spirited defence' and are well able to cope with intense academic debate and criticism. However, the candidate may be presenting an image that is far from how s/he feels inside, and may come away from such an experience rather bruised. Such candidates may see the long-term costs of such (bruising) public performances to be too costly to their well-being.

These possibilities clearly require further exploration. In a more positive vein, Table 13.1 shows that the viva has an encouraging effect for the majority of candidates. Fifty-three per cent of candidates reported increased perceptions of academic competence as a result of the viva, and 57 per cent reported increased confidence in the publishability of their PhD research. Kali, an English candidate, reported the positive effects of the viva on his feelings of academic competence: 'I felt vindicated. Until yesterday I did always feel that this isn't good enough or this isn't going to go through. Yesterday it felt really good.' For Dan, a chemistry candidate, the viva was particularly important because he reported receiving very little feedback from his supervisor throughout the course of his PhD: 'It was a pat on the back, because to be honest my supervisor isn't one to even go as far as a "well done" the odd time. He doesn't get excited about anything like that. I wrote the whole PhD thesis and not once did he ever say any of it was good, not any section or any piece.' For many candidates the viva is regarded, usually retrospectively, as being a rewarding experience.

13.3 Post-viva tasks

Candidates' post-viva tasks will depend on the examiners' recommendation of award (see Chapter 1 for details of what recommendations can be made).

Award forthwith with no or minor corrections

The data presented in the previous section demonstrate that despite a successful viva outcome, some candidates feel that the viva has impacted negatively upon their self-perceptions. Irrespective of outcome, a debriefing shortly after the viva provides an opportunity for candidates to discuss their feelings and concerns. A debriefing is particularly useful if the supervisor was present at the viva as s/he can then provide feedback about performance, this can reassure candidates, many of whom have performed better than they think they have.

> Actually she said that she thought I was very calm [in the viva] and I did very well. She thought at certain points that I would have been justified to tell them that their questioning was kind of out of line, because she thought some of the questioning was kind of within their agenda as opposed to my research . . . she thought they were pushing the issue . . . She said, 'You were very good to stay calm and so focused and not to get kind of rattled by their focus' . . . My co-supervisor, she was lovely, she took notes for me on the basic discussion and she basically said she thought it was a very high-level discussion.
>
> (Carla, PhD student, Art History)

Some candidates who have minor corrections to do report being unclear about the required amendments; a debriefing with the supervisor may help to clarify the nature and extent of them and also the timescale.

Referral

- If candidates have major corrections to undertake, it is important for the candidate to discuss these changes with the supervisor and/or the internal examiner.
- Candidates and supervisors need to discuss arrangements for the corrections and the nature and extent of support to be provided by the supervisor.
- In some cases where candidates have to undertake major corrections the relationship between the candidate and supervisor may become strained or break down. In such cases the candidate should consult the departmental postgraduate students' tutor to discuss support.
- Candidates who have to make major changes are entitled to written feedback about the corrections, and the supervisor should ensure that these are made available (see section below about access to examiners' reports).
- Institutions vary in the time allowed to candidates for major corrections. Leonard (2001) suggests that candidates should always accept the longest length of time that they are offered. Candidates can, after all, resubmit as soon as they are ready, but extensions to the deadline may be problematical. It is important to ensure that the latest date for resubmission is clear to all parties.

Candidates required to have a second viva

Sometimes, a candidate whose thesis is referred has to undergo a second viva following resubmission. In such cases, feedback from the supervisor and/or internal examiner following the first viva can help the candidate to improve their performance in the second. Examiners' reasons for requesting a second viva vary. Overall, however, they tend to mirror the purposes ascribed to first vivas (see Chapter 2):

- *Examination.* If the rewriting is substantial the examiners may want to examine the candidate on the rewritten version in order to authenticate the revised thesis, to test the candidate's knowledge and understanding, to enable the candidate to defend the (new) ideas, and so on. Examination may also be regarded as important if the candidate's performance in the first viva was deemed to be poor.
- *Development.* If the revised version is approved by the examiners, they may want to discuss aspects of the work that may be developed for publication.
- *Ritual.* Some examiners feel a second viva offers 'closure' on the PhD process. Relatedly, some examiners may see that a second viva acts as a 'reward' to (now successful) candidates for their extra work. The second viva may, therefore, offer ritualistic (and developmental) opportunities to the candidate that were not possible at the first one.

Are candidates allowed access to the examiners' reports?

Before the introduction of the Data Protection Act 1998, candidates in many institutions were not allowed, officially, to see the examiners' reports. Some of our respondents were very unhappy about this: 'This I am incensed about. It is not university policy to issue them. I feel this is extremely bad educational practice' (PhD student, History). Many people argue strongly that it is appropriate for candidates to have access to written comments on their work: after all, it has taken three or more years of hard work to complete it. Some candidates have sight of the reports unofficially; this was the case for 28 per cent of our questionnaire respondents.

The Data Protection Act has changed the situation somewhat. Although the Act lends itself to differences in interpretation, institutions seem to accept that candidates can have access to their examiners' reports under the terms of the Act. There may, however, be time restrictions, and in some cases a fee to pay. For example, at Lancaster University (Park 2004) the *Framework of Best Practice in the Doctoral Viva* states: 'Under the data protection legislation, students have a right of access to their Post-Viva Report after Senate approval of the examiners' recommendation is confirmed and the examination (including any revisions) have been completed'. In general, it seems that whereas candidates can request access to their examiners' reports under the Data Protection Act, many universities are not keen for candidates to see them, and will not allow access without a formal request.

13.4 When candidates are unhappy about the examination process

It is important that candidates know the range of options available to them if they are unhappy with aspects of the examination process. Unhappy PhD examination experiences do not go away overnight: years later many candidates are able to recount the anger and frustration that they felt, and often still feel, if their PhD examination went 'wrong'. As such, it is important for candidates who feel unhappy with their experience of being examined to think carefully, as soon after the viva as possible, about whether they want, or indeed can, take any action. Too frequently, candidates, and sometimes supervisors, are unaware of their institutional appeals and complaints procedures. This was the case for a candidate who wrote to Morley *et al.* (2002: 263):

> I completed [the PhD] and had a viva without any preparation or information about what to expect . . . I was awarded an M.Phil. without any feedback as to why . . . my supervisor never made any further contact with me (ever) and I was too pissed off to contact him and received my certification through the post. I didn't know of any appeal procedure until you mentioned it on Friday.

Whilst appeals should not be undertaken lightly (see Box 13.1), it is important that candidates, supervisors and examiners know the appeals and complaints procedures in the institution where the examination is taking place.

Appeals

Grounds for appeal

Grounds for appeal should be set out in institutional policies. Typically, grounds for appeal against examination decisions are permitted on the following grounds (see Box 13.1 for further discussion of these with examples):

- There were circumstances affecting the candidate's performance of which the examiners were not aware at the oral examination.
- Procedural irregularities occurred in the conduct of the examination, which were of such a nature as to cause doubt as to whether the examiners would have reached the same conclusion had the irregularities not occurred.
- There is evidence of prejudice, bias, unfair or inadequate assessment in the examination process.

However, the precise grounds for appeal vary between institutions, so do check the relevant institutional policy.

It is worth noting that candidates may not challenge the academic judgement of the examiners. Furthermore, in some institutions an appeal may not usually be submitted on the grounds of inadequate supervision during the period of study: if students have complaints about supervision these complaints should be lodged during the period of study and before submission of the thesis. It is also important to note that if a candidate wishes to appeal then s/he usually needs to submit a case within a limited timeframe (again, this varies depending on the institution). It is therefore important to check the institutional regulations about the appeal procedures and timescale as soon as possible after the viva. Discussion and advice about appeals and complaints is provided in Box 13.1.

Possible outcomes of appeals

Usually, the range of possible outcomes of appeals is as follows:

- The appeal is rejected and the examiners' recommendation is upheld.
- The appeal is accepted and one of the following courses of action is taken:
  - The examiners are asked to reconsider their decision in the light of the reasons stated in the appeal. The examiners are asked to report back to the appeal board.
  - The candidate is given permission to revise the thesis and resubmit for re-examination within a specified time limit (see Box 13.1 for an example).

- The examination is declared void and a fresh examination is conducted (see Box 13.1 for an example).

However, institutional policies do vary, so check the policy of the institution where your examination takes place.

Box 13.1 Case study

IF CANDIDATES ARE UNHAPPY ABOUT THEIR PHD VIVA AND/OR THE EXAMINERS' RECOMMENDATION, WHAT CAN THEY DO ABOUT IT?

by Kath Twaddell, Lancaster University

If your viva 'went wrong' in any way the first thing to do is write down your own recollection of the experience. What happened? What did you feel was inappropriate or wrong with the experience? You will forget the details very quickly, and if you do end up wanting to make an academic complaint or an appeal then accurate details are extremely important. The next step is to relax and calm down – go for a walk, have a bath, raid the fridge – whatever. Then think about what happened and what you want.

Grounds for appeal/complaint
Before going any further you need to be aware that you cannot question academic judgement. The grounds for your appeal or complaint cannot be that you and your supervisor think that you ought to pass your PhD. Whilst this rule may make no sense for work that is at the forefront of its field and fulfilling the criteria of 'originality', and so by its very nature may be challenging established 'academic wisdom', the rule still applies. So far, the courts in this country have agreed with universities on this point; if the examiners say it is not good enough academically then there is nothing that you can do about it. If you want to make a case for an appeal you need to:

- show that at the time of the exam your performance was affected by circumstances that the examiners did not know about (and that you had a good reason for not telling them); or
- find a procedural error in the way that your examination was conducted; or
- prove that there was an unrelated issue or bias at work that prevented the process operating fairly.

However, you cannot claim that an examination was unfair solely because the outcome was not a pass – this comes back to challenging academic judgement, which is not allowed. Some students do try this tack though. I had a conversation with a student that was deeply frustrating for both of us on this issue. The student claimed that his thesis ought to have passed without the need to resubmit, and because it did not he felt that the examiner was biased against him. The student had no evidence of bias other than an outcome that he disagreed with. As such, the student had no case for appeal as he was questioning academic judgement.

So, if it is not about an academic judgement, but there was something wrong with your viva (in your opinion), what do you do? After recording all you can about the event, the next thing to do is decide whether you want to make a complaint or an appeal. An *appeal* involves questioning the outcome – in such a case you will have failed or at least been referred (given a set amount of time for a rewrite). A *complaint* involves your being unhappy about the conduct of the viva but not necessarily objecting to the outcome. Obviously an appeal will probably also involve some complaining.

What can be the benefits of complaining?

There will probably be one of two reasons why you would make a complaint rather than an appeal. The first is that although the process of the viva was not good, the outcome was acceptable. The second is that you are not eligible for an appeal under the institution's regulations, but anyone can complain about anything at any time.

Let us consider more closely these two reasons for complaining. In the first case, although the outcome of the viva was favourable – or at least not unreasonable – you feel that there was something wrong with the viva itself. In this situation, you are not asking that the outcome/the decision of the examiners is changed. Your reason for complaining may be to alert the university to a problem with a particular examiner or procedure. Your complaint may be an attempt to prevent other students having to go through the same bad experience as you. If you are considering lodging a complaint, think carefully about your reasons. For example, if you found the viva unpleasant, reflect upon why you found it this way. If the viva was academically rigorous and this made you feel uncomfortable about your work – which is something that you will have become very attached to over the past few years – then there is not much wrong. However, if the examiners' conduct in the examination did not give you a fair chance to defend your thesis, then you may have grounds for a complaint. For example, I dealt with a student who came out of her viva with a positive outcome in terms of being known as 'Dr', but she was also pale and shaking. During the viva she had not been given a chance to answer the questions that were fired at her in quick succession, and this had led to the answers that she was able to squeeze into the conversation being rushed and badly thought out. When it became obvious that she was not happy or comfortable with this approach, comments were made about her needing to be made of 'tougher stuff' if she were going to be an academic. It was difficult in this case to determine whether the conduct of the viva was unfair, because many students find the viva nerve-wracking and difficult. However, her complaint was investigated and her case, and others like it, eventually led to a revision of the viva guidelines in that institution to include more guidance about the conduct of the oral examination.

A second reason that you may complain rather than appeal is that you may not have grounds for appeal. For example, some institutions allow an appeal only if you fail outright. So if you are allowed to resubmit for an MPhil rather than a PhD, this would not generate an appeal. However, this may be an outcome that you feel is not justified. Consequently you are in a situation that you feel requires an appeal on the grounds of the decision and yet you cannot appeal. Such situations can be difficult as the institution could say that you are attempting to make a backdoor appeal via the complaints procedure (which you are) and throw it out without investigating. You need to be clearly complaining about the conduct of the viva which, you feel, led to an unsound outcome. Depending on your institution's regulations your complaint *may* then lead to a changed outcome, although it may only lead to allowing you the chance to appeal. In either case it is the first step of a process that could lead to a change in your situation, if that is what you want.

What can be the benefits of appealing?
Before you launch into an appeal you need to decide what you want, what is the best possible outcome for you? Here you need to be realistic. Outcomes can vary from nothing changing to your getting what you want. Appealing can be very stressful; one of the reasons to seek advice is so that you do not go into an appeal with a no-hope case.

Apart from nothing happening, what else is possible? First of all you should be clear that an appeal board cannot simply award you the PhD. To get the PhD you need to prove that whatever went wrong made a material difference to the outcome *and* to prove that, given a fair chance, you can meet the standard. For example, I supported a student whose external examiner had spent a good 20 minutes of the viva questioning the student about the sexuality of her supervisor and how that had negatively impacted on the thesis. This account was supported by the internal examiner who seemed to be somewhat surprised by the line of questioning. It turned out that the examiner and the supervisor had long been on opposite sides of a disciplinary argument – which did raise side issues about the wisdom of selecting that particular examiner. This was an open and shut case; the examiner was considering issues that were irrelevant to the thesis and also offensive. However, the institution could not automatically pass the student, as there was no evidence that she would have passed had the viva been fair. In this case, the best possible outcome was for the viva to be declared void and to give the student a new viva with a different examiner as soon as possible (and never to employ the original examiner again).

There are other options open as well. One difficult case that I dealt with involved a student who had experienced various personal problems throughout the course of his PhD. Unfortunately he was ill during much of his third and fourth years so he did not see as much of his supervisor as he should have done. To compound his problems, just before his viva someone close to him died. All of this was evidenced; there was no doubt that this student had experienced four pretty terrible years. On examination, the examiners judged his work to be below the necessary standard for a PhD – he failed. At appeal, there was great sympathy for his situation; the appeal board had information that was, properly, not available to the examiners. We were able to get him 12 months to rewrite with a suspended start date to enable him to have a break and get back on his feet. In some exceptional circumstances, then, students who fail outright (don't panic, this is very rare) or who are permitted initially to resubmit only for MPhil, may be given the chance to resubmit for PhD if they are successful in their appeal.

Generally, appeal boards have a significant amount of power and flexibility so it is worth asking for your preferred option even if it seems unusual. However, make sure that you think about the consequences of getting what you want in an appeal. If you know that you cannot stand another 12 months working on your thesis then do not ask for it, even if it means accepting an MPhil. These are hard choices and an appeal may not be easy, that is why my advice to you, if you are thinking of appealing or complaining, is to seek guidance that takes into account your institution's regulations and your particular situation.

Appeals and complaints procedures and regulations
Practically, complaints and appeals will probably be dealt with slightly differently. In some institutions you may be able to attend a hearing through the appeals procedures and not through the complaints procedure. In other institutions it may be the other way around. There seems to be little consistency so you need to check your own institutional regulations. Whether it is an appeal or a complaint there may be time limits imposed by the institution, so make sure that you check this out promptly after the viva. There are also variations between universities in terms of the instigation of appeals. In some institutions the candidate needs to instigate the appeal procedures. In others, the institution has a mechanism that generates an appeal automatically if a student fails outright or is recommended for an award lower than that for which s/he was registered.

Because institutions vary in terms of their regulations and procedures, it is important to be informed about the regulations of your institution. Dig out the handbook that you were given all those years ago – the institution's Students' Charter, the Quality Assurance Agency's guidance on postgraduate student assessment – anything that may be of relevance. I would also advise going to your students' union advice centre or equivalent. Despite the work that students' unions do with, and for, postgraduate students, many people see the students' union as being for undergraduates only. It isn't. If the students' union cannot help you, they will say so, but it is worth trying.

It is also wise to find out about your particular situation from the point of view of the institution's paper trail. Ask to see your university file. Under the Data Protection Act 1998 you have every right to make a 'subject access request' to see anything that has ever been written about you by members of the university; this should include examiners' reports, although there may be issues about the timing of the access (see earlier section in this chapter). The university can charge you £10 for this, but generally they do not.

No matter what the specifics of the institutional regulations are, the appeal and complaints procedures should follow the principles of natural justice as codified in the Human Rights Act 1998. This basically includes advice regarding best practice in procedures. The procedures should be: accessible (easy to find and not written in Latin, for example), transparent (easy to follow), timely and open. In the case of an appeal, openness involves your seeing what the appeal panel (or individual) sees, and seeing it in advance of any hearing so that you can defend yourself. It should also mean that you are given a proper chance to defend yourself either in person or in writing. There should be some level of independence in the procedure; if the examiner against whose decision you are appealing is the direct line manager of the person to whom you appeal, this is not independent. You should be fully informed of your rights – you might be able to take someone to a hearing with you for example. You should also be fully informed of the outcome of the appeal in writing, with reasons for that outcome set out clearly.

Remember, whether you appeal or complain in person, in writing or both, be specific, direct and brief in your approach. Make it clear early on in any communications whether you are complaining or appealing. It is also worth pointing to the specific regulation under which you are operating. Explain what the problem was and outline the grounds on which you are basing your case. For example, in the case of an appeal, explain how the problem affected you, your performance, the outcome. What material difference did it make? What evidence is there to back this up? Do not be put off by a lack of documented evidence – your word can count as evidence, but if you can find a document or comment by another party this will reinforce what you say. If you need to ask someone for something or to prompt a response, do it in writing and keep a copy – remember, emails count, telephone calls might not.

To end on a positive note

It is extremely rare that a student will fail a PhD on the viva alone, and whilst many students who pass consider the viva to be an extremely stressful experience, it is rare that they feel there was unreasonable conduct. In fact, some PhD candidates have been known to enjoy the viva!

At the time of writing, Kath was a student union advisor with particular responsibility for postgraduate students. She has recently moved to work for Lancaster University in the Student Registry.

The examples used in this piece are all based on real experiences, although some of the details have been omitted or changed to maintain anonymity.

13.5 Summary

This chapter has mapped out common post-viva feelings – these are complex and varied. The viva does not always mark the end of the PhD examination process, rather it is one stage of it. As such, we have also considered what tasks candidates might want, or have, to perform after their viva is over, this included a discussion of appeals procedures.

References

Anderson, P. and Williams, J. (eds) (2001) *Identity and Difference in Higher Education: 'Outsiders Within'*. Aldershot: Ashgate.

Argyle, M. (1992) *The Social Psychology of Everyday Life*. London: Routledge.

Baldacchino, G. (1995) Reflections on the status of a doctoral defence, *Journal of Graduate Education*, 1(3): 71–6.

Becher, T. (1989) *Academic Tribes and Territories*. Milton Keynes: Open University Press.

Becher, T. and Trowler, P.R. (2001) *Academic Tribes and Territories*, 2nd edn. Buckingham: SRHE/Open University Press.

Becher, T., Henkel, M. and Kogan, M. (1994) *Graduate Education in Britain*. London: Jessica Kingsley.

Blaxter, L., Hughes, C. and Tight, M. (1996) *How to Research*. Buckingham: Open University Press.

Blaxter, L., Hughes, C. and Tight, M. (1998) *The Academic Career Handbook*. Buckingham: Open University Press.

BPS/UCoSDA (British Psychological Society/Universities and Colleges' Staff Development Unit) (1995) *Guidelines for Assessment of the PhD in Psychology and Related Disciplines*. Sheffield: UCoSDA.

Brause, R.S. (2000) *Writing your Doctoral Dissertation: Invisible Rules for Success*. London: Falmer Press.

Broad, A. (2003) Nasty PhD viva questions. http://www.cs.man.ac.uk/infobank/broada/cs/cs710/viva.html (accessed 9 June 2003).

Brookes, A. (1997) *Academic Women*. Buckingham: SRHE/Open University Press.

Burnham, P. (1994) Surviving the viva: unravelling the mystery of the PhD oral, *Journal of Graduate Education*, 1(1): 30–4.

City University (2003) Research student oral examinations: checklist for chair. http://www.city.ac.uk/researchstudies/rdcforms.htm (accessed 2 June 2003).

Committee of Vice-Chancellors and Principals (1988) *The British PhD*. London: CVCP.

Cottrell, S. (1999) *The Study Skills Handbook*. Basingstoke: Palgrave.

Cryer, P. (2000) *The Research Student's Guide to Success*, 2nd edn. Buckingham: Open University Press.

Deem, R. and Brehony, K.J. (2000) Doctoral students' access to research cultures – are some more unequal than others? *Studies in Higher Education*, 25(2): 149–65.

Delamont, S., Atkinson, P. and Parry, O. (1997a) *Supervising the PhD: A Guide to Success*. Buckingham: Open University Press.

Delamont, S., Parry, O. and Atkinson, P. (1997b) Critical mass and pedagogic continuity: studies in academic habitus, *British Journal of Sociology of Education*, 18(4): 533–49.

Delamont, S., Atkinson, P. and Parry, O. (1997c) Critical mass and doctoral research: reflections on the Harris Report, *Studies in Higher Education*, 22(3): 319–31.

Delamont, S., Atkinson, P. and Parry, O. (2000) *The Doctoral Experience: Success and Failure in the Graduate School.* London: Falmer Press.

Denicolo, P.M., Boulter, C.J. and Fuller, M.I. (2000) Sharing reflections on the experience of doctoral assessment: the voices of supervisors and examiners. Paper presented to the British Educational Research Association National Event, Reading, 2 June.

Durling, D. (2002) Discourses on research and the PhD in design, *Quality Assurance in Education*, 10(2): 79–85.

Georges, A. (1996) Applied Ecology Research Group. The research thesis: what examiners look for. http://aerg.canberra.edu.au/eduthes4.htm (accessed 2 June 2003).

Grix, J. (2001) *Demystifying postgraduate research: from MA to PhD.* Birmingham: University of Birmingham Press.

Hartley, J. and Fox, C. (2004) Assessing the mock viva: the experiences of British doctoral students, Studies in Higher Education, in press.

Hartley, J. and Jory, S. (2000) Lifting the veil on the viva: the experience of psychology candidates in the UK, *Psychology Teaching Review*, 9(2): 76–90.

Higham, M. (1983) *Coping with Interviews.* London: New Opportunity Press.

Hoddell, S., Street, D. and Wildblood, H. (2002) Doctorates – converging or diverging patterns of provision, *Quality Assurance in Education*, 10(2): 61–70.

Institute of Education (2003) Preparing for the oral examination. http://www.ioe.ac.uk/doctoralschool/info-viva.htm (accessed 2 June 2003).

Jackson, C. and Tinkler, P. (2000) The PhD examination: an exercise in community building and gatekeeping?, in I. McNay (ed.) *Higher Education and its Communities.* Buckingham: SRHE/Open University Press.

Jackson, C. and Tinkler, P. (2001) Back to basics: a consideration of the purposes of the PhD viva, *Assessment and Evaluation in Higher Education*, 26(4): 355–66. http://www.tandf.co.uk

Jackson, C., Leonard, D., Tinkler. P. and David, M. (2002) The PhD – gender dimensions and feminist issues, in D. Leonard (ed.) *The Politics of Gender and Education.* London: Institute of Education.

Johnston, S. (1997) Examining the Examiners: an analysis of examiners' reports on doctoral theses, *Studies in Higher Education*, 22(3): 333–47.

Leonard, D. (2001) *A Woman's Guide to Doctoral Studies.* Buckingham: Open University Press.

Loughborough University (2003) Regulations for higher degrees by research and notes for the guidance of research students, directors of research, supervisors and examiners.

Metcalfe, J., Thompson, Q. and Green, H. (2002) *Improving standards in postgraduate research programmes: a report to the Higher Education Funding Councils of England, Scotland and Wales.* http://www.hefce.ac.uk/pubs/hefce/2003/03_01.htm (accessed 27 February 2003).

Millar, R., Crute, V. and Hargie, O. (1992) *Professional Interviewing.* London: Routledge.

Morley, L., Leonard, D. and David, M. (2002) Variations in vivas: quality and equality in British PhD assessments, *Studies in Higher Education*, 27(3): 263–73.

Mullins, G. and Kiley, M. (2002) 'It's a PhD, not a Nobel Prize': how experienced examiners assess research theses, *Studies in Higher Education*, 27(4): 369–86.

Murray, R. (2002) *How to Write a Thesis*. Buckingham: Open University Press.

Nottingham Trent University (1998) *Research Degrees: Regulations and Guidelines*.

Okorocha, E. (1997) *Supervising International Research Students*. London: SRHE/Times Educational Supplement.

Park, C. (2004) Levelling the playing field: towards best practice in the doctoral viva, *Higher Education Review*, in press.

Peelo, M. (2000) Learning reality: inner and outer journeys, *Changes*, 18(2): 118–27.

Phillips, E.M. (1994) Quality in the PhD: points at which quality may be assessed, in R.G. Burgess (ed.) *Postgraduate education and training in the social sciences*. London: Jessica Kingsley.

Phillips, E.M. and Pugh, D.S. (2000) *How to Get a PhD: A Handbook for Students and their Supervisors*, 3rd edn. Buckingham: Open University Press.

QAA (Quality Assurance Agency) (2001) *National Qualifications Framework*. http://www.qaa.ac.uk/crntwork/nqf/ewni2001/contents.htm (accessed 1 August 2003).

Quale, J. (1999) Return of the runny bottom: my PhD viva experience. *Psychology Postgraduate Affairs Group Quarterly*, 31: 45–6.

Ramazanoglu, C. (1987) Sex and violence in academic life, or you can keep a good woman down, in J. Hamner and M. Maynard (eds) *Women, Violence and Social Control*. London: Macmillan.

Research Councils/AHRB (2001) *Skills Training Requirements for Research Students*, Joint Statement of the Research Councils/AHRB. http://www.gradschools.ac.uk/aca/jointskills.html (accessed 18 January 2002).

Royal Society of Chemists (1995) The chemistry PhD – the enhancement of its quality. http:www.rsc.org/lap/polacts/phd.htm (accessed 30 March 2003).

Shaw, M. and Green, H. (2002) Benchmarking the PhD – a tentative beginning, *Quality Assurance in Education*, 10(2): 116–24.

Spender, D. (1981) The gatekeepers: a feminist critique of academic publishing, in H. Roberts (ed.) *Doing Feminist Research*. London: Routledge & Kegan Paul.

Stanley, L. and Wise, S. (1993) *Breaking Out Again*. London: Routledge.

Thomas, K. (1990) *Gender and Subject in Higher Education*. Buckingham: SRHE/Open University Press.

Tinkler, P. and Jackson, C. (2000) Examining the doctorate: institutional policy and the PhD examination process in Britain, *Studies in Higher Education*, 25(2): 167–80.

Tinkler, P. and Jackson, C. (2002) In the dark? Preparing for the PhD viva, *Quality Assurance in Education*, 10(2): 86–97.

Trafford, V. (2002) Questions in a doctoral viva: views from the inside. Paper presented to the UK Council for Graduate Education Research Degree Examining Symposium, London, 29 April.

Trafford, V. and Leshem, S. (2002) Anatomy of a doctoral viva, *Journal of Graduate Education*, 3(2): 33–40.

UK Council for Graduate Education (2001) *Research Training in the Creative and Performing Arts & Design*, Dudley: UK Council for Graduate Education.

Underwood, S. (1999) *What is a PhD? Towards a Discussion Paper*. Lancaster: Higher Education Development Centre.

University College London (2002) MPhil and PhD regulations and procedures: the Grey Book. http://www.ucl.ac.uk/Registry/UCLStaff/Grey_Book/Vivaprocedure.htm (accessed 30 April 2003).

University of Brighton (2002a) Form PhD 10(B), Recommendation of the examiners on a candidate for the degree of Doctor of Philosophy.

University of Brighton (2002b) Research degree student processes: Notes of guidance for university staff.

University of Cambridge (2003) Guide to examiners for the Ph.D., M.Sc., and M.Litt. degrees.

University of Glamorgan (1998) Research degrees and diploma regulations.

University of Hertfordshire (2002) Award of research degrees: handbook for examiners.

University of Manchester (2000) Notes for the guidance of examiners.

University of Oxford (1997) Submission of theses: notes for candidates.

University of Oxford (1998) Memorandum for examiners for the degree of Doctor of Philosophy.

University of York (1997) The degrees of MPhil and DPhil: notes of guidance for students, supervisors and examiners.

Wakeford, J. (2002) Raging against the machine, *Education Guardian*, 7 November.

Wallace, S. and Marsh, C. (2001) Trial by ordeal or the chummy game? Six case studies in the conduct of the British PhD viva examination, *Higher Education Review*, 34(1): 35–59.

Winter, R., Griffiths, M. and Green, K. (2000) The 'academic' qualities of practice: what are the criteria for a practice-based PhD? *Studies in Higher Education*, 25(1): 25–37.

Wolfe, J. (2003) How to survive a thesis defence. http://www.phys.unsw.edu.au/~jw/viva.html (accessed 30 April 2003).

Wood, E.J. and Vella, F. (2000) IUBMB updates PhD standards, *BioEssays*, 22(8): 771–3.

Index

The Society for Research into Higher Education

The Society for Research into Higher Education (SRHE), an international body, exists to stimulate and coordinate research into all aspects of higher education. It aims to improve the quality of higher education through the encouragement of debate and publication on issues of policy, on the organization and management of higher education institutions, and on the curriculum, teaching and learning methods.

The Society is entirely independent and receives no subsidies, although individual events often receive sponsorship from business or industry. The Society is financed through corporate and individual subscriptions and has members from many parts of the world. It is an NGO of UNESCO.

Under the imprint *SRHE & Open University Press*, the Society is a specialist publisher of research, having over 80 titles in print. In addition to *SRHE News*, the Society's newsletter, the Society publishes three journals: *Studies in Higher Education* (three issues a year), *Higher Education Quarterly* and *Research into Higher Education Abstracts* (three issues a year).

The Society runs frequent conferences, consultations, seminars and other events. The annual conference in December is organized at and with a higher education institution. There are a growing number of networks which focus on particular areas of interest, including:

Access
Assessment
Consultants
Curriculum Development
Eastern European
Educational Development Research

FE/HE
Graduate Employment
New Technology for Learning
Postgraduate Issues
Quantitative Studies
Student Development

Benefits to members

Individual

- The opportunity to participate in the Society's networks
- Reduced rates for the annual conferences
- Free copies of *Research into Higher Education Abstracts*
- Reduced rates for *Studies in Higher Education*

- Reduced rates for *Higher Education Quarterly*
- Free online access to *Register of Members' Research Interests* – includes valuable reference material on research being pursued by the Society's members
- Free copy of occasional in-house publications, e.g. *The Thirtieth Anniversary Seminars Presented by the Vice-Presidents*
- Free copies of *SRHE News* and *International News* which inform members of the Society's activities and provides a calendar of events, with additional material provided in regular mailings
- A 35 per cent discount on all SRHE/Open University Press books
- The opportunity for you to apply for the annual research grants
- Inclusion of your research in the *Register of Members' Research Interests*

Corporate

- Reduced rates for the annual conference
- The opportunity for members of the Institution to attend SRHE's network events at reduced rates
- Free copies of *Research into Higher Education Abstracts*
- Free copies of *Studies in Higher Education*
- Free online access to *Register of Members' Research Interests* – includes valuable reference material on research being pursued by the Society's members
- Free copy of occasional in-house publications
- Free copies of *SRHE News* and *International News*
- A 35 per cent discount on all SRHE/Open University Press books
- The opportunity for members of the Institution to submit applications for the Society's research grants
- The opportunity to work with the Society and co-host conferences
- The opportunity to include in the *Register of Members' Research Interests* your Institution's research into aspects of higher education

Membership details: SRHE, 76 Portland Place, London W1B 1NT, UK Tel: 020 7637 2766. Fax: 020 7637 2781. email: srheoffice@srhe.ac.uk
world wide web: http://www.srhe.ac.uk./srhe/
Catalogue: SRHE & Open University Press, McGraw-Hill Education, McGraw-Hill House, Shoppenhangers Road, Maidenhead, Berkshire SL6 2QL. Tel: 01628 502500. Fax: 01628 770224. email: enquiries@openup.co.uk –
web: www.openup.co.uk